A TASTE OF
TEXAS
RANCHING

A TASTE OF
TEXAS
RANCHING

COOKS & COWBOYS

TOM BRYANT & JOEL BERNSTEIN

TEXAS TECH UNIVERSITY PRESS

This book is typeset in Goudy Old Style and Copperplate Gothic. The paper used in this book meets the minimum requirements of ANSI/NISO Z39.48-1992 (R1997). ∞

Cover photograph courtesy of the Southwest Collection, Texas Tech University, Matador Ranch photograph file #64.

Unless otherwise stated, photographs were taken by the authors.

Designed by Lisa Camp

Library of Congress Cataloging-in-Publication Data
Bryant, Tom (Thomas A.), 1934–
    Taste of Texas ranching : cooks and cowboys / Tom Bryant and Joel Bernstein.
        p. cm.
    Includes index.
    ISBN 978-0-89672-348-1 (pbk. : alk. paper)
    1. Cookery, American—Western style. 2. Cookery—Texas. 3. Ranches—Texas. I. Bernstein, Joel H. II. Title.
        TX715.2.W47B79   1995
        641.5978—dc20   95-41872
                                            CIP

Printed in the United States of America
11 12 13 14 15 16 17 18 / 9 8 7 6 5 4 3 2

Texas Tech University Press
Box 41037 | Lubbock, Texas 79409-1037 USA
800.832.4042 | ttup@ttu.edu | www.ttupress.org

CONTENTS

FOREWORD

By Elmer Kelton

It has been said that changes in ranching operations between the end of the Civil War and the beginning of World War II were less pronounced than the virtual revolution that has occurred since. Yet a few elements in ranching—particularly love for the life—have remained much the same as in those first free-wheeling days. Those areas of change, as well as the elements that have not changed, are reflected in the experiences of Texas ranch people quoted by Tom Bryant and Joel Bernstein in this book.

I feel a kinship to the authors' subjects, having grown up on a cattle ranch in Crane and Upton counties and having invested forty-two years of my adult life as an agricultural journalist in almost daily contact with ranchers and farmers.

My father, Buck Kelton, went on the McElroy Ranch payroll as a working cowboy in 1929, soon becoming the ranch foreman and eventually general manager. Born into a cowboy family in 1901, he vividly remembered his first sighting of an automobile, and he lived to watch the live telecast of men walking on the moon. Probably no generation in history ever witnessed so much elemental change as his. Some of it, he deplored. Most, he accepted. A little of it, he led.

Though the open range had already been compromised by barbed wire, Dad came upon the scene when many ranches still had only an outside fence and probably a horse trap. Most pastures were huge, so cattle-working methods had not changed much except that outside strays were no longer a significant factor.

Ranches of any size still kept a cowboy crew far from headquarters much of the year, accompanied by a chuck wagon and a large remuda of horses so the men could change to fresh mounts several times a day. Rounding-up was accomplished by spreading riders across the target area, usually miles wide, and pushing the cattle ahead of them to a specified gathering point. Most sorting and branding was done in the open, calves roped out of the herd and dragged to the fire where branding irons awaited, heated to a red glow.

By the time I was old enough to stay on a horse and tag along, more often in the way than being of real help, the huge pastures had been divided and divided again. I can remember the last days of the McElroy's traditional mule-drawn chuck wagon. Shortly after Dad became foreman he bowed to practicality and bolted the chuck box onto the rear of a flat-bed truck. The truck could carry a larger load and move more easily from camp to camp. He also retired the ranch's working wagons in favor of pickups for greater mobility. One of the few times I can remember riding in a McElroy wagon, I was just a toddler, and I fell out. That set the pattern for my cowboying career.

The chuck wagon in its various configurations was used twice a year during the thirty-six years Dad remained on the ranch. The first was for a week or ten days of branding at the end of August and early September, when we youngsters could be utilized as part of the working crew. The second and longer roundup was in November and December, for a final branding and shaping-up of the herd before winter set in. Because of school, we kids could participate in that "works" only on weekends, but we looked forward to the adventure. We were never paid, nor did we expect to be. I loved the cowboy life regardless of my shortcomings.

We considered the roundup fun—albeit hard work—but certain not-so-fun preparations had to be made ahead of it. Plenty of mesquite firewood had to be gathered and piled at each campsite so the cook could concentrate on what he was hired for. All the working pens were checked to make sure the gates swung, and any holes in the corral fences were patched so calves could not slip out. The chuck box and all the pots, pans, and utensils were scrubbed. Because the Dutch ovens were thoroughly greased at the end of each roundup so they would not rust in storage, this thick coating of lard had to be removed with soap and hot water—hardly the stuff of a Zane Grey novel.

We could always count on roundup help from neighbors like the Clark brothers and Hawley VanCourt, which we reciprocated when they worked. In addition, Dad hired several day-working cowboys to finish out a crew of ten to a dozen men and four Kelton kids. The wagon cook—hired by the day—would be someone he had known for years, like Tom Grammer or Hub Castleberry or Jiggs Plummer. All these men had been working cowboys and knew ranch routine backward and forward.

There were certain unwritten but well-understood rules in camp. You never rode a horse up close enough to stir dust around the wagon. The working hands ate first, visitors afterward. When you finished eating, you scraped your plate clean and dropped it and your utensils into the cook's "wreck" pan so he did not have to scout the area looking for stray hardware. You rolled up your own bed, and if camp was to be moved, you dragged it close to the wagon or even loaded it to help the cook and his swamper, if he had one. You never loafed around the cook's fire. In wintertime, the cowboys built a loafing fire of their own in the evening, a little way from the wagon. Many an outlaw horse was ridden around that fire, many a wild cow roped and brought to ground, at least in the stories that were told.

Most of the year the McElroy—along with other outfits—fed its regular hands at ranch headquarters. The company had an L-shaped combination bunkhouse, lobby, dining room, and kitchen and kept a full-time cook.

On a smaller ranch my mother might have been expected to cook for the hands, as my grandmother did for many years in the Midland area. The McElroy hired couples for the kitchen, however. The woman did most of the cooking, while her husband was expected to fill in as a general handyman around headquarters and to aid windmill man Cliff Newland when he needed help. Being a woman, the headquarters cook never went out with the chuck wagon.

Dad was extremely frugal in many ways, an advocate of buying a new nail only when a bent one could not be found and straightened. But he never scrimped on groceries for the hands. Having grown up working for various outfits, a few of which fed poorly, he strongly believed that a well-fed man was a happy man and a better worker.

Dad was an innovator. The McElroy was a large ranch of more than 220 sections, or close to 150,000 acres. In the early years we sometimes saddled up long before daylight and rode many miles before we even got to the pasture where the day's work was to be done. When we finished, we had to ride all those miles home, often killing more time going and coming than we spent working cattle. Though horse trailers were still something of a novelty, Dad began tinkering with them as potential time-savers. The first he built were rough but practical, constructed of lumber atop an old truck chassis. We would load the horses into a trailer and drive to the scene of the work, be home by mid-day, then go out and work another pasture in the afternoon. Trailers enabled Dad to get double the work done with fewer men and fewer horses.

This efficiency became particularly important to him and to other ranchers as World War II pressed the younger cowboys into military service. Family members and neighbor help became a critical necessity, and ranchers employed every labor-saving device and shortcut they could think of. A lot of work had to be left undone. More and more of the unavoidable was scheduled on weekends, when schoolboys were available and men with regular jobs in town could come and be cowboys for a day.

Several of the ranchers interviewed for this book noted today's common practice of employing family men, who tend to be more stable and stay in one place longer. Prior to World War II, a majority of working cowboys were bachelors. Most ranches did not have facilities for families, beyond those for their foremen and perhaps some camp men. But labor shortages during and after the war gradually brought ranchers to accept the necessity of furnishing adequate family living quarters. Today, married cowboys are the norm rather than the exception.

The McElroy Ranch as I knew it is gone, sold off and broken up. If it were still together, some of its operating procedures would probably be as I remember them, but much would be different. Even before it broke up, Dad's successors began using motorcycles instead of horses for some of their routine cattle work, and the venerable chuck box had been retired. My old friend and mentor Paul Patterson said he went out once to help round up a pasture, and the whole crew was taken to town to eat dinner at the Dairy Queen.

My son Steve's father-in-law, Binks McCutchen, operated a sheep ranch in Coke County. For years he did not own a horse. When he needed to pen his flock, he tolled them in by honking his pickup horn and rattling a feed sack.

In Granddad's time, a good cowboy was one who could ride well, handle a rope, and savvy the cow. Today he is likely to spend more time in a pickup than on horseback. The cowboy—and even more so the ranch operator—is expected to know more than a smattering about nutrition, animal health, and genetics. Granddad never heard of artificial insemination and embryo transplants. Dad knew of them but never used them. Today's cowboy and rancher know, and chances are good that they are doing some AI, at least. The cowboy is expected to be something of a mechanic, an electrician, and a welder. Today's heavy reliance on livestock performance records, as well as the IRS demand for precise bookkeeping, may require the cowboy or the ranch operator to operate a computer and manage a spreadsheet.

In olden times, ranchers knew they had made a profit if they had more money in their pockets at the end of the year than at the beginning. The business end of ranching has become infinitely more complex. It has been said that because of tight margins, a ranch more often makes or loses it in the office than in the pasture.

Costs of production have risen far more than prices for cattle, sheep, or goats, wool or mohair. For instance, ranchers have to sell two to three times more calves or lambs to pay for a pickup than they did thirty or forty years ago. Yet, there is little they can do to graze significantly more animals on a given acreage unless the land is put into cultivation or into something like the Savory method of intensive pasture rotation. Indeed, in the interests of range conservation and good land management today's ranchers are probably carrying *fewer* units of livestock on a given acreage than they once did. They can only hope that better nutrition and genetics will help offset in weight what may have been lost in numbers.

Today's ranchers have suffered much unjustified criticism from self-appointed environmentalists, especially in public lands states, who charge them with overstocking and ruin of the range. Most environmentalist criticism has more to do with a political agenda than with genuine concern over welfare of the land. Those making the charges are usually urban dwellers who would not know sideoats grama from burro grass. The truth is that most of today's ranchers are better land managers than their fathers and grandfathers simply because they have the advantage of several generations' time and experience. Their livelihood depends upon taking care of their animals and environment. If they hope to pass the land to their descendants, it would be foolish not to preserve and improve it so they can leave it better than they found it. Many professional range conservationists agree that except in the area of brush encroachment, a very difficult and costly problem to combat, western ranges today are in better overall condition than they have been in a hundred years.

There is no question that cowboys and cowgirls are far fewer than they used to be, but they are still out there. As John Erickson has said, you just don't see many from the interstate. They remain for the same reason most ranchers do: they love the life. Cowboys are not in it just for the pay, because that has never been high enough to be any real attraction.

That said, ranch owners sometimes have even less to show for their labors than the people who work for them. It is the freedom, the lifestyle, which keeps them in ranching when other investments of capital and labor would almost certainly pay larger financial dividends.

Given the many formidable challenges—some old, some new such as stringent environmental and work-safety regulations—it seems almost a wonder that ranching even survives. But it appeals to something elemental, especially in those people born to the land, to the work. Love of the land and of livestock has been a hallmark of ranch folk from the beginning. That element has not changed, though so much else in ranching has. There have always been those who would suffer any hardship, any sacrifice, to hold onto the ranch lifestyle. Thank God they are still out there.

The people in this book do not seem likely to give up anytime soon.

PREFACE

It is difficult to discuss Texas, the largest state in the contiguous United States, without delving into the influence of the Spanish and Mexican cultures. Texas is separated from Mexico by the not-so-wide Rio Grande, and for many years, Texas was a part of Spain (1519-1685 and 1690-1821); and France (1685-1690); and Mexico (1821-1836); was a Republic (1836-1845); was in the Confederacy (1861-1865); and finally became a permanent part of the United States (1865). Texas has a long and colorful history.

Before the white man, Texas was inhabited by Indians. The eastern woodland tribes were somewhat sedentary; they grew crops, hunted, and fished. The plains tribes, on the other hand, were nomadic and followed the buffalo, which provided for all their needs. Among the eastern Indians, the Caddo, originally from Louisiana, are said to have given Texas its name.

Texas means friend, or friendly people. As we traveled throughout the state interviewing ranchers, we were almost always warmly received, treated with that old southern hospitality for which the people of Texas, our friends, are so famous.

Of course, the first white men probably found Texas not quite so friendly. After America was discovered, Spain's colonization of Cuba began, and in 1528, Spain sent an expedition of 300 men to explore what would become Florida. No one is sure what happened to that expedition, but four years later, four survivors, including one Cabeza deVaca, were found wandering around in western Mexico, having walked over 6,000 miles across what today constitutes Florida, Alabama, Louisiana, and Texas.

We crossed and criss-crossed Texas in modern vehicles, and could only wonder what old Cabeza must have gone through in his trek. As the Comanche and Apache Indians quickly learned, Texas is no place to be afoot. Besides the high plains and deserts, there are over 1,000 species of cactus in the state and uncounted rattlesnakes; both give residents plenty to be wary of even today.

Life in Texas under Spain and then Mexico was fraught with hardships. The territory was huge and not easily traversed. The Indians, a powerful presence on foot, were an even greater force once the Spanish introduced them to horses. One old rancher, formerly a Range Rider on the Rio Grande, said that when the Indians got horses, it was like putting wings on a wildcat—it allowed them to cover so much more territory and go and come as they pleased.

Besides bringing over good horses and cattle, which wandered and escaped and proliferated and stocked the Texas ranges, the Spanish built a series of missions from which to operate. One of the first in Texas was the San Antonio, built in 1718. But San Antonio was a long way from Mexico, and the Texas Indians were not easy to domesticate. In 1772, Spain pulled its forces off the northern frontier.

Almost a half-century later, in 1821, Mexico revolted from Spain, and in 1825 passed colonization mandates which encouraged immigration. Five years later, after 30,000 Americans had settled in Texas, Mexico became nervous and rescinded the mandates. But it was too late. Americans had come and they liked Texas. They intended to stay. So, in 1835, the Texas Revolution began.

The battles for Texas were long and bloody, and after the Alamo fell and its defenders were massacred, Texas—in fact all of America—was furious. Its fallen heroes were revenged on the grassy plains outside present-day Houston, when General Sam Houston's army overran the Mexicans with cries of "Remember the Alamo." The Mexicans were defeated, Texas gained its independence, and Texans have been independent, hardy, and tough—yet friendly—ever since.

We found Texas fascinating—the great expanse of the country, the diversity of the land and the people. Texas has come a long way in the last century. Houston is now a leader in the space industry. Austin, the capital city, is a burgeoning mecca for computer technology. Texas has a thriving fisheries industry, as well as timber, mining, and agriculture. Though it is clearly a state with much to see, we concentrated our visits, and this book, on ranching.

Ranching in Texas is as old as Texas itself. One of the missions of the Spanish was to build ranches, so the cattle and horses they brought over were the best available. And Texas proved a perfect place for those animals to survive and breed and expand. Less than two hundred years after the Spanish first invaded Mexico, North American Indians were capturing and using horses, descendants of those Spanish imports. And Texas and Mexico were literally crawling with cattle.

It was the cattle that created Texas' large ranches. And it was the Mexican vaquero that worked those ranches and gave birth to the American cowboy. It is no small coincidence that much of the equipment used by the cowboy today comes from Mexico and Spain. Most of the language associated with the cowboy originated in Mexico and Texas. Early American cowboys, unable to speak Spanish and probably not caring, quickly adopted their own language of the plains, which has become synonymous with cowboys the world over.

The lariat, the primary tool of the cowboy, comes from the Spanish "la reata," chaps from "chaparajos," and of course most everyone in the world knows what a sombrero is and that rodeo, now a professional sport, comes from the Spanish meaning to round up or encircle. Practically all cowboy equipment has a Spanish origin and name. Most of it has been bastardized by the Americans, but the origin cannot be denied. The Spanish and the Mexican influence on cowboy culture is overwhelming; nowhere is this more true than in Texas.

It is correct to say that Texas was built around a horse culture. After Texas gained its independence and the settlers began to Americanize the state, counties were laid out and county seats designated in the center so that residents could reach the courthouse from any direction by horseback in one day's ride. When the immigrants began to clear the land, they couldn't help noticing the abundance of wild cattle. For a man on horseback, wild cattle are money on the hoof. It became a simple matter of gathering up these cattle and starting a controlled breeding program, or after the Civil War, to gather up these wild cattle, these Longhorns, descendants of Spanish fighting bulls, and drive them to the markets in the north.

Thus began, in Texas, a decade of the most glorious years in the American West: the cattle drives. Texas Longhorns not only had long horns, they had long bodies and long legs, perfect for long drives. The Texas descendants of the Spanish Andalusians already had cow sense in their veins, following centuries of selected breeding for the bullfighting ring. Bullfighting horses got cow-smart quickly or they got gored. The survivors became world-class cowhorses, the propagators of the Texas cowpony, and later, the American Quarter Horse, now the main working horse on most ranches around the country.

Given the changing times of the latter part of the twentieth century, we found that while most ranches keep good horses, fewer and fewer ranches depended on the horse as their primary tool in handling cattle. This takes nothing away from the Texas cowboys. There are probably still more working cowboys in Texas than anywhere in the world. But the times, they are a-changing, and Texas is no exception.

Western novelist Elmer Kelton grew up on a ranch and later retired from years as a columnist for the respected *Livestock Weekly* in San Angelo where he makes his home. "I think my Dad was probably one of the innovators," Kelton states, referring to the changing use of horses on Texas ranches. "He was a very innovative man. During World War II, you couldn't hardly find a cowboy. Most young men were off fighting the war. Dad built a trailer to haul horses before you could find a horse trailer anywhere. But he figured that if we could haul a horse to the back side of the pasture and push the cattle where we wanted them to go, we'd save probably a half day's riding. That half day could then be used in fixing fence or any one of a thousand other chores needing daily attention on a ranch."

And so it began, this change from constantly using horses, to hauling horses and using them half as much. This story is one that was repeated many times on as many different ranches. Like most American industries, ranches have had to downsize workforces and maximize efficiency. They have to watch every dollar. Ranches must get maximum efficiency out of employees' time, minimizing costs and maximizing profits just to stay in business.

We found ranches diversifying their operations. Many Texas ranches have discovered that hunters are a cash crop. Hunters are easily managed, they don't tear up the land, they don't eat much, and you don't need horses to herd them around. Hunters provide many Texas ranches with the wherewithal to remain in the cattle, sheep, goat, and horse business.

Ranches in Texas, almost without exception, are privately owned, deeded land, whereas in other western states, a ranch may own only a few hundred or thousand acres, and lease grazing rights on thousands of acres of public lands. On these public lands, private citizens still have the right to hike or camp, hunt or fish. Not so with private land in Texas. That seems to rile some city folk, who have indicated they want access to those lands. And that is a thorn in the flanks of many West Texas ranches.

The trouble seems to have started with the Reagan administration's war on drugs. The border patrol was beefed up and began intense patrolling of the Mexican border. Most of the land along the Mexican border is private, so the border patrol supposedly approached ranchers along the border and asked permission to patrol the property, promising to repair the roads in return. The ranchers thought this sounded too good to be true, and, of course, it was.

Before the United States government could "fix" the ranch roads, they had to prepare an environmental impact statement (EIS). In the proces, several species of rare plants, insects, and rocks were discovered. Suddenly, the government was telling ranchers no cattle could be run on those sections because the cows might step on an endangered spider or a rare flower or fossil. To a rancher who depends on running cattle on his pastures to make a living, this prohibition was deadly.

Several ranchers told us that, for that reason, they are very selective in who they let on their ranches. Some wouldn't allow any poking around or any photography. A couple granted interviews only at night, in town, in a private place. Far from being rude or ridiculous, they were just being cautious. They had seen that the government could keep them from using their own land. They were damn worried—and with good reason.

Some of the most beautiful country in the world is in West Texas. The plains, the high mountains, the catcus, the flowers, the trees, and the brush are a breathtaking sight. People from town have discovered West Texas and they want access. There are lawsuits on file to gain access to those mountains, most of which are privately owned. Ranchers in West Texas have organized the Trans Texas Heritage Association and are fighting back. Some are packing pistols, and we were told of one rancher who blew up a bridge to prevent trespassers from crossing his property.

Still, for the most part, we were well received. After we explained our purpose and intent, normally our hosts relaxed. Many times we were told there was no story there, but after a cup of coffee and some small talk, our hosts filled tapes and notebooks, provided us with photographs, meals, a place to stay, and a favorite recipe. We include recipes in our stories to present a total picture of each ranch.

And each ranch is totally different. Visit one ranch and they'll raise one kind of cattle, or sheep, or goats, or horses, and they'll eat entirely different food than the next ranch thirty miles down the road. We found this fascinating. Each ranch is a mini-culture, depending on the background and heritage of the owners. And food, like dress and language, is a part of that culture. In Texas, the Spanish influence is strong in dress, in language, and, of course, in food.

Tex-Mex eateries are popular across America. Tex-Mex food is Americanized Mexican food. It is not as hot or fiery as "real" Mexican food, but it can peel paint in the hands of certain cooks. The cooks we found in Texas were like cooks on most ranches anywhere. Ranch cooks are what the ranch can find. Man, woman, boy, or girl, whoever gets the call, gets to cook. It makes for interesting conversation, interesting eating and—we hope—interesting reading.

Another thing we found in Texas was the growing popularity of cowboy heritage. From Austin to Abilene, from Waco to El Paso, every city seems to have its annual cowboy festival. Many of these get-togethers include cowboy poetry, cowboy music, and cowboy cooking. Many cities and towns sponsor chuck wagon cooking competitions, with prizes running into the thousands of dollars. As one ranch cook told us, "Gives us cooks a chance to make some real money."

We find it fitting that cowboy cooks and traditional cowboy fare is becoming more popular than ever. And we also find it fitting that it all started in Texas. Where the cowboy was born. Where ranching began. Where the cattle drives originated. And where the chuck wagon was invented. If Texas ain't western, then there ain't no West. Welcome to "A Taste of Ranching, Texas." Ride with us for a while and get a feel for the people, places, and food that put the cowboy in Texas and a little bit of Texas in all of us.

INTRODUCTION

BY TOM BRYANT

I was just a gangly teen the first time I visited Texas. It was 1952 and my oldest brother, Gene, was in the Air Force, stationed at San Angelo. I drove with some members of my family from our home town in Thomasville, Georgia, to San Angelo in a new '52 Chevy four-door sedan. I've never forgotten that trip. We crossed the Sabine River between Louisiana and Texas about four in the morning. I was wide awake. I'd heard great stories about Texas all my life, and I didn't want to miss a bit of it.

After the Civil War, many Georgia soldiers returned home to find no home at all and headed for Texas to start a new life. It was common to find notes posted on doors and gates with the simple inscription "GTT" (Gone To Texas). Fathers and mothers in Georgia often complained that Texas was taking their babies as more and more young boys left to join the burgeoning cattle industry that was gearing up in South Texas and would make history for the next twenty years with its long drives up north.

I was spellbound back in '52 as I watched the sun come up behind us, casting long shadows of the wooded forest of East Texas across the road. East Texas is not at all different in climate, crops, or forest from Georgia, Alabama, Mississippi, or Louisiana, and it all looked like home to me. Gradually, the woods gave way to brush-covered hills as we motored west, and along about Brady, the self-proclaimed "center of Texas" where the ninety-eighth meridian separates eastern woodlands from western plains, we entered West Texas, a true high-plains country. It was all new to me, and totally exquisite.

By the time we reached the high, open plains of San Angelo, I was convinced that Texas was *where* I wanted to be and a cowboy was *what* I wanted to be. But alas, cooler heads prevailed, and at the end of our visit I was strongly encouraged to get back in the Chevy, return to Georgia, finish my education, and "make something out of yourself."

Well, I did get the first of those jobs done, but I haven't quite finished working on the last. After five years of college, eight years in the Army, ten years of public service, twelve years of cowboying in Montana—with ten years of writing—in 1993 I fulfilled a childhood dream. I was GTT. It was one of the most memorable experiences in my life. Now, I've done a little traveling. I've been so far east I ended up in the West and I've been so far west I was in the East, but I've never been anywhere like Texas. Texas, my friends, is hard to describe.

The simple geographical expanse of it is overwhelming. Texas is more than 800 miles across from east to west and about the same distance from north to south. It is part of a long slope of mountain ranges that run from the foothills of the Rocky Mountains to the Gulf of Mexico. This plain is cut by many great rivers, the largest being the Red River, which forms the northern border, and the longest, the Rio Grande, which separates not only Texas from New Mexico, but Texas from (Old) Mexico.

Water is plentiful in East Texas with the Sabine, Trinity, Brazos, Neches, Guadalupe, and San Antonio rivers providing for lush crops and fat cows. An annual fifty-plus inches of rain each year keep East Texas green and growing. But the farther west one travels in Texas, the less surface water you see and the less rainfall you encounter, with some counties in West Texas getting by with twelve inches or less each year. West Texas is true high-plains country, with some counties qualifying as true desert. Here, water becomes a precious commodity and farmers and ranchers spend most of their time, money, and effort trying to keep an adequate supply of it for livestock and crops.

While this lack of water might act as a determent to some, to me it holds a special attraction. The plants and animals and the people of West Texas have to be especially tough to survive in this dry climate. Nothing comes easy here. Workdays must be planned carefully; nothing is wasted. The distances between residences are great, and people here still must be inventive and ingenious to survive.

Throughout Texas I met people who demonstrated that old pioneer spirit—make do with what you have or do without. But the sparseness of the population of West Texas bred people even more inventive and independent than anywhere I had visited before. In these final days of the twentieth century, over 164 years after Texas gained independence from Mexico, it was both interesting and paradoxical to find people still struggling with many of the same problems our forefathers did when they originally settled this country—trying to survive in a hostile environment, facing unknowns every day, and having to face many of the problems alone. Texas, as always, continues to be a very special place.

On the day of the winter solstice, I was visiting with one of my new Texas friends, market economist and financial advisor R. E. McMasters, Jr., of Marble Falls, with one of our Montana friends, Patty Bowers, who provided spiritual support on the Texas trip. R. E. lives near one of the most enchanted places in the world—Enchanted Rock State Park near Fredericksburg. He invited us along for a visit.

R. E. says he makes a point to visit Enchanted Rock on both times of equinox and solstice. In the March 25, 1992, issue of his newsletter *The Reaper*, he wrote the following of his visit during the vernal equinox, which pretty much sums up what I experienced on December 21, 1993: ". . . Once I climbed to the top of this granite dome [Enchanted Rock], I knew immediately why it is so powerful. In fact, Enchanted Rock is the most powerful natural structure I have ever seen.

"This seventy-acre, 325-foot high paramagnetic pink granite dome is the second largest exposed batholith in the United States! It sits at the center of a horizon-to-horizon, 360-degree, concave, earthen paramagnetic dish from which it arises. . . . It was no surprise to later learn that a far greater portion of this huge granite dome still lies beneath the earth, that the exposed Enchanted Rock itself was much like the tip of an iceberg.

"With these tons and tons of paramagnetic pink granite serving as a solar collector and as a transmitter/receiver of the magnetic lines of forces of the earth [Ley Lines], I knew immediately its power was awesome. Geologists call En-chanted Rock an inselberg, an island mountain. The outcrop of the Enchanted Rock batholith covers ninety square miles . . .

"I jogged on down to the Visitors' Center and talked to a park ranger. There on the wall, in bold letters, placed over an outline of the State of Texas, was the following statement regarding Enchanted Rock: 'This is the place where Texas began. Enchanted Rock is a part of the basement or bedrock structure of Texas. Around this core, the rest of the state slowly formed. The foundation is stable, it is ancient. . . . Native and modern Americans have sensed the special qualities of this place called "Enchanted." It represents the roots of a continent and the birthplace of Texas.'"

At the top of Enchanted Rock, R. E. recited some special psalms and a prayer, forging a special bond between me, Enchanted Rock, and Texas. My home and my horses are in Montana, where I'll always live. But my heart, some very special memories, and some very special friends, remain in Texas.

I returned to Montana refreshed in spirit and renewed in dedication to working and producing a special book about a special state, about special people in a special land. I hope you enjoy the reading and the recipes as much as I have enjoyed gathering them for you. I want to especially thank all the wonderful people who allowed me to visit their homes and who took the time to share with me a portion of their lives and their lifestyles.

I want to thank my extended family for their continued understanding and support of my unusual and unconventional lifestyle. Thanks especially to my sisters, Dorothy, Ruth, and Nelle, and to my brothers, Gene, Ken, James, and Joe, for their financial and moral support, without which this book never could have been written.

I am grateful to my friend and packing partner, Steve Brawley, for taking care of the barn and the horses while I was in Texas. And to his wife, Alta, for putting up with my shenanigans and bringing me food when I was weak and stern stares when I got too bold. And to the Brawley Bunch, a.k.a. the Bryant's Barn Crew: Bucky, Dustin, Sarah, Chris, and Chance, the self-proclaimed "Toughest Man in the Barn."

And a heartfelt thanks to Patty Bowers, who encouraged me every step of the way on this book project; who forced me to stay focused; who prayed for me daily; and who endured the vicissitudes of my mid-project aberrations. I owe her dearly for reading and correcting the manuscript, and for never faltering in our friendship.

A special thanks to my partner, Joel, for his continued cooperation, diligence, and support. And thanks to our Montana editor, Carola Kronfoth, for reading, revising, and transcribing the manuscript.

As they say in Texas, y'all are the greatest. And researching and writing this book has been the greatest fun of all. Enjoy.

INTRODUCTION

BY JOEL H. BERNSTEIN

More than thirty years ago, when I bought my first place in New Mexico, in an attempt to truly fit in, I guess, I adopted some of the attitudes of my neighbors. And one of the most pronounced of these attitudes was a certain hostility to Texas and Texans.

The reasoning behind this outlook is pretty vague, but Texas is so big, and Texans do seem to dominate places where they congregate, so that I think New Mexicans—there are barely 1.6 million of us—are a little bit overwhelmed.

Even after leaving the Southwest and spending twenty years in Montana, when I returned to the "Land of Enchantment" in 1990, I still carried with me my old prejudices. And they lasted until I headed east to write this book and I had to come face to face with this contemptible race of people about whom we spoke only with scorn. Well, I'll be the first to admit that not only was I wrong about Texas and the good folks who live there, but I was *very* wrong.

As I traveled around Texas and visited with ranchers, cowboys, cowgirls, and cooks, on big outfits and small ones, the thing they all had in common was hospitality, a willingness to help me, and enormous pride in being Texans. Maybe it's that deep-felt pride that puts people off. But as I got to know these people, I came to admire them, and, at least superficially, understand what it means to be a Texan.

Texas is so big, and anyone even slightly familiar with ranching and the history of the West knows that modern ranching had its start in Texas. My own trip to the Palo Duro Canyon (now a state park), along the eastern edge of the Texas high plains just south of Amarillo, where I viewed the restoration of a line shack used by the first commercial cattle ranch in the Texas panhandle back in 1876, jump-started my own thoughts about ranching and Texas. This is where it all started. It put me in mind of the rich heritage and traditions of ranching, and why it is so darn American, and why Texans, particularly the ranchers, are such a proud lot.

I first visited the Lone Star State in the mid 1960s when I was rodeoing in West Texas. To be honest, I thought the country was pretty barren, both dry and desolate. In fact, my traveling partner and I couldn't wait to get out of there. Now, with the hindsight of years of ranching in the West, it looks completely different to me. I can finally see the rich grasslands and better appreciate the space and the solitude. And the people. And the size. Probably the old XIT, more than any ranch in the United States, captures the sense of size. With 3,050,000 acres spread in the Panhandle, the ranch covered parts of ten counties. Many of the old-time cowboys say the brand stood for "Ten in Texas." In all likelihood it was actually picked for its utility. The cowboys could burn the XIT on a calf with five strokes of a straight five-inch iron, and it was sure a hard brand for rustlers to alter. The XIT had as many as 150 cowboys riding its range. They rode 1,000 horses, herded 150,000 head of cattle, and branded 35,000 calves each year. That's Texas big. But, as you'll read in the following chapters, even though it has been broken up into smaller ranches for many years, ranchers and cowboys still speak fondly of the old XIT.

Much of the XIT's history is preserved at the Dallam-Hartley Museum in Dalhart where Dessie Hanbury, now in her eighties and the daughter of one of the old XIT cow bosses, will give you a full rundown. She was so generous and helpful that it set the stage for my entrance into Texas ranch history.

It seems that no matter where I go in ranch country, from Alberta, Canada all the way down to the Mexican border, the people are open , giving of their time, and so very proud of what they do. They don't complain about bad weather or gripe about the falling cattle prices. They accept what is and go on about their business, a business that is every bit as much a way of life as it is an economic endeavor. Time after time, as I arrived at a ranch and was barely out of my vehicle, the head man ushered me into his pickup for a tour of the ranch, a tour that was filled with history, ranching information, environmental data, and pride. Not false pride, but pride in the land and the accomplishments of generations of strong, resourceful ranchers. Seeing all the cattle, horses, and wildlife in that big open country sometimes made me feel like I was living in another time. Maybe a better time.

This book is, in part, a tribute to all those Texans who learned to live and prosper in a tough land. I can never thank them enough for their help and generosity. They frequently fed me, often gave me a good bed to rest my weary bones, and engaged me in much more good conversation than anyone is entitled to.

Tom and I are also very lucky that, with the help of Carole Young at Texas Tech University Press and the folks at the wonderful Ranching Heritage Center in Lubbock, we have a real Texas connection for this volume. Somehow that just seems fitting. And a big thank you to Jeanne Warren, our editor from Hickory Creek, Texas, for making the writing of these two cowboys make some sense.

And to mi amigo, Tom Bryant, one of these days we're going to have to start traveling together again so that we can share some of these great ranch experiences as they happen.

Texas advertises itself as being "like a whole other country." They might be right, but we're all damn lucky that they're willing to share it with the rest of us. See you all again, real soon.

THE ROUND-UP COOK

BY JIM FISHER

(We found this poem printed in several different publications. We don't know who Jim Fisher is, or if he is even still alive. We do know that this poem was written more than fifty-five years ago, and that it is a wonderful introduction to the many cooks who still keep all those ranchers, cowboys, and cowgirls well fed. We join the salute to these mainstays of America's ranches.)

Yep, that's him over there by the wagon
That bald-headed, mean-lookin' cuss.
With the sugar sacktied round his belly,
There now: he's a-lookin' at us.
I'll bet that in all o' your ramblin'
You ain't seen a more poisonous look.
Some day he'll jest swell up an' bite his own self.
But say! That ol' buzzard c'n cook.

He never stays long with no outfit,
I've knowed him t' rare up an' quit
When a Circle Bar rep fetched a bottle fr'm town
An' he didn't get any of it.
He'd quit if we tried t' hooraw him,
F'r he's jealous an' tetchy as sin;
But he'll roll outa bed an' dig up a hot meal
If a puncher is late gittin' in.

I reckon there ain't no more like him,
He's a cross between angel an' skunk,
An' I'd rather be stuck in a Mexican jail
Than be around him when he's drunk.
But he sure can make doughnuts an' biskits,
An' his blackberry cobbler's a dream;
An' no other darn cook on this sheep-stinkin' range
C'n match him at handlin' a team.

He ain't got no sweet disposition;
Most anything makes him git sore,
But I seen him move camp with four knot-headed bronks
That had never wore harness before.
An' the hell of it was that he made it,
An' them bronks wasn't showin' no grief;
An' when the first riders had made it t' camp
He was there with hot coffee an' beef.

Fr'm Miles City clear up t' Benton,
An' fr'm Billings t' Malta—an' back,
His marrow gut mulligan, biskits, an' pie,
An' his "son of a gun in a sack"
Has built him a rep with the cowboys;
So when the boss went t' Chinook
An' found him there broke, he just brung him along
F'r we shorely was needin' a cook.

If you drink the last drop in the bucket
An' don't go an' git him some more;
Or don't put your plate in the round-up,
He'll jest paw the ground up, an' roar.
He'll roar if you trip on a guy rope,
An' have fits if the stove wood is damp;
But I ain't seen a cook fr'm the Pecos t' here
That c'n beat him in settin' up camp.

He'll jest tie the lines t' the brake bar
An' git t' unlashin' the stove,
An' he's got 'er all set up an' smokin'
Before the last tent peg is drove.
An' he's shovin' a roast in the oven
While the wranglers is stretchin' the fly;
An' as soon's he c'n git in the mess box
He's turnin' out biskits an' pie.

If the cavvy sh'd mud up the water,
'R the wrangler is slow gittin' wood,
You c'n hear him a-cussin' clear out t' the herd,
An' believe me, ol' timer, he's good.
But when they have turned loose the round-up,
An' the boys hit f'r camp on the fly,
They are sure of roast beef that'd melt in y'r mouth
An' plenty hot biskits—an' pie.

He always gets drunk when they're shippin',
An' stays that way; damn his ol' soul!
An' the boys has t' rustle the grub f'r themselves
Till the wagon is ready t' roll.
An' it's hell jest a-gittin' him sober
An' I know it is true, f'r a fact,
That he'll never get sober, an' ain't worth a dam'
Till he's drunk all the lemon extract.

But he'll move when it's mud to the axles;
An' he'll put up his tent in a storm.
An' he'll fix up hot coffee, an' move things aroun'
T' let the boys in t' git warm.
An' he don't never need any pilot,
F'r he knows the whole range like a book.
So he works when he wants to, 'r quits an' gits drunk—
F'r the ornery ol' buzzard c'n cook.

THE CHUCK WAGON

The chuck wagon: a mess wagon that carried the cooking outfit, food, and supplies when cowboys drove the herds up the cattle trails of the West or gathered their own cattle during the fall and spring roundups on the home ranch. Simple. Except the chuck wagon, one of the most vivid symbols of the cowboy west, was so much more. The wagon was the cowboy's "home on the range," and more often than not, the centerpiece of the drive or roundup.

A relatively recent creation, the chuck wagon is credited to Texas cattle baron Charles Goodnight. In 1866, Goodnight reworked an old Army wagon, selected primarily because it had extra heavy duty iron axles. The design became so popular that cattle outfits all over the West began to copy it, each ranch making only slight changes. Eventually, the idea became a commercial success and chuck wagons were produced by several wagon builders, including the Studebaker Company, which sold the wagons for $75 to $100.

On the trail, the chuck wagon followed behind the remuda, or extra herd of saddle horses, as it trailed the main herd. It was the moving "throne" for the cook. Generally, they were ordinary four-wheeled wagons, without springs, with a "chuck box" built on the back, with drawers and shelves for food storage, and cooking and eating utensils. The tailgate lowered onto either one or two legs; this table was a working surface for the cook. Under the table was a large "roundup pan," or "wreck pan," for the dirty dishes. It was considered a major breach of etiquette for any cowboy to forget to put his dirty dishes in the roundup pan after a meal.

Under the wagon body, the cook and his helper had a "cooney"—a dried cowhide used to carry firewood when it was available, or buffalo or cow chips when necessary. Sometimes inside the wagon, but more often tied securely to the side, was the priceless water barrel, which usually held two or three days' supply of water. Extra ammunition, first-aid supplies, sewing materials, and the cowboys' extra clothing and bedding were also carried in the wagon.

The wagon itself was drawn by four horses, mules, or oxen, and it was a darn heavy load to pull. The cook was responsible for carrying at least a month's supply of food plus all the gear and odds and ends that always seemed to be needed on a long trail drive. Flour, sugar, dried fruit, roasted coffee beans, pinto beans, salt and pepper, onions and potatoes, lard, baking soda, vinegar, molasses, salt pork, and a sourdough keg for making "rising bread" constituted the staples. When you add to that the tool box, cast iron skillets, the Dutch ovens, extra wagon wheel, lanterns, axle grease, branding irons, horseshoeing gear, hobbles, and ropes, you can only imagine the size of the load that had to be hauled hundreds of miles during the several months on the trail, often crossing rivers, deserts, and sometimes meeting up with a band or two of hostile Indians.

Some drives were better off than others. The more fully equipped might have a "bed wagon," driven by the cook's "flunky" to carry the cowboys' bedrolls, and maybe even a "hooligan wagon," which only carried firewood and water. Such outfits were the exception rather than the rule; the main chuck wagon was normally the only traveling commissary on the trail to the railheads or the northern ranges.

Once the drive had moved out, the entire crew maintained a routine to ensuring stability for an extremely hard and dangerous job—at the going rate of a dollar a day.

The cook's day began before first light. In darkness, he lit his lantern, built the cooking fire, put on the five-gallon coffee pot, and set up the Dutch ovens. Then he began to prepare the morning meal.

The basic meal on the drive was bread, meat, and beans—all washed down with gallons of piping hot coffee. On the northern ranges the bread was made of wheat flour, while in Texas and most of the southwest, cornmeal was the primary ingredient. Boiled rice loaded with raisins, called "moonshine," or "John Chinaman," was an occasional treat. "Salt hoss" (corned beef) also was available from time to time, and hoecake and flapjacks were always a popular item. Dried fruit—apples, peaches, and prunes—were served at least once a day. On every chuck wagon you could find gallon cans with some sort of syrup, usually "blackstrap molasses." The cowboy's sweet tooth is legendary.

Nobody argues with the idea that the cowboys had to have their java, or "mud," to get the day going. The coffee was almost always Arbuckle's, which came with a stick of peppermint packed in each one-pound can. The can usually bore an "XXX" brand. The cans cost eight cents a pound, if bought by the case. In the north it was sweetened with cane sugar, but on the southern ranges they used sorghum molasses. This particular regional variation originated late in the nineteenth century, when southern cattle prices fell so sharply that the owners couldn't sell range cattle for any price. Tough times called for strict economic measures; virtually all the southern outfits cut their sugar rations and began to provide their crews with the cheaper, readily available molasses.

Canned goods, also called "airtights," were pretty rare among the provisions on the wagons. Every now and then a trail boss might let a cook carry a few cases of corn, tomatoes, peas, or even milk, but these cans added too much weight and expense to an already heavy and costly load.

Cooks were paid considerably more than the riders, and were hired long before the drovers were ever signed on. The savvy trail boss often paid his cook wages for a month or two before he was to actually start the drive, to be certain that he could hold onto him. It was not unheard of for one ranch to try and steal the cook from another wagon outfit.

The cook was king and no one—not seasoned trail hand nor casual drifter—dared question the authority or overstep the welcome of the cook's domain. Everyone showed him respect. Because the outfit was usually gone so long, much depended on the cook, who was probably the drive's doctor as well as the father figure for many of the young cowboys. Consequently, he was indulged whenever possible. A drover could "mess" with the cook for only so long before the trail boss would step in and put an end to the problem, whatever it was. No boss wanted his cook to pick up and ride off some hundreds of miles away from the home range. Hungry cowboys, being paid so little to risk their lives, wanted and expected to be fed well. The trail boss had to see that they were well served. There were plenty of horse wranglers and punchers, but the number of first-rate wagon cooks was in short supply. So many of the cooks, maybe because they knew they were needed and perhaps because they worked such a rugged schedule, were pretty irritable. But they were, it seems, all colorful characters.

Meal service was simple. The cook set out the eating utensils, cups and plates on the raised deck, lined up the cans of salt, sugar (when it was available), and pepper, and yelled, "Come and get it," or some less printable invitation.

The men scrubbed up at a wash basin provided by the cook, using a community towel, that soon became pretty soggy and damn dirty. Each man helped himself to a plate, cup, and eating utensils, then lined up and took the meals from the various Dutch ovens. Maybe there was a "Sonofabitch stew," sourdough biscuits, red bean pie, or a vinegar cobbler. Hot tallow made good "sopping" for the bread or biscuits. After the plates were filled, the cowboys often sat on the ground, cross-legged, and ate, coffee cups on the ground beside them. There wasn't a whole lot of chatter at mealtime, but when they did talk, it was usually about the drive, the cattle, or the horses.

After the meal, the dishes were placed in the "wreck pan," and if time permitted, a quick smoke around the fire. Soon it was back into the saddle and on with their work—a twenty-four-hour, seven-day-a-week job.

As soon as the punchers left the cooking area and were back with the herd, the cook and his helper washed the dishes, tossed the bedrolls into the wagon, loaded the gear, hitched the team, and headed for the next camp, always on the lookout for good water and fuel, making sure that wherever they set up the next camp, it was an easy distance for the cattle to make before the next meal. If the trail boss or cook had been over the trail before, they might arrange for a specific spot up ahead. Once the site was selected, they set up camp and began preparations for the next meal, waiting for the herd to arrive with the hungry cowhands. The firepit was dug, pots and pans arranged, ingredients sorted, coffee started over the fire, and the Dutch ovens prepared. The process went on three meals a day, every day, for months. And despite the long day, the cook was often the last man to crawl into his bedroll at night. Before turning in, he would perform one final chore—pointing the tongue of the chuck wagon toward the North Star so the trail boss had a fix on direction in the morning. No matter how late the hour, before sunup the cook got started so the cowboys could have their breakfast as the light began to appear ever so faintly on the eastern horizon.

Today, the big cattle drives are over, and the cook spends most of the time at the ranch headquarters kitchen, where the facilities are convenient and modern. But the cook still rules the realm and still wants to be treated with respect. The meals are more varied, better balanced, and far more nutritious. Hungry cowboys have to be fed. There is no substitution for the good solid food. Ranch work remains hard, the weather is still unpredictable, and the hours haven't changed a whole lot. Good food has a way of making a cowboy, at least for the moment, forget that he is bone weary.

Matador Ranch chuck wagon (photo courtesy Southwest Collection, Texas Tech University, Matador Ranch photograph file #64).

GRUB PILE

WALT COBURN

From out the mess-tent's grimy door,
Making the cowboy's heart grow sore, Morn after morn, in the same
old style, Comes the cook's call of "Grub Pile."
To each cowboy it means the same,
No matter what may be his name;
In the morn's chill air it sounds a mile— That rasping cook's call of
"Grub Pile." How harsh it seems to the waking ear When one more
dream would be so dear! Ah! naught will ever reconcile The soul
to that old call, "Grub Pile."

From *Rhymes from a Roundup Camp*, Gem Publishing Company, Los Angeles,
California, 1926.

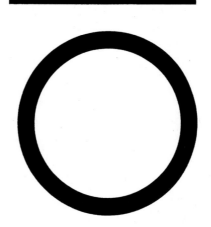

BARBER RANCH

CHANNING, TEXAS
DALE AND MARY ANN BARBER

SHOWING FOR FUN AND PROFIT

Driving around the Channing/Dumas area after dark leaves you with the impression that someone forgot to turn out all the Christmas lights. When the sun comes up, you are aware that all those lights are on one of the giant gas plants that are such an intricate part of the area's economy. The first gas well in the massive Panhandle-Hugoton Field was discovered just a few miles from the Canadian River in 1918. That 2,600-foot discovery well produced about five-million cubic feet of gas daily. This area still has one of the world's largest natural gas fields, produces two-thirds of the country's helium, and is in the center of the nation's largest grain sorghum producing region.

The Hartley County seat of Channing started out as the headquarters for the gigantic XIT Ranch and the original headquarters building still stands on Main Street. In addition to the XIT, the Matador Ranch also had an office in this city that is now not much more than a wide spot on the road between Dalhart and Amarillo. This country was home, too, to the old LX Ranch, another sprawling empire that covered some forty-five miles between Dumas and Amarillo—twenty miles wide and a range of over 1,000 square miles.

The Barber Ranch lies right in the middle of this rich country, on a Texas ranch road between Channing and Dumas. The Canadian River Breaks begin on the southern edge of the ranch, where the flat farm lands give way to the rugged terrain carved out by this once mighty river.

Dale and Mary Ann Barber have been at the ranch together since 1970. They met in Lubbock when Mary Ann was at Texas Tech and Dale, fresh out of college, was stationed at Cannon Air Force Base. They married in 1968, while Dale was still in the service.

Dale Barber of the Barber Ranch.

Dale comes from central Texas, where his dad ran a good-sized ranch. At Texas A&M, Dale earned a degree in veterinary medicine, though he never actually practiced this profession after he separated from the military.

THE FAMILY RANCH AND THE FAMILY

Mary Ann was raised on the old Edlin Ranch, and after college and the military, Dale and his bride decided life on the ranch would be more rewarding than setting up a new veterinary practice. So, when things broke right for the young couple, they headed back to Channing and the Edlin Ranch.

Today they have four children—two out on their own and two still at home. Brett, who is in his mid-twenties, lives in Lansing, where he shows cattle for the Agriculture School at Michigan State University. Terri, who is in her early twenties, works for the International Brangus Cattle Association and lives in San Antonio. Jason and Justin, twins approaching their teens, are at home and learning about the ranch, showing cattle, and rodeoing.

THE REGISTERED HERD

The Edlin Ranch was started in 1904 by Mary Ann's grandfather, who had come west from Kentucky. The ranch has been in the same family for over ninety years, and just as when Mary Ann was growing up, it is still a Hereford

Mary Ann Barber with her show Herefords, Barber Ranch.

operation. The family started running a registered herd in the 1950s. Mary Ann says that, "I always wanted to stay in ranching. If I wasn't in ranching, I'd probably be dead. That's all I wanted to do . . . I can't imagine doing anything else." Her mother, Anna Belle Edlin, still lives on the ranch, in a nice home of her own.

The Barbers run about 150 mother cows, producing valuable and highly regarded breeding stock, which they sell to other ranchers. They show throughout the West, and sell to ranches both inside and outside Texas.

Because the herd is relatively small and calving isn't a major production, the Barbers calve throughout the year, with their primary seasons being August to October and March and April. The calves are tattooed when they hit the ground, then branded when they are weaned. They use the Bar O brand. The O was the original Edlin Ranch brand; the bar over the O, Dale's addition.

THE COSTS OF TECHNOLOGY

As on most ranches, particularly when the family has been at it for some time, the Barbers have mixed feelings about the changes that are taking place and the future of Texas ranching.

According to Mary Ann, "everything has gone up in costs. It's harder to make a living and it's harder to make ends meet." Items like feed costs and taxes have skyrocketed. Dale remembers a time when you heard stories of ranchers buying a new pickup for ten calves. "Today you'd spend $20,000 for a good used one."

And there are other changes. "We still raise cattle, but to me it's changed a lot. It's so much more mechanized," says Dale. There are procedures like artificial insemination and embryo transplants, "that you didn't even dream of even twenty years ago." A veterinarian by trade, Dale has an interesting perspective on this new age of genetic engineering. He thinks that, "in the very near future, you'll be able to raise all steers or all heifers . . . "

But ranching is still enjoyable to the Barbers. Mary Ann says that the quality of life that they remember is still there and they both agree that a ranch is "still the best place to raise children."

And for all the mechanization, the Barber Ranch still gets most of its cattle work done from the back of a horse. They raise some and buy some, but they do have a couple of mares to breed so they can always raise a couple of foals.

WHY REGISTERED CATTLE?

Registered herds aren't as popular today as they were ten or fifteen years ago. "There are probably fewer families who do it as we do it," Dale explains. "Mainly it's a plaything for rich people, where we actually make our living from it." It's definitely cheaper and less work to run commercial herds, but "we've always run registered cattle and we enjoy doing it. We enjoy raising bulls and heifers and showing cattle." Mary Ann says she enjoys the competition because they are, in fact, competing against other people who raise bulls, "and the people that raise the best cattle are the ones that will survive."

Showing is very important for a registered breeder because it gets their cattle known. Their pickup becomes increasingly important as the Barbers travel the thousands of miles each year from Denver to Odessa to Fort Worth to San Antonio to Houston to Albuquerque—mile after mile after mile. They also haul the twins to the junior shows; in a few summer months they can easily clock 10,000 miles. All four of the Barber kids have participated, and, Dale says proudly, that "it's the life for all of them." Yet the ranch isn't big enough for all of the children to come home and make a living on the land.

PROUD OF THE CATTLE

The Barbers take great pride in their ranching operation and, in particular, the quality of their cattle. Though showing cattle is a necessary part of their business, it is also a part they enjoy. The show cattle are the ones that they actually take on the road. Dale tells of a trip to a show in Odessa, Texas, where a fellow came up to their cattle, looked them over, and asked if they had anything like it for sale back home on the ranch. When Dale told him that they had a half-brother to the steer, the cattleman said he would write out a check for one of them right on the spot. Mary Ann points out that, "If we stayed home and didn't haul and show and get them (the cattle) out to the public, nobody would know what we've got. It's the best advertising in the world."

RANCH KIDS AND CITY KIDS

Raising ranch kids can be a little trying if they are torn between the ranch and the city activities at their school. Unlike a lot of children who live in the city, the Barber children didn't compete much in sports. "We spend a lot of time with them showing, cattle and horses," their parents pointed out. "You can't hardly do both, and we get more and more coaches who want all the kids' attention and won't let them do both." Their daughter, Terri, is a good example of the pull between school activities and the ranch. She was forced "to either or. The coach put it that way." So she quit sports and continued showing her cattle.

The twins, as their visible bucking barrel clearly shows, are involved in 4-H rodeo.

KEEPING AT IT

Ranching is far from static. A good rancher is always trying to make things better—or at least not let the present problems overwhelm him. "You always look to the future and make improvements. We have prairie dogs and a turpentine weed that'll both take over the country if you don't have some kind of control." And, of course, they are always trying to improve their herds.

Each day is full. On an average summer day, Mary Ann explains, "one of the boys and I don't do anything . . . but work on show cattle. We wash and rinse them, train them, and break them to halter. And the other boy goes with Dale and they tend the A.I. (artificially inseminated) cattle . . . . We breed everything artificially, at least in the spring."

For Dale, farming takes up a good part of the summer, and chores like feeding the cattle, especially the weaned calves, and the twice-a-day feeding of the show cattle, are time consuming. You get the feeling that Dale doesn't mind these chores; he sees farming as a necessary part of ranching, and by far the most enjoyable part of their operation at the Bar O.

As we drove around the ranch in the pickup, Dale was obviously at home with the rugged terrain and the openness of the range. Everything fit into place. We talked about the land, the deer, and the quail, which the Barbers can hunt right on their ranch. Mary Ann is not a hunter because she's "too much of an animal person to hunt." She even jokes about selling her cattle to "only good homes." And when you see this attractive woman working in the pens with the stock, you just sense the commitment and pride she has in her work. In with several big steers, she is as relaxed as when we sat around the kitchen table over a cup of coffee.

RANCH QUAIL FOR DINNER

Mary Ann learned to cook from her mom, who cooked for pretty large crews, especially the harvest crews, when more farming was done on the ranch. Nowadays, Mary Ann cooks for the family and the occasional visiting judging teams from the various colleges, particularly Texas A&M, when they stop by. She likes to cook prime rib, but one of her very favorites, and a particular favorite of Dale's, is their "Smothered Quail." "It just falls off the bone—it's really good," says Mary Ann. You might not have the ready access they have to these delicate birds, but it's worth a little extra effort. Now go and get that quail and start cooking.

SMOTHERED QUAIL

6 quail
6 slices raw bacon or salt pork
1 cup butter
A few drops hickory smoke
Salt and pepper

Quarter the quail and split the breast. Salt and pepper to taste. Place the quail in a cast iron Dutch oven and put the raw bacon or salt pork over the quail, add a cup of butter and a few drops of liquid hickory smoke. Cover and cook at 250°F for six to eight hours.

Serve with vegetables and potatoes.

Serves four.

THE BAYLOR RANCH

SIERRA BLANCA, TEXAS
JANE BAYLOR AND
CATHI BAYLOR RUSH,
CO-OWNERS AND COOKS

SCRATCHING OUT A LIVING ON THE WEST TEXAS PLAINS

To be truthful, we did not visit the Baylor Ranch headquarters. We did however, visit the Scratch Ranch, which is leased by the Baylor family of Sierra Blanca and encompasses some 258 sections of fine West Texas ranching country. Our first stop in Sierra Blanca was at the county extension office, where the secretary, Ruthie Vance, told us that the Baylor Ranch was gathering cattle. She suggested we might be welcomed at the Scratch, and made a few phone calls to pave the way.

"The Scratch is twenty-eight miles north," Ruthie advised, then threw in the clincher: "You can't miss it." We pointed the RV north on Ranch Road 1111, wondering what kind of outfit would have part of their ranch called "Scratch." There had to be a story there somewhere. We mused about it as the RV rocked and rolled up FM 1111, a beautiful road that follows the contours of the country, taking the visitor past sotol, prickly pear, rainbow cactus, red yucca, cane cholla, dagger, sage, and a hundred other kinds of plants that dot the West Texas range.

We did not meet another vehicle on the twenty-eight-mile drive. Only an occasional horse or wandering cow reminded us that other creatures inhabited this part of the earth. Solitude is a way of life in West Texas, its high desert climate unlikely to attract many long-term residents.

THE SCRATCH

The one-lane dirt road to the Scratch Ranch is marked by a single sheet of thin metal, about two feet by eight inches. The inscription reads "Scratch." That's it. No welcome. No "No Trespassing." No nothing. Just "Scratch." The

Scratch headquarters, once an elegant home, is now a weathered and worn cow camp, lonely and forlorn in the cold harshness of winter. The elm trees are bare and the wind rattles the doors and shutters. A cow bawls in the distance and a horse whinnies from the horse trap. No humans are in sight. The fall roundup is underway.

A helicopter buzzed in from across the desert, hopscotching over the sagebrush. The pilot of the Robinson R-22, Scott Autry of Midland, is a modern day waddy specializing in gathering cattle when he's not checking pipelines or conducting deer surveys. Scott says gathering cattle with a helicopter is no different from gathering them by horseback. "You can just see more country, therefore you see more cattle, especially in this brush. These cattle are pretty spooky, so you gotta hang back. I love it. I've got the best job in the world. I work with the greatest people in the world, cowboys and cattlemen."

Scott kept the cowboys and cattlemen busy all afternoon, pushing cattle out of the brush with the R-22 while the cowboys rounded up strays, opened and closed gates, and fixed fences that the runaway bovies had ignored and run through. Meanwhile, the cowboys' dinner arrived in a Chevy Suburban, escorted by the Baylor Ranch cooks, Jane Baylor and Cathi Baylor Rush, accompanied by Cathi's four-year-old son, "Buster" James.

While Buster unwound from the trip, Cathi and Jane filled us in on the Baylor operation. "No one knows where the name 'Scratch' comes from," they started. "There used to be a well here called the Scratch Well. Our grandparents (James E. and Norfleet "Norty" Baylor) leased the Scratch Ranch in the early 1940s, about 165,000 acres, from the University of Texas."

As big as the Scratch Ranch is, the Baylors only have a small full-time crew—three men at the present, plus the manager, Cathi and Jane's brother, Tom. The ranch runs Angus-based F-1 crosses, using Brangus, Simmental, and some Gelbvieh bulls on their cows. "We try to keep an Angus base in our cows," the Baylors say. "We think Angus and Angus crosses are the way to go in this country."

This West Texas country takes a tough, self-sufficient cow to survive. Jane and Cathi say that in the high desert, they don't have the problems with flies, ticks, or diseases that are common in the lower, wetter country of eastern Texas. The soil here is very rich, and when it rains, the grass is strong and the cattle do well. The main problem on the Baylor Ranch is lack of water.

"There's no surface water on this ranch," Cathi says. "We do have dirt tanks which fill with water when it rains, but they dry up when there's long periods between rains. We have twelve wells and over one hundred miles of pipe. We've got a few windmills, but mostly electric, submerged pumps. We've put in one solar-powered pump, but so far that's proven to be an expensive project that we're taking a hard look at."

STARTING FROM SCRATCH

"Papa [Jim Baylor] was an old-time cow trader and ranched all over southern Texas with his father, J. E.," Cathi says. "He ranched at Carrizo Springs, Alpine,

Jane Baylor (left) and Cathi Baylor Rush (photo courtesy Baylor Ranch).

and near Durango in Mexico for a while. There was a time when they were burning up the roads between the three ranches. Ma [Barbara Baylor] wanted a permanent home. She got tired of traveling back and forth, so they settled here [at the Home Ranch] because of the good water.

"The Baylor Ranch has been their home for fifty years now. Jim still goes out every day to check the water and the pipelines. He's better then the mailman because it doesn't matter if it's 104 degrees or raining or snowing or sleeting, he's out checking the cows and the water. In the winter we call him "Nanook". Ma and Papa worked hard all their life and built up a pretty good ranch."

That's a tradition that the Baylors continue today. "I used to work more than I do now," Cathi says. "I still keep twenty five cows of my own and a few brood mares. But I don't get out ahorseback much anymore. None of us do as much riding as we'd like. The men are just too busy with water lines and fences. There's so much work that has to be done every day and only so many hours to get it done, it doesn't leave much time for riding, like we all love to do."

"We used to take lunch to the cowboys out in the pasture when we were working cattle, and still do at times, but it usually works out better to eat either

Jim Baylor (second from left) and Baylor Ranch cowboys (photo courtesy Baylor Ranch).

Left to right: Norfleet Baylor, Alvin Blalack Sr., J. E. Baylor, Mr. Ford from Kansas, Arthur Eardly, Pitt Martyn, and unknown—taken at Baylor Ranch, Carrazo Springs, Texas (photo courtesy Baylor Ranch).

at the main house or at the Scratch," Jane adds. "They fix themselves a big breakfast about 4:30 [A.M.], then eat lunch about 12:00 or 1:00, but sometimes don't get to eat until 4:00 or 5:00 [P.M.], depending on how things go with the cattle. By dark they're so doggone tired they don't want to eat." Understandable.

"It's hard to get this crew gathered up in one place," Cathi continues. "Usually they're all going separate ways. But like at this gathering, they're all here and it's easier for us to come over for lunch. These are a good bunch of guys. They don't do the dishes, but they always eat everything we set out."

On this day the girls set out pork chops, beans, cheesecake, iced tea, lemonade, homemade cake, and coffee. Coffee, the girls admit, is not their thing. "Coffee is a disaster with us," they say in unison. "We don't drink coffee so we don't know how to make coffee. We've asked several people [how to make coffee] but everybody gives us a different story so we just guess each time."

Jane and Cathi admit that cooking is not their favorite thing, but it's a job that has to be done, so they just double up and share the chores. They've been at it long enough that they've each developed their own expertise and have proven that two cooks don't necessarily spoil the broth; they just have to know who is doing what. Jane and Cathi have years of experience of cooking together.

COOKING FROM SCRATCH ON THE SCRATCH

"We've got so many old family recipes," Cathi says, "we've been talking about doing our own cookbook. We do 'most everything from scratch. Ma always said, 'You're cheating if you use anything from a box.' We cheat once in a while. In fact, we cheat a lot when we're cooking for ourselves. But when we're cooking

for crews, we try to feed 'em right. But grandma didn't cheat. Ever. Everything she cooked, she cooked from scratch."

Cathi and Jane live together in El Paso and do their shopping there. They buy in bulk, and because they're used to feeding hard working cowboys, they don't buy wimpy food. "You come here, you're gonna get cholesterol," Jane says. "We use real butter. Ma had a sign in her kitchen that said, 'Good food is made with lots of love and lots of butter.' There's been three generations of women cooking on this ranch and we ain't about to change our ways. We use a lot of our mother's and our grandmother's recipes. Some are well over a hundred years old."

"Jane is the one who will cook for fun," Cathi says. "I really don't like to cook; I just like to eat. Once in a while I'll bake a pie or a custard for dad. I do like to garden. My husband said all I can do is grow gourds. We do eat a lot of squash. I'll also cook main things like meat and potatoes, but I'm not at all domestic; I just like the ranch life."

BUT THE TIMES, THEY ARE A-CHANGING

After graduating from high school in 1973, Cathi attended New Mexico State University in Las Cruces and got a degree in Agricultural Education. Jane graduated from San Angelo State University and has been a steady part of the ranch since 1968. Even though Cathi is now attending University of Texas at El Paso, working on a teacher's certificate, both girls keep their hands in the ranching activities, because they say they love the life and the country.

"It usually starts raining in July," Jane says. "When we get rain, it really makes a lot of grass. And it's so pretty. There's a little yellow flower here we call yellow-top which is real good as horse and cattle feed. Our elevation here is about 4,500 feet, and even the summers are not bad. It'll get up to a hundred [degrees] and more, but it's dry. And I love it when it snows in the winter. It's so pretty. It covers the cactus and the sagebrush. It's just beautiful."

And remote. "Mom and I broke down one time [going into town from the Scratch]," Jane says. "And we didn't see another vehicle on that road until the school bus came by the next morning. We spent the whole night in that car." That gives a good indication of the sparseness of population around Sierra Blanca, a fact that has not gone unnoticed by some big cities.

"Used to, when it rained here, it was the most beautiful smell in the world," Jane continues. "So fresh and clean and pure. It was just intoxicating. Now it smells like New York City garbage, but it's worse [it's nauseating]. It's New York City sludge. Sewage. It's so sad. They ship it out by trains. They've bought an entire ranch and they use it just for a dumping ground. If it was only manure, it wouldn't be so bad. But this stuff is full of toxins and carcinogens, so we don't know what it's going to do to our kids. We're trying to get organized to fight it. We don't know how far we'll get, but we've got to do something. Our ranch is twenty-five miles from town, and when it rains, we can smell that sludge. It smells just like what it is. Shit. New York City shit. It just makes us sick."

The girls say that no one around Sierra Blanca was paying much attention when the company pushed the paperwork through to get the sludge dumping permits. Now the state of Texas is trying to open a nuclear dump site, but the local citizens are closely studying and monitoring that situation. "Once clever. Twice, never," they swear.

MEANWHILE, BACK AT THE SCRATCH

As the December sun starts to sink in the south, the cowboys come trailing in from the desert, pushing several bulls ahead of tired horses. The bulls are bawling and slinging slobber and pawing up the dry earth. Posturing. Making a stand. The cowboys close the gate behind them and peel off toward the saddle shed. It's windy and cold even though the sun has been shining brightly. The cowboys are wrapped in canvas and leather, hats pulled down low and tight, faces windburned, ruddy, and red. Exhaustion is near. Talk is limited.

After saddles are stripped and horses fed, the men file by a big cooler in the back of a pickup, and each grabs a can of cowboy Kool-Aid. They're covered with dust and stained with sweat, wanting nothing more than a meal and some rest. After guzzling a couple of beers to get their electrolytes back in balance, they grab plates, pile them high, and flop down in any available chair to eat, mostly in silence.

Dan French, who is running the work crew this fall, is happy with the day's work. He is talkative. "I'm the cowboss, I reckon," he says between mouthfuls. "But don't tell anybody. When you've got a crew as good as this one, they don't need no bossing. But the cattle today were pretty tawdry. We had some go through a few fences. I told the guys this morning, 'Just forget everything you know about cowboying. This [gathering with helicopter] is different. It's more like out-of-control team penning. Just hang back.'"

Thirty-four-year-old Tom Baylor is the ranch manager. Big and tall and tough, he's also still able to carry on a conversation after a hard day in the West Texas wind. A cowboy and rancher all his life, he's used to the demands of the job. "This is the third time we've used a helicopter to gather," he states. "It works out very well. Saves us a heck of a lot of time. We've got some big pastures here. One, the Sampson, is over 60,000 acres alone."

Tom says that during spring and fall roundup, he hires cowboys who do day work. The men provide their own horses, saddles, and transportation to the job and back. "They're all good, experienced hands. They know their jobs. They know cattle and they learn the country. We had a good gather today and we expect to have another one tomorrow. When we need cowboys, we hire the best."

Tom is constantly working on the wells, even drilling a few new ones and laying more water lines to provide more water for the ranch. More wells means he can extend the pastures. He is a very careful rancher, rotating pastures and resting them frequently. Additional wells will bring more land into use. Drinking-water on the Scratch is packed in from ranch headquarters. "The water here is full of gypsum," Tom says. "You can tell anyone who grew up here. They've all got gypsum stain on their teeth."

Minerals in the soil help grow trophy horns on the many antelope and deer of the Scratch and the Baylors have converted that natural resource into a cash crop. "Hunting is a big part of our business," Tom states. "We guide lots of antelope hunters. Several of our antelope have made the Boone and Crockett Record Book. Cathi and Jane cook for the hunters. We feed 'em breakfast, pack 'em a lunch, and feed 'em dinner. We have lots more antelope than deer."

And rattlesnakes. "We kill rattlesnakes all the time," Cathi says. "We were taught, 'You see one; you kill it.' We kill 'em with guns, rocks, sticks, pipes, anything we can get our hands on. Snakes are bad on livestock. I've seen horses and cows that were bitten on the nose and it's not a pretty sight. Their nostrils swell up and they can't breath and die a horrible death. We kill every snake we see."

There are those who eat rattlesnake, but not the Baylors. They much prefer beef. "It's all bone," Cathi says of rattlesnake. "It's not something I want to eat. Tom and I ate some one time. We didn't like it." On another occasion Tom, who is bilingual, was dining with a Mexican family and used the salt shaker extensively. Later he was told that the shaker contained ground-up rattlesnake. The family believed the potion would prevent cancer. Tom said it must be working because he feels fine. You'll feel fine too after sampling these fabulous recipes from the Baylor Ranch that have been handed down through four generations.

JANE'S GRAHAM BISCUITS

3 cups graham flour (whole wheat)

1 cup white flour

1 cup sugar

1 cup Crisco

2 eggs

2 teaspoons baking soda

2 cups sour milk (we use buttermilk, or 1 cup plain yogurt and 1 cup whole milk)

Throw all the ingredients in a large bowl. Use your hands to mix it well. Turn out on a well-floured surface, adding a little more flour as you prepare to roll it out. Use a rolling pin and roll out dough, cut and put on ungreased cookie sheet. Bake at about 375°F.

These are great for breakfast. Split them in half, toast and butter them, serve with your favorite preserves.

CATHI'S BAKED CUSTARD

4 cups milk

9 eggs

1 cup sugar

1 teaspoon almond extract

1 teaspoon vanilla

Scald milk, remove from heat. Separate egg yolks. Beat yolks and sugar together. Pour hot milk into egg mixture. Add almond extract and vanilla. Pour into loaf pan. Place pan in a larger pan with about an inch of water in it. Bake for about an hour at 350°F, until set.

Beat egg whites with a pinch of cream of tartar and sugar to taste (about one-third cup), until stiff. Pour meringue over custard. Return to oven and bake until meringue browns. Cool and refrigerate.

"My grandmother put peach leaves in the milk when scalding, when available. When she did this, she did not add almond extract. I've never tried this. The vanilla is my addition."

THE BC RANCH

Alpine, Texas
Becky Smith,
Cathy Fortenberry,
Karen Waggoner

RANCHING IN THE TRIANGLE OF THE BIG BEND COUNTRY

Alpine, the county seat of Brewster County, is a cornerstone in a beautiful triangle of mountainous towns in some of the best ranching country in the world—the very heart of the Big Bend country. Even by Texas standards, ranches in this largest county in the largest state in the contiguous United States run large. Brewster County encompasses more than 5,935 square miles—that's more geographic land area than in the entire state of Connecticut. The town of Alpine, founded in 1882, is surrounded by ranches, mountains, and mines, and is the home of Sul Ross State University. Alpine, Brewster County, and the Big Bend country are unique in every way. It was here we found one of the most interesting and beautiful ranches we visited—the BC.

The BC Ranch is located just on the outskirts of Alpine, but don't bother asking for directions. You may not be welcome. Not that the owner is antisocial, for you'll not find a more congenial person on earth than Becky (Rebecca) Smith. It's just that she's quite serious when it comes to running her ranch. Lately, she's been overrun by visitors—not your average, gawking tourists, but journalists.

The BC is doing wonderfully under Becky's careful guidance. The ranch has good looking cattle, sturdy fences and gates, and well-maintained pastures and buildings. The BC also has an all-female crew. That, in itself, makes it different from all other ranches we visited. It was that fact, picked up by various news networks, which prompted a stream of writers and camera crews to deluge the ranch. The media attention was so constant that it interfered with ranch work; that it did not sit well with Rebecca Smith. She'll tell you in a heartbeat that this ranch is her life and is a way of life for her segundo and cook, Cathy

Fortenberry, as well as their top hand, Karen Waggoner. The story of the BC is one of love and hardship and determination and the hard work of the ranching life.

Rebecca Smith was not born into ranching, but she is one of the most astute ranchers we visited in Texas. She told us she was born June 17, 1931, in the great state of Alabama, and graduated from Birmingham Baptist Hospital School of Nursing in March, 1953. For the next ten years, Becky nursed and spent a tour in the Air Force Nurse Corps as an operating room supervisor. She says she chose nursing as a career because of the unlimited job possibilities it offered.

In 1964, Becky came to Alpine, Texas, to visit friends and says she fell for the old adage: "If you wear out a pair of shoes in Big Bend country, you'll always come back." "I did and I'm still here. Just packed up and moved here." At first she continued nursing in the local hospital, then started filling in at the Alpine Veterinary Clinic, and eventually became a full time veterinary assistant. It was there she met the original owner of the BC Ranch, eighty-one-year-old Perry Cartwright.

"He loved those white-faced cattle," Becky recalls, choking back tears. "He loved the Herefords above all others and he instilled that love and appreciation in me. He brought a little dogie bull calf to the clinic and told me, 'I have something for you, if you want it.' Out in the back of his pickup, with all four legs tied up, was the prettiest red calf with the prettiest white face you'll ever see. He was a stocky little thing but I picked 'im up and took 'im inside and weighed 'im. It was the first calf I'd ever touched. He weighed fifty-four pounds and he was all mine."

Her nurturing instincts and nursing training kicked in. "We made him up a formula and I named him Perry. We had the best time. I beam just sitting here thinking about him and some of the stuff he pulled. I put him in a pen behind the clinic and came over every four hours to feed him; at 10:00, 2:00, and 6:00 at night, rain or hail, sleet or snow. I raised that calf just like he was a baby."

Which was good not only for Perry, the calf, but for Perry, the rancher, and as it turned out, good for the nurse. "He had no wife and no children and had been through good times and hard times on this ranch. He taught me everything I know about conservation, about the breeds, grazing capacities, pasture rotation, how to look at a cow or calf or bull and tell about their general health and well being. Perry Cartwright was more than a cowboy: he was a cowman. He was my mentor and I'll never forget him. He was way ahead of his time, ranching in this country. I've been using his methods of ranching for years and some are just beginning to be accepted out here." Like creep feeding calves and caking cows.

"There's lots of poisonous weeds in this country, and if you don't supplement your cows in the winter, sooner or later you're going to get your tail in a crack." Becky once lost nearly a third of her herd because of a deadly combination of salt with copper, coupled with cows eating secenici weed. She has a hard time talking about those hard times, so she is wont to concentrate on the good times. Like things she learned from Perry.

BC Ranch crew, (left to right) owner and operator Rebecca "Becky" Smith, Karen Waggoner (sitting on gate), and foreman Cathy Fortenberry (photo courtesy Becky Smith).

"We feed our cows alfalfa cubes. They love it. We found some of the older cows weren't doing so good on the breeder cubes. They're too hard for those older cows to handle. But with the alfalfa cube, their saliva melts it right away and you can just see the contentment on those old girls' faces."

Becky takes equally good care of her younger cows. "I personally calf out the first-calf heifers. Cathy and Karen feed and handle the cows, but I'm in there with those heifers during calving season." To make calving season easier on everyone, the BC feeds alfalfa hay about 10:00 in the evening. "It works," she swears. "I tried it and it works and I'm still doing it. We haven't had a half dozen calves born at night since we went on this program. It works well for us women."

Becky hired Cathy in 1980, when Perry was still alive. "I was getting older, too, and doing all the feeding and the calving and the calf pulling. I had to have some help." Becky says she'd known Cathy, a farm girl who loves to work outside, for several months. Her presence has been of great benefit to the ranch. "She keeps things tied together. She's the foreman."

Perry was ninety-two when he passed away in 1981, and in 1985 Becky hired Karen Waggoner, another friend who has proven almost indispensable. "She had a fantastic job with the power company around Dennison making good money, but she was laying her life on the line every day by working on power lines, hanging off towers, crawling down into cylinders. And she could weld." A handy skill around any ranch. In fact, some ranches require ranch hands be able to weld, and Becky needed a real ranch hand.

"She came down to visit one summer and said, 'I'll be back if you'll hire me.' I told her there was no way I could even pay her close to what she was making, but she said she didn't care. She had to get out of where she was. She's here now and has been a tremendous help. She's done all the welding on the ranch and she can drive trucks and tractors and can ride a horse with the best of 'em."

MULES HELP FEED THE CATTLE

Like many ranches in Texas today, less work is being done on horseback at the BC. Early on, they tried trucks. "Perry had always used pickups except for roundups. But they started making pickups lighter and lighter and more expensive. We were wearing out a truck every three years. This ranch is split. Four sections across the Fort Davis Highway are rocky and rough. It's a thirty-six-mile round-trip to feed cattle on this place. If we got three years out of a truck we were doing good. That's ridiculous." So the BC went to mules. Real mules.

"That lasted about a year. It was a dandy deal. Our wagon had rubber tires and we put bows on it so the feed would be covered. But if you're gonna have mules you gotta work the tar out of 'em and we weren't doing that. The longer we had 'em the friskier they got. Then they ran away. First time with the girls in the wagon and the second time with just the blue heelers enjoying the ride and the girls were afoot. So we went to Kawasaki mules."

Kawasaki mules? "Don't laugh. They're four-wheel, all-terrain vehicles that cost less than half as much as a pickup. They've got a little bed to haul feed or tools and they get more than twenty miles per gallon. They have saved this ranch a tremendous amount of money. I've got ranchers calling me from all over asking what I think about my mules." A lot, but not as much as she thinks about her Herefords.

"We run a commercial Hereford operation. We raise all our replacement heifers and we hand pick our bulls. I can tell a good bull prospect by his conformation. By the way he carries himself. A good bull has a certain pride in the way he walks. The girls see a good bull calf and call him a little hunk."

The ranch puts the big hunks out with the cows for about ninety days in May, June, and part of July. Calves are born from mid-February to early April, then the spring roundup gets underway—a period of intense work where all hands, including the cook, turn out.

"We use only horses during spring and fall roundups," Becky says. And only women. "That started the last year Perry was alive. He asked if I thought I could put together a crew for fall roundup. I just got on the phone and starting calling friends. That first roundup we had about fifteen women and it took us about twelve days to get it done. Now we still have about the same fifteen women come twice a year but we get the job done in three days." That takes a little organization.

"You've got to be organized. Roundups are a busy time." Another reason for not wanting visitors around. "I've got to figure out what to feed all these women while they're here. I've got to get the trucks lined up for shipping. There's chores for everyone."

Becky does the castrating and Cathy does the dehorning. "We used to use those old spoons (a dehorning tool) and it was a bloody mess. Now we use an electric dehorner and it works great. No blood. No flies. No maggots. Just a little scar which will hair over in a few weeks and you'll never know it was there. I love these cattle and I want them handled gentle."

Which is the very reason for the all-girl crew. "There's no animosity toward men," Becky says. "None. But women will follow my orders. They have more patience and they're gentler." And they're all friends. Translation: they work cheap. "I try to pay for their gas over and back. And I feed 'em and furnish 'em all the Miller Lite beer they can drink. We have a ball. There's nothing like friendship."

Except maybe running your own ranch. But that ain't all fun and fishing either. "We work hard and we play hard. I love to fish. Every summer I put my pontoon boat on Armstead Lake and go fishing. And I have family in Alabama I still like to visit. Even a rancher has to take a little time off."

But that's not as easy as it sounds. "We only get one paycheck a year, so we have to be careful. If I lose a single calf, that cuts into our profit. This isn't a real large ranch but it is a real good ranch. We just have to pay attention to what we're doing all the time. We're barely making a living. And that's all you do ranching. But it's a way of life. A hard life. But it's our life. It's great. We love it."

So that's the way it is on the BC; working hard and loving it. Riding and roping and relaxing are all parts of the cowgirl's life. And so is cooking. Cathy, the foreman, also guides hunters during deer season and feeds the crews on the BC. While we were visiting, she was guiding deer hunters, getting up at 3:30 in the morning and not returning until 10:30 in the evening. She sends us one of her favorite recipes which is a favorite at their all-girl roundups and should be a hit at your outfit too.

CATHY'S EASY BBQ BEEF BRISKET

1 beef brisket, any size
Liquid smoke
Garlic salt
Salt
Pepper

Place brisket in roasting pan, fat side up. Pierce brisket entirely with fork. Cover brisket completely with lots of liquid smoke, garlic salt, salt, and pepper as desired. Cover. Cook in 150 to 250°F oven. Cook very slowly, six to ten hours, depending on the size of the cut.

Pierce with a fork. When meat comes out with fork, it's done.

Let brisket cool completely, or chill. Then slice against the grain.

Reserve juice to pour over meat to prevent drying.

Serve with or without barbecue sauce.

BIG CANYON RANCH

SANDERSON, TEXAS
HERMAN AND MILDRED COUCH

BUILDING A BOUNTIFUL LIFE IN BIG CANYON

West of the Pecos River and the infamous old frontier town of Langtry—where Judge Roy Bean held court in his saloon—you enter the high, dry country of what is known as the Lower Trans-Pecos, an area of rocky limestone mountains and plateaus broken by the steep canyons of the Rio Grande and Pecos River. In the late 1800s, when cattlemen first came into this country, they found grass stirrup-high to a tall horse. A perfect place to live, ranch, and raise livestock.

Mid-afternoon, we wandered into Sanderson, a thriving center of agricultural commerce in lower Terrell County, and stopped at the Kerr Mercantile, the most prominent structure in town. We inquired as to cooks and cowboys in the area and were referred to the town's most outstanding rancher, Judge Harrison. Though his Honor was busy, his friend (and a descendant of one of the county's original cowboys), Will Murrah, introduced us to Herman Couch, manager of the Big Canyon Ranch, one of Terrell County's largest.

Herman Couch is eighty-five, retired, and lives in a beautiful home on the north side of Sanderson with Mildred, his wife of fifty-four years. Mrs. Couch was away visiting friends and Herman was entertaining a few friends of his own. He has a well-stocked bar just suited to the occasion. He's also a talented storyteller, and this day he's spinning a few yarns. Herman Couch has seen an awful lot of cowboying, a lot of changes in cowboying, tough times and tougher men, women, horses, and cattle. After seven decades as a cowboy in the Lower Trans-Pecos, Herman says he's about seen it all.

Herman Couch, Big Canyon Ranch, Sanderson, Texas, circa 1940 (photo courtesy Herman Couch).

Big Canyon Ranch cowboys, Herman Couch second from left, circa 1940
(photo courtesy Herman Couch).

TEN DOLLARS A MONTH AND FOUND

"I came out here in 1924," he says, pausing to take a swig from his tall glass. "I was fifteen. Just a big old kid. Didn't know nothing. Nothing but hard work. That's about all I've ever known. But I ain't done too bad. If I had to do 'er over, I don't know where I'd start." In this life, Herman started in Menard, "moving there when I was a year old. I was born at Zephyr, Brown County, Texas." His parents separated a year later and soon launched him into the big, wide world; ready or not.

"Damn near died in the first grade," he recalls. "Went to school in Fort McKavett. They had a little store, a saloon, and a school. That was it. And they had that damn diphtheria there that year. Everybody had it. Old doctor used to come around and give shots. Didn't take me long to get enough of that." So Herman left Fort McKavett after a single season and began cowboying. Well, not right from the git-go.

"I did just about anything I could to get by. Open gates. Cut wood. Pack water. Anything. I bet I opened a million gates for them Russell brothers when I first came here." When Couch came to the Big Canyon Ranch it was owned by N. H. Corder and R. R. Russell. The ranch was originally founded in 1886 by Andrew and J. J. Dull, steel manufacturers from Pittsburgh who traded rails to the Texas-Mexican railroad for land in the productive and beautiful Big Canyon, at the base of Iron Mountain, twenty-three miles north of Sanderson.

The ranch was sold in 1905 to a consortium that included the Russell brothers. When that corporation was dissolved, the ranch was split eighteen different ways, though it still is one of the largest in the county. When young Herman hired on at Big Canyon, the term "big" really suited it. "Back then all the sheep were under herders. There were no fences in this country. No trucks. We did everything ahorseback. My first job was helping a guy take care of the herders. They paid me ten dollars a month and I was damn glad to get it."

Herman lasted about a year as a camp tender, but hard times hit and he was cut loose. "Things were tough all over," Couch recalls. "I just hung around an old set of pens there by the road until some outfit came by with a bunch of cattle. It was old Monte Corder and he asked me what I was doing out here and I told him I was looking for a job. He said, 'You got a saddle?' I said, 'Yeah, I got one with an iron stirrup on one side and I don't remember what's on the other.' Well, he hired me right there."

WAGING WAR ON COYOTES

He probably felt sorry for a kid who didn't even know how his saddle was rigged. But though Herman had abandoned formal education, he quickly learned the cattle business. "They were shipping cattle to Oklahoma. They used to go up there in March and burn off that country and in April would ship up cattle to fatten up on that new grass. If they had more than three car loads, they had to send a man with the stock and they sent me. I stayed with them until '27."

It was then that the young cowboy took a hiatus and went west, to Tombstone, Arizona. "Got there just in time to see 'em kill two people so I just hopped another freight and come back to Texas." Couch cowboyed for the West Pyle Cattle Company near Longfellow until 1929 then returned to Sanderson and to working for Tom Russell. "He practically raised me."

Russell liked the young cowboy so well that Herman was allowed to run some cattle of his own. He later became foreman of both Big Canyon Ranch and Rocking R Ranch at Eldorado, Texas, which was then owned by the Russell Estate. It wasn't an easy life. "First lamb crop I had we sold for two dollars a head. Coyotes were so bad you couldn't hardly raise a lamb to market size. They were bad on calves too. People say a coyote won't kill a calf. I've seen 'em do it. Be two or three of 'em. They'll circle that old cow till she chases one, then the others will run in and get that calf. I seen 'em."

Herman said they also had Lobo wolves in the country at the time, though they were all but gone by the early 1930s. The coyotes were a different story. The ranches would hold drives in an attempt to kill them. "Be thirty-five to forty men, all ahorseback and all in a line," Herman explains. "We'd just make a sweep and shoot anything that moved. We killed lots of coyotes that way." Herman still has an old bolt-action 30.06 rifle, serial number four, that was given to him by W. L. Barler, a former Texas Ranger in Terrell County.

A MULE WRANGLER NO MORE

Herman is still in the sheep and goat business. He used to use the old sheep to make enough money to feed his cows. "Mr. Russell said, 'You just take this bunch of calves and pay us when you sell 'em.' So I did. When the steers were past two, I sold 'em for fifty dollars a head and had the rest free and clear.

"I seen lots of changes. Lots of 'em. We used to drive everything to town to ship. Sometimes them calves be halfway here before we got 'em settled down. And them mules. We like to have never got them dirty buggers shipped."

When Herman became foreman of Big Canyon, the ranch was famous—or perhaps infamous—for its mules. "They'd make us use damn mules to wrangle on. Scary as hell. Them mules'd get to going along in the dark, hear something on one side and maybe spook sideways into a hole on the other side. I didn't like 'em. Mules will kill coyotes, but they'll damn sure kill lambs, too. I got rid of all of 'em."

Herman says his mule drive would going pretty good for a ways, "then one of them dumb mules turned his head sideways and brayed and the whole bunch scattered like quail. We finally got 'em rounded up and headed back to town. They had just paved this road through here and them mules wouldn't cross that blacktop. No way. They'd balk and bray and break and run. We wore out some pretty good horses before we got rid of them mules."

BAD BRONCS AND A BAD BREAK

Some pretty good horses have caused Couch some pretty good wear and tear over the years. "Back during the war [WW II] you couldn't hire a cowboy nowhere," Herman recalls. "The army had 'em all. There was just me and one boy working this whole outfit. We was worming sheep and I went to jump a big old ditch and the horse didn't quite make it and throwed me off and broke this leg." Herman pulls up his pants to reveal a human leg shaped like to a dog's hind leg, featuring a seventy-degree angle just below the knee.

"I musta laid there four to five hours before the boy come looking for me. He said, 'I can't get no truck or nothing over there, what're we gonna do?' I said, 'If you can help me get on that damn horse, we'll go in that way.'" Herman laid around for three months, healing himself. He only recently sought medical advice. "One doctor wanted to go in and build me a new leg, but it don't bother me much; just a little here lately."

GRANDMA TO THE COOKIE GREMLINS

Recently, Herman and Mildred and the two other life-tenants at Big Canyon, Lewis and White, leased the ranch to the Couch's son, Tom. For the last twelve or thirteen years, the Couch's have lived in Sanderson and say they only go to the ranch when needed. Herman says Mildred is one of the best cooks in either of the two counties and has always enjoyed cooking, a fact that she readily confirms. "Times were pretty hard fifty-four years ago," Mildred begins. "But when we first married, Herman and I were working for the same ranch we now have an interest in.

"We were paid forty dollars a month, but we never worried about being poor. I didn't mind the cooking and the housekeeping. I've worked hard all my life. Cooking and cleaning was my part of the ranch chores. I cooked for fifteen to twenty men when extra labors were needed. I cooked on a big wood [burning] stove; no running water and no electricity, but somehow I always came up with plenty of food."

"Grandma" Couch continues to cook for large numbers. "We have a son and a daughter [both adopted], five grandchildren and one great-granddaughter. They are the light of our lives. I don't see how people live without children." When access to her grandchildren is not imminent, Mildred bakes big batches of cookies and distributes them to neighborhood youngsters. "Oh yes," she continues, "I bake for all the kids. We'll have 'em over and have a big party. They call me 'Grandma.'"

And so will you after you sample her favorite "old cake". This is from a cook who cooked for years over a fireplace and has never owned a microwave oven or a dishwasher.

ORANGE CHIFFON CAKE

2¼ cups flour

1½ cups sugar

3 teaspoons baking powder

1 teaspoon salt

½ cup cooking oil

5 egg yolks, unbeaten

¾ cup juice from two oranges (water can be added)

3 tablespoons grated orange rind

1 cup egg whites (from about 7 or 8 eggs)

½ teaspoon cream of tartar.

Preheat oven to 325°F. Sift flour, sugar, baking powder, and salt into mixing bowl. Make a well in the mixture and add oil, egg yolks, orange juice, and rind. Beat with a slotted spoon until smooth.

Beat egg whites and cream of tartar in large bowl until whites form very stiff peaks, or three to five minutes with electric mixer at high speed. DO NOT UNDER BEAT.

Pour egg yolk mixture slowly over beaten egg whites, folding just until blended. DO NOT STIR. Pour into ungreased tube pan. Bake fifty-five minutes at 325°F, then increase heat to 350°F. Bake ten to fifteen minutes more, or until top springs back when lightly touched.

Turn upside down over neck of bottle or funnel. Let hang until cool. Loosen from sides of pan with knife or spatula. Hit pan on table to loosen.

(This is a mighty good recipe from a mighty good cook. But wait, there's more.)

FROSTING FOR CAKE

⅓ cup soft butter or margarine

3 cups sifted, powdered sugar

3 teaspoons cream or orange juice

1½ teaspoons vanilla

Rind of one lemon, grated

Blend butter and sugar. Stir in cream or orange juice and vanilla. Beat until creamy. Spread on cake.

"I have had this recipe for over fifty years. Got it off a sack of Betty Crocker flour and have used it and modified it and loved it. It is a treasure to me." And it will be to you. Enjoy.

BOIS D'ARC RANCH

MARATHON, TEXAS
BIDDY AND PAT MARTIN

RANCHING IN THE HISTORIC MARATHON BASIN

East of Alpine, in the center of Big Bend country, the landscape opens up into the Great Marathon Basin. The town of Marathon is home to about 800 residents, though this number balloons during tourist season. Marathons lies at the crossroads of Highways 90 and 385, a major route to Big Bend National Park.

Geologists say that primitive man lived in this Chihuahuan Desert region centuries before the white men arrived. When settlers came to the Marathon Basin, the area was controlled by Indians, and in 1879, the United States Army established Fort Pena to patrol the frontier. The town of Marathon grew up in 1882, around sidings of the Texas and New Orleans Railroad, and was named by a ship's captain who said the area reminded him of Marathon, Greece, an ancient town on the plains northeast of Athens.

We pulled into Marathon one sunny afternoon shortly after Thanksgiving and parked in front of the predominant landmark in town, the Gage Hotel. Texas cattle baron Alfred Gage, who owned a 500,000-acre ranch in the Marathon Basin, figured he needed a proper place to stay whenever he left his residence in San Antonio to visit his holdings around Marathon. Mr. Gage apparently liked to travel in style, and built the Gage Hotel in the early 1900s. It features thirty-seven rooms, a huge kitchen, a separate dining area, and a cool "placita" (court yard). Today, the Gage Hotel is on the National Register of Historic Places.

J. P. and Mary Jon Bryan of Houston purchased the Gage Hotel in 1978. They have kept the Old West decor and have managed to maintain the feel of Texas hospitality and history. The Gage was, and still is, a popular place for cowboys and cattlemen to meet and exchange tales of ranching. It was there we met third-generation Texas rancher Biddy Martin. He was talking to a second-generation rancher who was hard of hearing and didn't talk much. But Biddy did.

RUNNING SHEEP, CATTLE, AND GOATS, AND FIGHTING THE COYOTES

Biddy's father was called "Bit" Martin; a nickname for little bit, a common Texas phrase. Biddy was called "Little Biddy," which was mercifully shortened to Biddy. "I was born on a ranch near Del Rio in 1928," Biddy begins. "Dad worked on ranches all his life and we moved to Glenn Springs where he went to work for Boye Babb. I started drawing a man's wages in 1939. Working sheep. All horseback. Made $2.50 a day. Not a helluva whole lot of money. Just a helluva whole lot of work. There's always something to do to a sheep." And goats.

"We had lots of goats. They had to be worked too. We'd work sheep just like we would cattle. We'd go out with a chuck wagon and a crew, stay two or three days in one spot, then move to another. [There was] always something to do." Biddy said after the drought of the 1950s, a lot of ranches sold off their sheep. Lack of water has always been a problem in the 4,000-foot-high Marathon Basin, but coyotes were the clincher in many ranchers' decisions to sell.

"Coyotes put a lot of people out of the sheep business," Biddy recalls. "It was a domino effect. When everybody had sheep, everybody killed coyotes. When a ranch sold their sheep, the coyotes went to the next ranch and would make it twice as hard on that outfit. I figured if my neighbor wasn't killing coyotes, at least he was feeding 'em. It made it easier on everyone."

Another big concern of stockmen all over the West at the time was screw worm infection. "If a critter got cut or scratched, blow flies would lay eggs, which hatched out as maggots. Maggots eat the flesh of animals and will kill 'em quick." During that period, ranches employed lots of cowboys and cowboys used lots of horses and did lots of riding and lots of roping.

"Those things killed lots of livestock," Biddy recalls about the screw worm days. "I was foreman on the Gage outfit and we'd hire students from Sul Ross [State University in Alpine]. We'd have a different crew every day—all those that didn't have classes and those that were cutting classes. They were good hands. They were mostly ranch-raised boys who knew their way around stock. My own two boys were in high school at the time and even they were in the crew.

"I remember doctoring cattle on the Gage Ranch all day. If you didn't ride at least thirty miles per day, you weren't getting much done. Sometimes we'd change horses two, three times a day, and most always two times a day. We'd try to get back over the same ground once a week to see if we'd missed anything. We had 101 windmills on the ranch and had a full-time windmill man. I remember one time he quit and I'd ride cattle half a day and and fix windmills half a day."

Ranching partners Pat and Biddy Martin, Bois d'Arc Ranch, Marathon, Texas.

THE WAY IT WAS

Ah, the good old days. Nowadays, Biddy spends a lot of time drinking coffee at the Gage. The sun was a distant memory when we left the hotel that bears the name of the brand he rode for all those years. We met back there the next morning at daybreak, as the sun cast long red streaks over the few clouds hanging above the hotel. "Beautiful sunrise, ain't it," he says. "I love to see the sun come up. Lots of people ask me, 'Did you see that beautiful sunset?' I tell 'em, 'Yea, but did you ever see it come up?' Lots of people never do."

We ask if he thinks it is going to rain. "If it was anywhere but Marathon, it'd already be raining," he replies. Biddy knows his country. He came to the Marathon Basin in 1937 and married Pat Shely in 1948. After coffeeing up at the Gage, we adjourn to the Martins' modest house in town.

Pat Shely Martin was born in a hospital in San Antonio because her mother was small and the family was concerned about the delivery of the child. Pat's paternal grandparents came to the Marathon Basin in 1901 and settled at a springs south of Marathon. Her grandfather was one of the first county commissioners of Brewster County. "Our brand (the Heart Half Circle) was recorded in the 1920s by my grandfather, T. M. Shely, and his sons," Pat tells us. "My father, Charles Shely, retained the brand and now we have it on our ranch."

Pat's mother was born in a jail cell in Alpine. Her grandfather Shoemake was a deputy sheriff in Alpine and her grandmother cooked for the prisoners. "He cowboyed around Alpine a lot of years," Pat says of her maternal grandfather. "Then he got into the law. He was in the customs service and was stationed at El Paso. I remember him telling about laying on the canals watching for smugglers."

Pat says the Shelys came to Texas from Tennessee after the Civil War and settled around San Antonio. In the early 1900s, her grandparents drove sheep into New Mexico. "Grandmother said when they got to the summer pasture, it was still freezing cold and there were dead, frozen sheep lying all over the bedground. She told grandpa, 'I ain't staying here.'" So the Shelys moved southeast of Marathon at the end of a railroad siding near Bois D'arc Springs. "My mother and father were married there in 1918," Pat recalls. "They had sheep, and when I was about ten, they brought in Angora goats. The goats weren't used to this country and would get tangled in the catclaw trees and couldn't get out. We'd have to ride every day and get the goats out [of the catclaw]."

YOU CAN FIND A COWGIRL, BUT A COWBOY? MAYBE

At first, Pat and her cousin Fred, who lived nearby, would ride stick horses around the yard and in the pasture by the house. Pat says it wasn't too long before she was riding with the men, doing the same work. There was no discrimination when it came to work; only when it came to business. "I used to get so mad. Whenever a buyer or anyone important came, I'd have to go to the house."

And the house was not where this little cowgrirl wanted to be. Still isn't. "I'm not a housekeeper. I never was. Even now I'd rather be out with Biddy, even if it's just opening gates or something like that." On one occasion, Pat probably saved Biddy's life. He tells the story. "We had a big old Brangus bull that kept getting out on the neighbors. He'd get out and we'd go get him and he'd get out again. I was gonna ship 'im so we went out to gather 'im up and he ran into a little thicket and we couldn't get 'im out.

"I was on a young horse and rode in front of him and he came out of there and caught that horse by surprise and hit it right in the brisket. Picked us both up and carried us about seventy-five or eighty feet and dumped us in a ditch. I never thought about quitting that horse. I've always been hurt worse by getting off a horse than staying on and I wasn't about to get down with that damn bull there. I stayed on. I landed under the horse. It knocked the wind out of me and I knew I was hurt bad. I'd never been in a hospital before, but I knew that's where I belonged."

Pat was rode her good grey mare over and Biddy pulled himself up on the stirrup leather, then walked alongside the horse to the truck. He indeed needed to go to the hospital. "I broke every rib on my right side and bruised my hip so bad, it still ain't right." Biddy says he has no animosity against the bull; such wrecks are all a part of a cowboy's life. While it is a life that he he loves, he also recognizes it's not for everybody.

"You can't hardly find a good cowboy today. It don't pay enough. Cowboys today cowboy because they like it. It's just like being a rancher. We ranch because we like it. It's our life. If I could work cattle every day, that's what I would do. I don't care about driving around in a pickup." But after the bull wreck, Biddy had to spend more time in a pickup, so he bought the best. A new Dodge. With power everything. As they say in the auto business, loaded.

RIDING THE EVER-CHANGING RANGES

"We spend so much time in a pickup anymore, I figured we might as well get a good one. 'Course it cost more'n the house did." Biddy and Pat have three houses. One on the main ranch, one in town, and one at their other ranch. They split their time between the three places, while their son runs the ranch. They run Brangus crossbred cattle and take in deer hunters during season. Does Pat cook for the deer hunters? "No way. Those guys are on their own. I hardly cook for Biddy, even though you can't tell that by looking at him. I just don't do housework. I'm an outside person. Supper around here is likely to be a pot of beans, some potatoes, and beef. I fry a lot of steak and make mashed potatoes and gravy. I look for something fast and easy."

The Martins say that they have witnessed many changes in ranching in their lifetime, and continue to look for less time-consuming ways to work. "We never had a horse trailer when I was young," Pat remembers. "We did everything ahorseback. I was raised during the Depression, but I don't remember being poor. We had a big garden and always had fresh meat. We didn't go to town very much. Now we practically live in town."

Biddy says the biggest change he's seen in ranching is the type of cattle. "Used to be, everybody here ran Herefords. Now it's mostly Brangus or Brahman or some crossbred from those breeds. Eared cattle. And we haul horses a lot more than we used to. Everybody's got trailers now. The biggest thing was the eradication of screw worms. We don't have to ride as much, don't have to doctor as much, don't need as many cowboys. We do still need good cowboys. We always will."

And those cowboys will always have to eat. Here's Pat's favorite recipe. She says it's easy to fix and people seem to love it. She calls it Mississippi Mud Cake. We call it Marathon Mud Cake. Eat and enjoy.

MARTIN'S MARATHON MUD CAKE

2 sticks butter or margarine

½ cup cocoa

2 cups sugar

4 eggs, slightly beaten

1½ cups flour

Pinch of salt

1½ cups nuts, chopped

1 teaspoon vanilla

1 cup miniature marshmallows, or
  enough to cover top of cake

Melt butter and cocoa together. Remove from heat and stir in sugar and eggs. Mix well. Add flour, salt, nuts, and vanilla. Mix well. Spoon batter into a thirteen-inch x nine-inch pan and bake at 350°F for thirty-five to forty-five minutes.

Sprinkle marshmallows on top of warm cake and let stay a few minutes in oven with the heat turned off. Cover with frosting.

MUD CAKE FROSTING

½ stick margarine

1 box powdered sugar

½ cup whole milk

½ cup cocoa

1 teaspoon vanilla

Soften margarine and add milk, cocoa, powdered sugar, and vanilla. Beat until mixture is smooth, then ice the cake. Yum, yum.

BRIDWELL WEST RANCH

ADRIAN, TEXAS
GENE AND ETHEL ELLIS

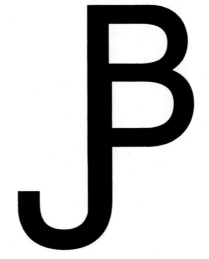

RANCH COOK AND CORPORATION

The Llano Estacado, or staked plains, is one of those dominating geological areas of the West. The area has been the subject of a number of major photo essays. It is also the site of one of the most dramatic scenes in *Lonesome Dove*, the place where Gus McCrae holds off Blue Duck's comancheros by killing his own horse and using it for a barricade. Almost all of the Texas Panhandle lies within its boundaries. The fortress-like appearance of its escarpment causes very distinct weather patterns. Nomadic Indians and untold numbers of buffalo herds dominated this huge plain when Vasquez de Coronado's expedition first explored the area in 1541. It wasn't until well into the nineteenth century that it became a center for cattle ranching. Much of the fabled XIT ranch was contained within its borders, and today cattle ranching is still an important industry on the flat, grassy plain.

As you rise out of New Mexico and reach the Llano Estacado, one of the first ranches you come to, after leaving Glenrio on the road to Amarillo, is the Bridwell West Ranch, a large cattle outfit. Heading north through the main gate off Interstate 40 and onto a dirt road to the headquarters, there are horses and cattle grazing freely. If you ever wanted to see the "wide open spaces," this would be as good a place as any to start. In addition to the horses and cattle, this ranch is loaded with mule deer and quail.

Along the road, you pass loading and shipping corrals, and windmills; only occasionally do you feel the intrusion of man. The first building you'll see is the ranch headquarters; otherwise, the environment is virtually unchanged.

Once you arrive at headquarters, you are taken by the number of horse and stock trailers and pickup trucks, the barn, the corrals, and the old bunkhouse, all setting off the main house on the ranch where Gene and Ethel Ellis live. Gene is foreman and Ethel does the cooking. They've been on the Bridwell West for more than ten years. This outfit is owned by the Bridwell Oil Company of Wichita Falls, Texas, and it is one of five that the company owns in the Lone Star State—three in the Panhandle and two near Wichita Falls.

Before coming to the Bridwell West, Gene and Ethel were working on the company's Romero Ranch, west of Dalhart on the New Mexico border. They've had more than a twenty-two-year association with this company, and they certainly seem to be enjoying their life and their work.

STAYING CLOSE TO THEIR ROOTS

Gene and Ethel Ellis, after all these years, are still close to their roots, which are just across the border along the western edge of New Mexico. Ethel comes from Tucumcari and grew up a city girl. "I was raised in town. I'd have sworn I'd never be out like this when I was a girl. And all my friends would have told you that, too."

Gene is from a farming and ranching background near the tiny town of Amistad, New Mexico. The couple met at a dance in Nara Visa, almost halfway between their two home towns. They've been married nearly thirty-five years and have four children—three boys and a girl. Their oldest son, Rodney, now runs the Bridwell's Romero Ranch, and Jeff has his own place down near Hagerman, New Mexico. Trenton is a senior at Adrian High School, and their daughter, Star, lives with her husband and two children in Tucumcari.

THE RESTLESS BREED

The Bridwell West Ranch is a cow/calf operation sprawling over nearly 100,000 acres. They cross Hereford and Brangus cattle and run between 2,000 and 2,500 mother cows. The ranch is set up with five camps plus the headquarters. Each of the camps has a married cowboy, and at the moment the cowboys all have children. Being married with children isn't a prerequisite for getting a job on the ranch, although Ethel says, "We like to have married cowboys because it seems to work better in an isolated area like this." Gene adds, "It's harder to keep single boys on the ranch. They want to run to places."

The Bridwell is a ranch that is always busy. Calving starts around December first, branding begins in mid-March, and shipping takes place in the fall, around the first of October. Most of the cowboys' wives have jobs off the ranch and aren't readily available to help out. Besides the seasonal calving, branding, and shipping, there is the day-to-day work of feeding when it's necessary, mending fences, checking water, and breaking ice in the winter. Most of the cowboys watch over five-hundred head of cattle; they have to make sure none of the

cows get out on the highway—the ranch is split by I-40 and Gene says he's "real particular about not getting cattle on the highway."

The cowboys and their families do pretty well at the Bridwell. Gene points out, "There's so much variation in cowboys, but depending on their responsibilities, I usually start them at $700 a month and move them up as they go along." They do get regular raises, and, of course, they also get a house, their utilities are paid, they are supplied with two steers a year for meat, and they get a pickup and gas for ranch use. Unheard of a decade or more ago, today's cowboys are provided with a health program and a retirement plan, where the company puts aside money for each cowboy who has been with the ranch for at least seven years. "The Bridwell pays good and the hands are treated very good," observes Ethel. Gene says that the retirement plan is an incentive for the cowboy to stay, because, "I don't like to break in new hands. It takes quite a while for a boy to get to know the country . . . "

Maybe because of the working conditions and the foreman, the cowboys on this ranch have a tendency to stay around a bit longer than at some other ranches, where they just draw straight wages in the bunkhouse. Three of the punchers have been with the Bridwell for over five years. Gene is pleased because five years for a cowboy to be on one place is a long time. "They're a restless breed," he notes.

The ranch also hires quite a few day cowboys when they ship and brand. These hands are often local guys who have a small place of their own or work at some other job. They earn between fifty dollars and seventy-five dollars a day, which is pretty good pay in the cowboy world. And they're fed well, as you'll soon see.

COURTESY, SELF-CONFIDENCE, AND LOYALTY

When asked what he looks for in a cowboy, Gene Ellis doesn't give the usual qualifications—riding, roping, working the cattle. Instead, Gene says he wants his punchers to be courteous, self-confident, and loyal. These might seem like traits from a bygone era, but Gene says, "I want them to be out there at their camps and make a decision and know that what they are going to do is right and not have to look over their shoulder." Ethel says that what Gene really wants, "is a self-starter." He adds, "I want to know what's happening, but I don't want them setting and waiting on me to make a decision on everything. Each one of the cowboys has so many decisions to make. I want them to go ahead and take care of it."

Gene only sees his cowboys about two or three times a week, but they stay in touch by two-way radio. These camps are pretty far apart, many miles from headquarters. The foreman is a good man to work for. "If I don't like what one of the cowboys is doing, I'll tell him. I don't mince words. But once they've been around me for a year or so, then they can pretty well take care of their country and I go by and see what's happening. If they have problems, I talk to them about it." The hands range in age from twenty-four to fifty. "There is no age limit as long as they're decent help and they want to work. A man who is a good cowboy is a good cowboy . . ."

IT'S A BUSINESS

The Bridwell West is still a ranch that "uses a lot of horses." They raise their own quarter horse colts and usually run close to fifty head. In a given year they may breed fourteen or fifteen mares. But lest you think that this is all a romantic tie to the past with little modern importance, Gene clears that up pretty fast. "This is a business ranch. It makes money. The only way I keep my job is to make money for the owners." He quickly adds, "These boys (cowboys) who work under me, they keep my job secure because they take care of their end of the deal." For example, they shoot for a better than 90 percent calf crop each year at weaning time. Although it varies a bit from year to year, this helps keep them in the profit range.

Working on a corporate ranch is a little different from working your own spread, Gene says. "There's a paycheck coming every month. If you're running you own place you don't get one. Corporate ranches are just as much work. We basically do the same things as if I'd owned it. They still budget me and everything is kept on computers." Ethel adds, "They keep close tabs."

Gene is very clear about the corporation. "These are business people. They want to make money out of the ranch. And it's not what you've done yester-day—it's what you do tomorrow. If I wasn't making them money they'd want somebody who could, somebody with different ideas who could make the thing work." But, he stresses that on the day-to-day operation of the ranch he is free to do things his way. One exception is selling the cattle and buying the bulls—this is done at corporate headquarters.

Horses (top) and bulls (bottom) on the range, Bridwell West Ranch, Adrian, Texas.

J. S. Bridwell bought this land and put together the ranch in the 1950s and early 1960s. He originally made his money as a wildcatter in the oil fields. This range was part of the old Matador and XIT in the last century.

FROM COWBOY TO FOREMAN

Gene Ellis brings a wealth of experience to the ranch. "I worked for lots of ranches over in New Mexico since we've been married." He worked in feedlots, and, as he describes it, "I just applied for a job—I was in my thirties—and from there on they just kept moving me up. I've produced for these people. You've got to make them some money someplace down the road, and if you don't there's something wrong. The ranching business has changed so much." He goes on to explain how things have changed. Not the traditional changes, like better equipment or higher costs. He sees it all in the cattle. He talks easily about bigger and heavier calves, greater health consciousness, and a more scientific approach to the ranching industry.

HEAVEN ON EARTH

Life on the ranch "is heaven," according to Ethel. "It's so nice not to have neighbors looking over at you—it's nice to be on your own." She sure doesn't sound like a city girl now. And sitting around the kitchen table over some coffee, you can feel the warmth of the home that Gene and Ethel have carved out for themselves on the ranch. But it's not all easy living for Ethel. During branding and shipping season, she's cooking for between thirteen and twenty-five very hungry cowboys. She cooks right in her own kitchen and the hands spread out and eat there, on the back porch, even in the living room. Cooking for cowboys, she says with her easy laugh, "is work—what can I tell you? But it's fun. I try to feed them real well and make it worth their day to come here. So many of the day cowboys like to come to eat." She says that she cooks meat, beans, potatoes, vegetables, and salads, all pretty basic stuff. "It's hard work. I do only two meals a day, breakfast and lunch. I have had to cook all three meals, and I don't like that. When we've had cowboys in the bunkhouse I've had to do that. But now we try to stay away from that." The day hands don't usually stay for the evening meal. "We've had college kids who did stay in the bunkhouse and we did cook all three meals for them. It just gets to be a really big job."

The day cowboys usually arrive an hour before daylight and they have breakfast at 5:30 A.M. They often stay until dark and return the next day. Cowboys are generally bone-tired during the branding and shipping, but they continue to be optimistic about their prospects. The notion of the "dying cowboy" is a strange one for these hands, who make their living astride a horse.

Gene thinks ranching still has a bright future. "As long as people eat, they're going to eat beef. A lot of people love beef. And we're going to be exporting it, too." The Bridwell West is strictly in beef production, with no plans to change. They ship their calves to the feedlots and from there they go to the factories. Of course, the Texas Panhandle country *is* feedlot country, and even Ethel says she is amazed by how many feedlots there are in the area.

THE COOKING IS IN THE TIMING

Cooking on the Bridwell West is typical of most large ranches. "These boys just aren't real picky" Ethel says. And Gene adds, "As long as there's good food, they're easy to please . . . and they don't mess with the cook because they appreciate what they get." Ethel says that in all her years cooking, she's never run into many that gripe. Other than scrambled eggs, she can't think of any food she's gotten complaints about. Gene jokes that Ethel got the job as cook because "nobody else wanted it." And Ethel points out that it's really getting hard to find ranch cooks. "I've cooked at every ranch we've ever been on. One of the most difficult parts of cooking on the ranch is timing. Having the food ready at the right time and cooking things the cowboys like to eat." Gene says that the work on the range can't be timed closely, and though he might predict he'll be in at noon, he often doesn't show up until three or four o'clock. "But I've gotten used to it," Ethel explains. "I've learned that you just go with the flow. Some people would really get irate—some of the women just can't put up with that, they can't cope with it. After thirty-some-odd years you just learn to work with it. I've even carried lunch to them out in the pasture when they can't get in." The cowboys are often so far from headquarters that they would rather just finish what they're doing out on the range instead of coming all the way in and then making the long trip back out for the rest of the day.

But if you want a wonderful pepper steak or a piece of Ethel's Black Forest Cherry Cheese Cake, you'd do well to get your work done and get on into headquarters and the kitchen. As she says, "Everything goes better if you're well fed."

BLACK FOREST CHERRY CHEESE CAKE

²/₃ cup unsifted flour

3 tablespoons unsweetened cocoa

1¹/₃ cup sugar

¹/₃ cup margarine or butter

3 8-ounce packages cream cheese, softened

2 teaspoons vanilla

¹/₈ teaspoon salt

1 8-ounce container sour cream

3 large eggs

1½ cups semisweet chocolate chips, melted

1 17-ounce can cherry pie filling

1 container Cool Whip or whipped cream

In a small bowl combine the flour, cocoa, and ¹/₃ cup of sugar. Using a pastry blender, cut in the margarine until the mixture is crumbly. Press into bottom of nine-inch springform pan. Bake in 350°F oven for twenty minutes. Cool.

In a large bowl, using mixer at medium speed, beat the cream cheese, vanilla, salt, and remaining cup of sugar until the mixture is smooth. Add the eggs, beat one minute, until just blended. Reduce speed of mixer to low and blend in the sour cream and melted chocolate chips. Pour this into bottom of prepared pan. Bake at 350°F for fifty-five minutes. Cheese cake will not sit in center. Cool completely on rack.

Cover cake and refrigerate for six hours or overnight. Fill the middle with whipped cream and spoon cherries around the sides.

PEPPER STEAK

1 large round steak
Flour
Salt and pepper
Shortening
1 can Ortega chilies, chopped
2 cans tomato sauce

Cut the steak into serving portions. Roll portions in flour and season to taste. Brown the steak on both sides in melted shortening. Drain the grease and cover the steak with the chilies. Add the tomato sauce and two cans of water. Simmer for 1½ hours until tender.

Feeds family of four.

CARTER RANCH:
H BAR C CATTLE COMPANY

DALHART, TEXAS
HOSS AND MARY CARTER

THE OLD AND THE NEW

Any time you are in the Dalhart area, you are in XIT country. And when you head west on U.S. 87, the local citizenry makes sure you know it. At the north end of Dalhart's underpass is the famous "Empty Saddle Monument," designed by cowboy Bobby Dycke and dedicated in 1940, honoring all the range riders of the past. Dycke created the sculpture after a widow asked that a horse bearing an empty saddle appear in the annual Dalhart cowboy reunion parade as a tribute to her husband, a former XIT cowboy. At that reunion, which started in 1936 and grows stronger each year, a riderless horse, carrying a wreath to honor all deceased XIT cowhands, is led through the parade. In the early years, one of the former XIT hands led the horse. Today, because all the former hands have passed away, a descendant of one of those cowboys is given the responsibility of honoring the memory of the XIT cowpokes.

Each year, in early August, Dalhart's usual population of around 6,500 hospitable Panhandle people, swells, as the "World's Largest Free Bar-B-Que" feeds more than 20,000 visitors. This is all to let you know that you are in cowboy country, with a history as far reaching as any ranching area in the United States.

Heading through the underpass on the way out to visit with Hoss and Mary Carter on their ranch northwest of town, it is easy to envision this once great cattle empire. Although today's ranches are smaller, the country remains ranch country.

The wind is blowing up a real storm as the ranch headquarters looms on the horizon, but the Carter house is warm and cozy, decorated throughout with a wealth of handsome and interesting antiques.

The H Bar C Cattle Company, the Carter's outfit, was at one time part of the XIT range; it became the Reynolds Ranch when the XIT was broken up. The Reynolds outfit covered some 300,000 acres. Eventually, the ranch became the Harding Ranch when Mrs. Harding, who was a Reynolds, inherited the place. Bob Harding took over from his mother, and Hoss Carter's father and Bob Harding went into partnership on the cattle. Hoss and Mary Carter came to the ranch to work for them. After his father died, Hoss took over the day-to-day management of the ranch. Mr. Harding was a bank president in Fort Worth, and left the ranch to the Carters upon his death. So from 1932, when Hoss's dad came to the Harding Ranch, there has always been a Carter presence. Hoss and Mary have been on the ranch for more than forty years.

THE ONE AND ONLY JOB

The Carters were married in 1950. Mary is from a ranching family in Colorado City, Texas, south of Lubbock, where her grandfather started ranching in 1880. Hoss is from Strawn, Texas, between Abilene and Fort Worth. As he describes it, his family "had quite a big ranch down in that part of the world."

The couple met in Strawn in grade school after Mary's family moved to town. "But we didn't date then . . . we waited a while," she adds with a big laugh. Neither Hoss nor Mary ever wanted to do anything but ranch. Mary says that, "I was probably looking for a ranching husband from the time I ever thought husband." Hoss says it never crossed his mind to do anything else. Mary is quick to point out that, except for his stint in the military, "he's never had but one job—this ranch." Now they have three children, all involved in ranching and cattle. Ike, the oldest, manages the Satellite Cattle Exchange in Amarillo, Ross is on a ranch near Clayton, New Mexico, and Kay and her husband Curt White, live on the home ranch and work alongside Mary and Hoss. The three married children have given their proud parents nine grandchildren.

The Carters have a yearling steer operation, running between 1,000 to 1,500 head, and they also have about 100 mother cows. They get their yearlings "from all over Texas." They buy them at about 400 pounds and sell them at 750 pounds. There is time between selling and buying the next herd when the range is virtually unused. As Hoss points out, "You don't ever want to overgraze your range because you've got to make a living off of it and it can't produce for you if you've overgrazed it. I think a person shouldn't abuse the land. If it's supposed to carry one head for ten acres, you should run one head for twelve acres. I think you should give the cattle a little bit more."

GETTING THE MESSAGE OUT

Hoss and Mary are not atypical in their concern for the land, and they have some interesting observations about why ranchers just can't seem to get their message across to the public, especially those who oppose ranching. Mary believes that "ranchers are just too busy working hard, doing their job, being

Hoss Carter with old ship's bell at headquarters, Carter Ranch.

with their families, and they really don't have time to organize and promote and put the word out. They try to live and let live and have a good day every day." Hoss adds that if the people who oppose ranchers and ranching "had a prairie dog in their front yard and a rattlesnake in their backyard, they wouldn't like it." Mary jumps right back in. "Ranchers try to keep everything in balance. Most country people like wildlife and want it to be in the natural habitat."

The Carters don't farm on the ranch. They did at one time, but Mary says "Hoss was not a farmer . . . we were not farmers. He sold the farm land and got out of farming." Hoss says that, by choice, he doesn't want to farm, although if he had to, he'd sure do it.

THE WEATHER—AGAIN

Neither Mary nor Hoss has had the urge to move from the Panhandle except "when the sand was really, really blowing." In 1953, when they moved onto the ranch, they had "lots of days like that, and if someone had brought the truck and backed it up we probably would have left. But every year since then has been better. That probably was the worst weather year—we were in a new place, away from home. We had electricity but no phone. The electricity was out a lot because the wind blew and the snow fell."

And, of course, everyone remembers the March blizzard in the winter of 1957. The Carters lost about sixty mother cows, eighty or ninety calves, and nearly one hundred and twenty yearlings. Mary says that was about the worst winter. At the ranch, the wind blew seventy-five miles per hour for nearly seventy-two hours straight. The temperature hovered around twenty-four degrees. "The storm smothered the cattle. It drowned them. They drifted to corners and the snow was so fine that they breathed it in and it drowned them."

STILL A HORSE OUTFIT

Like most good ranches, the Carter Ranch continues to work from the back of a horse. Some are raised on the ranch and some are bought. Their remuda numbers twenty-two head. They have a few mares, and as Hoss notes, "If you've got a daughter and a granddaughter you've got to raise some horses." Hoss is a solid horseman and Mary proudly points out that he is a roper—a calf roper for some years and then a team roper. And despite Hoss's modesty about his accomplishments with a rope, Mary says that he always roped. He even won the Stamford, Texas, Cowboy Reunion roping and Texas Oldtimers Rodeo Association team roping finals with Junior Hays from Channing as his partner. He has quite a few trophy buckles to show for the many years he's been swinging his loop.

A LIFETIME ON THE RANGE

Over the years, ranching has changed—sometimes for the better and sometimes not. Hoss notes that when you could buy a calf for twenty cents a hundred pounds and sell it for thirty or forty cents, you actually made more money than you do nowadays when you can buy a calf for eight-seven cents a hundred and sell it for $1.20. Ranching expenses have increased that much. But no matter what, "ranching is still fun. Just to get up and watch that old cow have that calf—watch that new baby and watch those yearlings grow. It's a pleasure to me." modernization has caused other changes. Hoss remembers when they drove their cattle eight to ten miles to the railhead. Today they just run them into a corral, back up a truck, and haul them off. Now they feed from the back of a pickup instead of a wagon and team. Both Hoss and Mary agree that they don't do as much "neighboring" as they used to. "Most of the neighbors have moved to town or died . . . and they have boys living on their ranch . . . that weren't raised on ranches and they don't know how you work. We like gentle cattle. Some of these boys you don't want on your place. You get a bunch of wild cowpunchers yelling and awhistling . . . that shouldn't take place." When the Carters look for cowboys, they want punchers who are all-around hands. They have to know how to fence, feed, fix a windmill, know sick cattle and how

Headquarters at the Carter Ranch, Dalhart, Texas.

to doctor them, and do a little roping, although "most of the time we drive our cattle into the lots. We don't doctor our cattle outside anymore."

At branding time, the calves are still dragged to the fire, but the yearlings, who can weigh around 400 pounds, are branded in the chutes. They'd need too many hands to hold them on the ground and even the horses would "give out dragging them to the fire." It's also harder to find good cowboys these days, at least where the Carters ranch. Mary tells of the time one of her sons was in high school rodeo and was beat in the roping by a kid who wore tennis shoes. "Needless to say he did not grow up on a ranch. I thought Hoss was just gonna pass out. You didn't want that kid in tennis shoes winning. You somehow wanted a ranch kid to win." Of course, this is a modern tale—of rodeo participants who aren't cowboys and are only good in their event. They are athletes, not cowhands, and they rarely ever make it to a ranch after the rodeo. For them, it's a sport, not a way of life.

CONTINUITY

Curt White, daughter Kay's husband, is from a "sandy land farming" background, and says that what he knows about ranching he learned from Hoss. "I wish I knew what he's already forgotten." Hoss says that in the three-plus years Curt's been on the ranch, "He's made a real good hand." The Whites have been married since 1981, and Mary says that having them back on the ranch "has been real nice"—a clear understatement. Continuity is the prevalent theme at this ranch. The headquarters where the Carter's house, the White's house, the old bunkhouse, and the garage are all neatly painted gray with white trim. The garage is decorated with all sorts of farm implements and antiques, as is the main house. Mary has always been interested in antiques. "I had a grandfather who came to Texas from Vermont, and he always had little treasures in his room. And as a young child I had to look at all the treasures at least once a month and hold them and cradle them. . . . I have never thrown anything away. I've passed a lot on to my children and I do a lot of refinishing. To take something that isn't any good and to make some good out of it is a great fulfillment. I used to go to a lot of auctions and farm auctions." Hoss shares her interest and enthusiasm for these treasures.

The Carter's collection includes crocks, a hobby Mary shares with JoWayne Summerour, a ranching friend. Together they make carved, beautifully painted Santas each year. Mary also does some sewing, including very attractive, decorative samplers.

WHAT THE FUTURE MAY HOLD

The Carters remain optimistic about the future of ranching, but Hoss makes an interesting observation about its future in the Panhandle. He thinks that "big industry seems like it wants to take over. The feedlot people run their own cattle to where anytime they need cattle to fill up their pens they can go to their ranches and get them. And they're running thousands of cattle on ranches they've bought or leased. It makes it tough on the little man—a man with maybe up to one thousand head . . . they're trying to choke them out."

Hoss follows these remarks with a wide grin, "My little granddaughters and grandsons will be doing what Curt and I are doing now." Mary cuts in, "If they so desire." But Hoss comes right back, "I hope to hell they're going to do it." He says he'd really be disappointed if his grandsons and granddaughters didn't want to ranch. Mary adds, "I want these kids to do things their own way, but I want them to have ranching in their hearts. I want them to love the land and love ranching and love the country." She chuckles and says she has one grandson who lives in Amarillo and likes to come to the ranch "to get a good night's sleep. The ranch is a healing environment, I think, from getting in a car and running and jumping all over town."

DOG DAYS

If there is a ranch in Texas, or anywhere else, without a dog, it's keeping pretty quiet. All ranches seem to have dogs and the Carter Ranch is no exception. They say that dogs are "something to go with you and help you. I guarantee you that my dogs help me. You've got a buddy." Mary says that they are your friends. Hoss once had a dog that could pen 150 calves. "I never had to saddle up. The dogs did the job. It was better than a horse. Those calves couldn't get around those dogs . . . I love dogs." Mary observes that people would be amazed if they realized how much the men and their dogs are alike. But the men aren't the only ones who value the dogs. "I wouldn't want to live out here without a dog," she says. They have three.

THE HEART OF THE RANCH

The kitchen and the dining room table are the entertainment centers in so many ranches. Mary's is a compact and wonderfully decorated kitchen, with crocks and other old implements and tools covering the walls. Years ago, she often cooked for crews of ten or twelve. Today she says her big crew is seventeen, when the whole family gets together. "I'm still into cooking big and I love company." Hoss says she is a great cook, and after trying a couple of her recipes you can at least get a handle on why he feels that way.

MONKEY BREAD

4 cups flour

1½ cups milk, scalded and cooled

1 package dry yeast, dissolved in ¼ cup warm water

2 egg whites

½ cup sugar

¼ cup Crisco oil

1 teaspoon salt

Add two cups of flour to the milk and yeast. Beat the egg whites until they are stiff and add one-half cup of sugar. Add this to the flour and milk mixture. Let this rise until it is double in bulk—about one hour. Then stir down and add the Crisco oil, salt, and remaining two cups of flour. Beat well and refrigerate at least six hours, or overnight.

To make into rolls: roll dough until it is one-half-inch thick. Cut with a diamond shaped cookie cutter. Dip in melted oleo or butter. Layer about twenty-four diamonds per tube pan, alternating the diamonds (so they don't stick together).

Let this rise about two hours. Bake at 350°F, thrity to thirty-five minutes or until golden brown. Turn it out on a rack, cool, freeze and reheat to serve.

RICE, CHILIES & CHEESE

1 cup rice
1 cup sour cream
8 ounces Monterey Jack Cheese
1 6-ounce can green chilies
Butter

Cook rice as per instructions on the box. When it is cooked, stir in the cup of sour cream. Layer one-half the rice mixture in a small casserole.

Cut the cheese domino size and wrap a green chili around the cheese and place on top of the rice. Use all the chilies with plenty of cheese. Then cover with the remaining rice. Dot with butter and grate the remaining cheese on top.

Cook at 350°F for twenty to thirty minutes.

(Mary recommends this be fixed with broiled steak, green salad, and monkey bread.)

DAUER HEREFORD RANCH

PANHANDLE, TEXAS
JOHN PAUL AND CHARLOTTE DAUER

MR. OUTSIDE AND MRS. INSIDE

On U.S. 60, heading northeast from Amarillo, just before the town of Panhandle, sitting behind a protective fence, is Thomas Cree's "Little Tree," the first tree planted in the entire Texas Panhandle. This area was once a sea of grass. In 1888, a pioneer settler by the name of Thomas Cree lugged a sapling bois d'arc from beyond the Cap Rock country and planted it by his dugout home. Over the years Cree nurtured and watered the tree. Cree has long since passed away, but the tree survived until 1969, when it was accidentally killed by agricultural chemicals. Fortunately, natural seedlings from the original tree were saved and are growing today.

This country hasn't changed all that much. Wheat and cattle have been joined by petroleum products as the mainstay of the small community of 2,355 people. But the land remains flat and treeless.

THE FAMILY

Just south of town, out on the big, sprawling prairie, John Paul and Charlotte Dauer oversee their ranch with its herd of Hereford cattle and rich farm land.

John Paul and Charlotte, both native Texans, met on a blind date in Brownsville, on the Gulf Coast. They were married in 1978, the second marriage for both, and there are now four children—Amy (22), Stephanie (21), Justin (19), and Micca (14).

Of the four children, it is the two youngest, Justin and Micca, who have been the best "ranch hands." As Charlotte points out, "Micca has been working cattle with her dad since she could ride in a car seat."

The Dauer Ranch is really part of three ranches: one run by John Paul's mother; one ramrodded by his brother Steve; and his own place. Together they run about 450 mother cows, both registered and non-registered Herefords. They calve in the spring and wean about November. Usually, the ranch tries to keep their steers until March, and when they can work it in between their farming chores, they brand in the summer. As on every other ranch, there is a seasonal rhythm to the activities and the everyday responsibilities.

The farming, an intricate part of most ranching operations in the Panhandle, consists of raising wheat, corn, and milo, as well as hay and silage for the cattle.

EACH TO HIS OR HER OWN PLACE

Charlotte and John Paul love their life on the ranch, but the woman of the house admits, "I'm not real active—I'm not out there riding a horse. I'm in the house working on the computer and cooking. I run the inside and he [John Paul], runs the outside." They both laugh at this admission as the cowboss continues, "And we don't interfere with one another." Charlotte jumps in with "It's wonderful. He loves for me to pay the bills. I take care of a lot of the business. But we're real compatible. . . . I just like more of the business end of things." She was a business education major at Texas Tech in Lubbock. John Paul, who looks every bit the Texas rancher, did his undergraduate work at Oklahoma State in Stillwater and then took the very well-respected ranch management course at Texas Christian University, where, he says, "I learned more than I'll ever use."

John Paul is a fourth-generation Texas rancher—his grandfather and father both ran outfits in the Panhandle area. Since his father passed away several years ago, John Paul is pretty much the manager of the Dauer Ranch operations, farming and running cattle on some 20,000 acres. Although he had cowboyed in his younger days at the Four Sixes, when "Bigun" Bradley was the wagon-boss, surprisingly, he says, he was a little disappointed by the experience and much preferred the family ranch where you could be your own boss.

THE WEATHER CAN GET YOU

Charlotte says she really likes living in the rural area of Carson County, away from Amarillo. In addition to managing the business end of the ranch, she teaches physical science and biology at Panhandle High School while the regular teacher is on maternity leave. This isn't her first teaching experience at the school. She is a rather frequent substitute teacher. In fact, the Dauers are very much a part of their community.

But she does laugh when she talks about the weather and the dirt road leading to the ranch and their house and what it was like during Thanksgiving, 1993. That was when the Dauers had to get in and out through their pastures. "The snow was so deep that it [the road] was like a tunnel. You couldn't even get in or out our front door." She also remembers the time that John Paul came in at about 10:00 A.M. and at that time it was snowing and blowing so hard that

John Paul Dauer with one of his bulls at ranch near Panhandle, Texas.

they decided to head the five or six miles to town to pick the kids up at school. The only way they made it to the pickup was to hold on to one another. Well, "the wind was so strong and the snow was getting so deep we couldn't make it. . . . We had to turn around. The only way I made it back into the house was to not let go of John Paul. The kids never did make it home that night."

Winter weather in this part of Texas can be pretty rough. John Paul says that in some years the winter storms kill a lot of cattle. At the ranch they do a considerable amount of winter feeding, especially when the snow is covering the ground. He recalls one year, around 1957, when he was still living at his mother's, just north of his present home, when "I could walk across the corral on dead cattle. It [the storm] killed all the horses but two and what were left—the fences just drifted over—just walked away. They found cattle from here down at the Palo Duro Canyon [about fifty miles south]. They just got on a road and drifted with the wind until they either gave out or found shelter.

What amazes me is how the ranchers could survive all that, financially. Like now, if I lost that many cattle, I'd be writing books or something." That last comment was accompanied by the widest grin . . .

The Dauers like the country around the ranch. They enjoy the flat country and its unlimited vistas. Of course, it can spoil you for other spectacular views. Charlotte says when they went to Hawaii and took a sunset cruise "the big deal was to see the sunset. Well, it was no big deal to us because we see the beautiful sunsets every day."

MICCA, THE VETERINARIAN

When they brand at the ranch, the Dauers and the hired men from the three ranches do it pretty much by themselves. "We don't drag em to the fire. We run 'em through the chutes. It's not as much fun. . . . It sure is more fun to drag 'em to the fire." But in this day and age, many ranches, particularly the smaller spreads, use the chutes to save on manpower, and in some cases, time. But this is still a ranch where most of the cattle work does get done by horseback.

John Paul and Charlotte think that Justin looks ahead to a ranching career and that Micca has her sights set on veterinary medicine. When Micca was just three or four years old, she was out with her dad when he had to pull a calf. Micca told the story to her baby-sitter and the other kids there. "My dad jumped out of his pickup and ripped his shirt off and rammed his arm up that cow's butt—it was gross and bloody." The baby-sitter tried to calm the other children by saying, "Micca, I'll bet that was a sweet little calf." Micca answered, "Nah, it was dead." So much for the mysteries of life.

THE LAST CATTLE DRIVE

This is ranch country with a long and romantic history. The last great Texas Panhandle cattle drive was organized at the N Bar N (N-N) headquarters, not too far from the Dauer Ranch. The ranch manager, J. L. Harrison, and the trail boss, T. L. (Tom) Coffee, hired 100 tough Texas cowboys and they drove ten herds, each with 2,500 cattle, for a total of 25,000 beeves, to the Miles City/Powder River country of eastern Montana. The drive took from April to September in 1892. The herd belonged to the Niedringhaus brothers, German tinsmiths who made a fortune in Saint Louis making enamel granite household wares. They had plowed a good part of their fortune into ranching.

But by the last decades of the nineteenth century, times were changing on the range. Between 1882 and 1886, the N Bar N had leased range in Carson and neighboring counties from the Francklyn Land & Cattle Company, a British syndicate backed by the Cunard Steamship Line. Later the range was owned by the White Deer Land Company. The N Bar N outfit had to leave this range because the White Deer Land Company wanted the land cleared of large herds. At the time, the Montana range was still wide open. By 1907, the 650,000 acres in Texas were offered for sale to small ranchers and farmers. This is the way some of the great nineteenth century Texas spreads were broken up.

FROM FAR AWAY THEY COME

The Dauer Ranch produces prized Hereford breeding stock. Buyers come from all over Texas and the adjoining states, and sometimes from across the country. While we were at the ranch, two cattlemen from Florida showed up and we all hopped into John Paul's rig and headed out to look over some bulls. The Florida buyers were big cattle operators, and it's a measure of the quality of the Dauer stock that they came this far. We eyed the young stock and mature bulls as the boss gave the bloodlines and other pertinent information. When we got back to headquarters and all the good-byes were said, no decisions had been made, but these Floridians sure did get to see some fine looking Hereford bulls.

COOKING PIES

Charlotte is a fine cook with a great sense of humor. At first she says that John Paul is "just your typical steak and potato man." And it sure is true that it seems like every cowboy and rancher in Texas favors steak and potatoes. But when we ask her what her favorite thing to cook is, she responds "sandwiches—beef baloney." On a more serious note, Micca says she likes her mom's pork chops, even though her parents insist Micca's favorite dish is chicken-fried steak, another Texas staple. If she had to cook just one thing, Charlotte says it would be her beef brisket. Yet, what she says she really likes is when her husband cooks steaks outside. She also says she doesn't bake pies, although John Paul vividly remembers her telling him once that she just baked a pie. "So I say, oh, good, what kind of pie is it? She said it was apple pie and I cut into it and it was cherry." Definitely not a homemade pie! But Charlotte has given us some wonderful Texas ranch recipes.

THE TEXAN HOTEL

One last note about Panhandle, Texas, and the life of the folks who live in this small ranching and farming community. Right in town is the Texan Hotel, a bed and breakfast, run by Clarence and Betty Rhyneheart, who try to give their guests a "touch of the past." And that they do, right down to the water basin and pitcher in the bedroom—although these are more for decoration than for actual use. The place is run with old-fashioned hospitality, something missing at the more sterile newer hotels and motels. The Texan Hotel gives its guests a definite touch of the Texas ranching tradition. You can really imagine the drovers coming in off the trail and staying at a hotel just like this one.

And to satisfy some of that hunger that builds up on a long drive, here are a couple of Charlotte's favorite recipes, including one that just about everyone associates with Texas, barbecued ribs. Yes sir, that is sure pure quill Texas!

TEXAS BARBECUED RIBS

2½ pounds of ribs
1 large onion, sliced
½ cup catsup
½ cup vinegar
2 teaspoons chili powder
1 teaspoon paprika
2½ teaspoons salt

Place the ribs in a baking dish in a 350°F oven. Mix the remaining ingredients; pour half the mixture over the ribs. Bake for forty-five minutes, then add the remaining mixture. Bake an additional forty-five to sixty minutes or to the degree of doneness desired.

MEXICAN DORITA DELIGHT

1 pound ground meat
1 onion
1 can cream of chicken soup
1 can cream of mushroom soup
1 can enchilada sauce
1 package taco sauce
1 can evaporated milk
1 small can green chilies
1 package Doritos
½ pound American cheese or Monterey Jack cheese

Brown the meat and onion together. Add salt and pepper. Add the soups, sauces, milk, and chilies. Line a thirteen-inch x nine-inch pan with Doritos. Pour in the meat mixture and top with the cheese. Bake at 350°F for twenty minutes.

THE FORD RANCH

MELVIN, TEXAS
FORREST ARMKE, MANAGER
AND SNAKE WRANGLER

A PARADISE FOR HUNTERS, HERDERS, AND OVER-EATERS UNANIMOUS

When you get to Brady, you are in the very heart of Texas. This county seat of McCulloch County was settled in the early 1800s along the old Dodge Cattle Trail. From Brady, it's 437 miles to El Paso, 401 miles to Brownsville, 412 miles to Texline in the corner of the Panhandle, and 341 miles to the Sabine River on the eastern boundary. Just north of Brady is the geological center of Texas, and just south is Calf Creek, where Jim Bowie, his brother, Rezin, and a few friends had an eight-day running battle with Tawakoni Indians. Bowie survived only to perish at the Alamo, but his legend lives on.

If you want to know more about Brady, see Kathy Roddie, Executive Vice President of the McCulloch County Chamber of Commerce. "There are lots of historic ranches in the area," she informs us, "but the Ford Ranch is probably the most interesting." She makes a phone call, gets us an appointment, and we were on our way. Kathy Roddie is right. The Ford Ranch is one of the most interesting ranches in the world.

To get there, take Ranch Road 2028 south and west of Brady toward the little town of Melvin. The Ford Ranch is before Melvin, but on the drive you'll pass the G. Rollie White Race Track, a very modern facility that looks out of place in the brushy hill country of central Texas. Mr. G. Rollie White, former owner of the Ford Ranch, was not only a futuristic cattle man, but a shrewd businessman and an incurable horse lover. You'll like the Ford Ranch before you even see it. We did.

We arrived in McCulloch County in the middle of hunting season and were told to come to the deer camp, off Ranch Road 2028, two-and-one-half miles down a fenced lane. A cluster of blue plywood buildings nestled under spreading live oak trees, the deer camp is at once inviting and comfortable; almost like coming back to a place you know and love. In other words, visiting the Ford Ranch hunting camp is a little like coming home.

No one came out to greet us, so we opted to enter the largest of the buildings, figuring it was the kitchen/mess hall. To the right was a large kitchen with two huge gas-fired ranges, a walk-in cooler, and groceries stacked to the ceiling. At the northeast corner, three men dressed in camo-clothing were reviewing a video on a small TV. They were with Terry Rohm of Wellington Outdoors from Madison, Georgia, we learned later, shooting footage of deer responding to various lures the company markets.

Across the room, at a large plywood table, sat Ford Ranch Manager Forrest Armke, pads and papers spread around him as far as he could reach. He peered over half-glasses and motioned to us. He was obviously very busy, but dealing with visitors is part of his job. At his behest, we pulled up chairs and took out our tape recorder and notebook. Forrest is revved up and kicks into high gear.

FROM THE WILD TO FORD TO WHITE AND BACK

"This ranch was founded by James Ford," he begins. "Mr. Ford was a cavalry officer stationed at Camp San Sabe. The ranch was surveyed out in 1842 and Ford operated it until 1894. At that time the ranch was purchased by Mr. G. Rollie White who became known as 'The Steer King of Texas.'" White, Armke states, started the ranch with his father, the senior White, and they bought and leased land and bought and sold steers; buying wild cattle in west Texas along the border and driving them to the ranch to be fattened.

It is interesting to note that on the back side of the Ford Ranch there still remains fence that was part of the world's longest fenced cattle trail—100 miles from Sonora to the railhead in Brady. The Fort Worth and Rio Grande railroads bought a 250-foot-wide right of way and fenced it the entire length, building holding pens and watering troughs along the route. Armke again, "Mr. White was fond of saying that he could get in his buggy and drive one-fourth of the way to Sonora [find all the cattle he needed], and buy all the steers he could run for a year."

But speculating on steers is about as bad as or worse than speculating on Wall Street and Mr. White went bust a couple of times. "One time," according to Forrest, "he shipped a bunch of steers to Kansas and the market fell apart, so he shipped 'em back to the ranch and fed 'em through the winter. Then shipped 'em back to Kansas and still lost money on them."

Mr. White was learning about the steer market the same way he was learning about water in Texas—success in both can be tough to come by. "In the beginning," Forrest continues, "they had only one stock tank on the 33,000-acre ranch. The year it dried up, they lost 600 mother cows. He then went to developing water, putting in wells and windmills. Mr. White did a tremendous amount of work on this place. He was a tireless worker and generous to a fault. Just a wonderful man."

Ford Ranch Family: (left to right) Ellen, Wade, Cord, Forrest, and Amy. Ford Ranch, Melvin, Texas
(photo by Forrest Armke).

G. Rollie White died in 1965 but his legacy lives on. "Eighty-five percent of his holdings went into a trust fund," Forrest says. "He did not have any children. His wife died in January [1965] and he died in February. Fifteen percent [of the White estate] went to a niece, Jo Lina White. She visited here a lot as a child and spent summers with Mr. and Mrs. White. The cattle and machinery here are hers. We're required to give five percent of our gross [ranch] earnings to charity every year before we can put a penny back in this ranch."

According to Armke, the White trust is administered by Bank One in Fort Worth and profits from the ranch are plowed heavily back into the local community. "That's the way he wanted it. Funds go to acceptable charities and organizations, such as volunteer fire departments and the G. Rollie White Auditorium at Texas A&M University. Mr. White was an 1894 graduate of Texas A&M and a big fan of the school."

And a big fan of big horses. "At one time he had over a hundred Belgians here. He didn't like farming, so he sold off a lot of prime farming land. But he kept a bunch of horses. He loved horses." About that G. Rollie White Race Track? "He donated that race track to the community. It was the first licensed race track in the state—held license number one. But it came under questionable management a few years ago and is inactive at the moment."

INTENSIVE MANAGEMENT OF INTENSIVE GRAZING

There's nothing questionable about the management at the Ford Ranch. They seem to have the best. Forrest Armke was raised around Blanco, Texas, to a farming and ranching family, and grew up dreaming about running his own ranch. He said he still harbors that dream, but has never been happier since being able to manage a progressive ranch like the Ford. "I came here in 1985. There was a drought in '84 and there wasn't much grass. We've made a lot of changes since then."

Some of the changes Forrest implemented include an intensive grazing and rest-and-rotation program. "Our pastures used to be 3,400 acres or better," he says. "We cut them in half and are cutting them half again into 800s. We split the pastures with solar-powered, permanent electric fence. We get more hoof action in the smaller pastures." Hoof action? "It may sound weird but it works. The action of the cattle's feet is like roto-tilling the soil. It softens it and allows the natural grass to grow much more quickly. If I hadn't witnessed it, I wouldn't have believed it."

Another intensive grazing benefit that Armke admits he had a hard time believing is the effect the program is having on pear, as in prickly pear cactus. "We're on our way to eliminating pear from the Ford Ranch." That's a pretty bold statement coming from the heart of prickly pear paradise. "We have found that there is a fungus that kills pear. That fungus is carried by a red spider and other bugs that live in [the grass at the base of] the cactus. In pastures that are rested, the grass grows and protects the bugs through the winter. In the spring, they carry a fungus that kills pear. It works. I've seen it with my own eyes."

MANAGING THE CASH CROP OF HUNTERS

Each fall Forrest takes those eyes for a ride in a helicopter to count deer and take photographs of the pastures. One of his favorite hobbies is photography. We just missed seeing him shoot a session with Suzy Smith of Outdoor Sportswear, who was at the ranch hunting and modeling a new line of camo-clothing. Hunting is a big sport in Texas and it is big business on the Ford Ranch. Armke manages the deer and deer hunters as carefully as he does his cows and cowboys.

"When I came here, the ranch was under nine separate hunting leases. In '85 we did away with that and in '86 started guiding our own hunts. This ranch has always had a wonderful deer population. In 1892 one of the biggest bucks in the world was killed here. He was called Moose and is now known as the Benson Buck or in some cases, the Brady Buck."

It was the Ford Ranch foreman, Jeff Benson, who hung "Moose" on the wall. "Moose was shot by a hunter in 1892 and got away," Forrest relates. "Word got back to Benson, who saddled a horse, rode into Brady, questioned the hunter, rode back, tracked, and found the buck. Benson was living in a twelve by twelve shack at the time [which is now the Armke kitchen] and he sold Moose's head for $100. The price of big bucks has gone up considerably in a century.

"We get $1,800 for a three-day hunt," Armke advises. "The hunter gets to kill one trophy buck and two does. It's a good deal all around." It's good for the ranch and for the general public because money from the hunts goes to the trust fund which goes back to the community. And the deer must be harvested. "I've talked to old timers," Forrest says, "who remember gathering cattle here and the place was crawling with deer." Literally. "Lots of the deer were so weak they couldn't jump a four-foot fence."

After his helicopter survey, Forrest figures how many deer to harvest. Some seasons they take 500 or more deer. Some years less. It depends on the weather and the fluctuations of mother nature. It once even depended on the hogs. Hogs?

"When I came here [wild] hogs were a big problem," Forrest says. "Big problem. They were taking about two-thirds of the deer born in some pastures. They took goats and calves. When a hog goes carnivorous, it's a terrible thing. They go right to the birthing ground. They take the placenta, then take the offspring. I declared war on hogs."

The war worked. The Ford Ranch is now one of the premiere hunting ranches in the world. "We have hunts here eight months a year," Forrest said. "My phone rings all the time. By January 1, we're booked solid for the year. We only allow hunting on weekends. We need to take a rest and the animals need to take a rest. We have quail hunters here from January to March, turkey hunters in April and May, dove hunters in September and October, and deer hunters in November and December."

A FAMILY AFFAIR ON THE FORD RANCH

That doesn't leave much time for cowboying, but Forrest, ever the efficient manager, has that part down to a science. "This ranch is run by myself, my family, and one full-time cowboy, Mark Morvan. My whole family cowboys and helps me take care of this ranch. Amy is twenty-five, Wade, twenty, and Cord, fourteen, and all work weekends and when not in school. When we need additional hands we hire day workers. The original cows here were Herefords, then Brahman-Hereford crossbreds. We now have quarter-bred black cows. That's your terminal cross out of the best bulls money can buy. We have big cows, and we have big calves that weigh 650 to 670 pounds at weaning. Our bulls are Red and Black Limousin and Montana-bred Angus. That's our livestock program."

It seems to be working well. Forrest says when they feed the cattle during the winter, he and Mark can move the herds from one pasture to the other with only the dogs to help them. "Used to be when a cow would break from the bunch, a cowboy would take down a rope and go after her. Now I just put the dogs on her. When she comes back, she not only goes to the herd, she goes to the middle of the herd. Those dogs educate cattle in a hurry."

Kinda like the cats educating the snakes around the Armke residence. "Yea, we have a lot of cats," Forrest tells the visitor. "The cats keeps the snakes away." Oh, really. "There's lots of rattlesnakes on this place," he continues. "I carry a long stick with a hook on the end with me at all times. When I see a snake I pick it up and put it in a barrel on the truck. I've put my daughter through seven years of college catching [and selling] snakes." Talk about innovative.

And the cats? "The cats tease the snakes," Armke answers. "They just strut around in front of a snake, just out out striking range and drive the snake crazy, till it leaves."

Forrest and family aren't thinking about leaving. "We're very happy here. Ellen and I have been married twenty-seven years. We have two sons and a daughter and we like to take off and ski during winters and whitewater raft in summer. We enjoy this lifestyle and we're doing what we enjoy." You can't beat that—even with a stick with a hook on the end.

And you can't beat the cooking on the Ford Ranch. We ate at the deer camp and the only complaint we heard was from one of the camera men from Atlanta. "Man, they really push the food at you here," he groaned. "I eat more here in a day than I normally eat in a week. The food is fantastic. The only thing wrong is it really puts the weight on you. But it is good, no doubt about it. Probably the best in the West." Truer words have never been spoken by a more sober man.

Forrest says his wife Ellen cooks most of the meals at the ranch. "When we work livestock, she feeds the whole crew. We saddle and unsaddle her horse while she whips out the food. She has lots of character and always has a verbal war going on with the cowboys. She cooks because we have to eat; but she cowboys because she loves it." Here are a couple of recipes from the famous Ford Ranch. Watch your weight.

ELLEN'S HOLIDAY YEAST ROLLS

3 cups flour
1 package dry yeast
1 tablespoon sugar
1½ teaspoons salt
½ cup plus 1 tablespoon warm milk
½ cup warm water
1 tablespoon vegetable oil

Sift flour into large bowl. Make indentation in center and add yeast, sugar, salt, milk, water, and oil. Mix well and allow to rise about two hours. Knead and choke off rolls. Place on baking sheet and allow to rise another two hours. Bake in preheated oven at 375°F fifteen to twenty minutes or until brown.

Makes approximately one dozen rolls.

FORD RANCH GRILLED MEAT

Any cut of beef or venison or turkey breast
Mixture of ½ soy sauce and ½ Worcestershire sauce
Apply to both sides of meat with brush or by drenching
Pinch of fajita seasoning
Pinch of salt and pepper

Place meat on grill, baste with melted butter to prevent drying. (A little oil can be added to soy sauce mixture.) Cook slowly, seasoning to taste, and cook to desired doneness.

FOUR SIXES

GUTHRIE, TEXAS

JOE PROPPS

THE COWBOY'S SPOKESMAN

Entering Guthrie it's pretty hard to tell whether or not you are actually in a town or on the Four Sixes Ranch. Guthrie is the county seat of King County, so there is a courthouse, but the ranch and the 6666 Supply Store dominate the area.

This is another of the legendary Texas ranches that began in the latter part of the nineteenth century through the vision and daring of one man: Samuel "Burk" Burnett. The Burnett ranches—there are four—now comprise over 480,000 acres near the north-central plains towns of Guthrie, Panhandle, Paducah, and Granbury. They are generally known as the Four Sixes because of the famous brand, 6666.

As with many such enterprises, all sorts of tales concerning their origins have been repeated, and these grow with each telling. The story here is that Burk Burnett won the original ranch in a poker game with a winning hand of four sixes. However, the ranch says that, in fact, around 1867, Burnett bought one hundred head of cattle near Denton, Texas, and they all had the 6666 brand. He bought the brand with the cattle and continued to use it. Why the original owner used the 6666 brand remains a mystery.

Burk Burnett is one of the more fascinating of the early Texas cattlemen. He was born in Bates County, Missouri, on January 1, 1849. His father farmed, but during the very bloody Ruffian and Jayhawk raids (1857 and 1858) that preceded the Civil War, the Burnett home was destroyed. The family headed for Denton County, Texas, just north of Fort Worth.

STARTING AN EMPIRE

This was still the time of the open range and Jerry Burnett, Burk's dad, entered the cattle business. Burk was just nineteen when he bought the 6666 herd, but by 1873, he drove 1,100 steers to market in Wichita, Kansas. And the very next year, he bought 1,300 more cattle in the Rio Grande Valley and drove them up the Chisholm Trail to the Little Wichita River. Burnett also began to buy land, for as little as twenty-five cents an acre, and he positioned his headquarters near Wichita Falls, Texas.

Throughout the 1880s, the Four Sixes continued to grow, but a severe drought nearly destroyed the grazing lands. Burnett needed more grass for his cattle. Burk joined with some other ranchers and convinced the Kiowa and Comanche tribes to lease them some pasture, nearly one million acres of reservation land just north of the Red River in Oklahoma. For Burnett, this resulted in 300,000 acres of grass and a new friend in the great Comanche chief, Quanah Parker. Their friendship was strong, and the Comanches named Burnett MAS-SA-SUTA, "Big Boss."

Near the turn of the century, the United States government told the ranchers that they had to leave the Indian lands because the land was going to be opened to homesteaders. The ranchers felt that this was very unfair, so Burnett went to Washington D.C. to make his plea personally to President Theodore Roosevelt, who had himself been a rancher in North Dakota. The President helped the ranchers obtain a two-year extension on their leases, giving them enough time to find new grasslands for their cattle.

In the spring of 1905, Teddy Roosevelt visited the Indian lands and the ranchers he had helped. Burk Burnett, his son Tom, and a small group of ranchers, including W.T. Waggoner, entertained the old North Dakota cowboy in wild Texas style, including an unusual bare-handed hunt for coyotes and wolves. But the West was changing and changing fast. Much of the open range was being fenced. Therefore, if a man intended to stay in the cattle business, he needed to get deeded land and as much of it as he could afford.

Burnett was keenly aware of the need to acquire land. So he bought the 8 Ranch in Guthrie from the Louisville Land and Cattle Company. This is the heart of the Four Sixes today. Then he bought the Dixon Creek Ranch near Panhandle from the Cunard Line. These two ranches plus some later additions gave Burnett about a third of a million acres—a solid base on which to build.

THE HEADQUARTERS

During the development of his ranching empire in the plains of West Texas, Burk Burnett lived in Fort Worth, making frequent trips west. As many tycoons did, and he was definitely becoming a tycoon, he even had his own railroad car to take him to Paducah, where he got off the train and climbed aboard his horse and buggy for the thirty-mile ride south to Guthrie.

To many, the crowning jewel of the physical plant at the Guthrie ranch is the main house. Headquarters is an attractive setup with red barns and outbuildings, the horse facilities, a series of homes for the ranch workers and the cowboys, and the house that Burk Burnett built in 1917 to be "the finest ranch house in West Texas." It certainly is that, and more. It is beautifully landscaped; the trees and bushes are so lush they make the house hard to see. The house was constructed with stone quarried on the ranch at an original cost of $100,000, a princely sum at the time. There are few ranches anywhere that have homes as large or as dominating and as attractively set as this "ranch house" at the Four Sixes.

A FAMILY TRADITION CONTINUES

Samuel "Burk" Burnett died in Fort Worth in 1922 at the age of seventy-three. He left a legacy that few have equaled. He is credited with starting the idea of all-steer herds. In 1875 he introduced blooded Durhams and Herefords to his ranch and was one of the organizers of the Texas Cattle Raisers Association. He was a member of its executive committee all his life. In 1907 the town of Nestorville, in Wichita County, Texas, was renamed Burkburnett in his honor. This man was truly a giant of the cattle industry. At his death, his will provided for the appointment of two trustees to manage his holdings. They and their successors ran the Four Sixes until 1980, when Burnett's great-grand-daughter, Mrs. Anne Windfohr Marion took over.

Burk Burnett had three children, but his son Tom was the only one who survived him. Tom was a good rancher, learning the cattle business first as a ranch hand and then working his way into management with his father. He was a top-notch judge of horses and cattle and well respected by other stockmen and the hands at the the Four Sixes. He developed the Triangle Ranches at Paducah and Iowa Park, Texas. His first marriage to Ollie Lake of Fort Worth produced a daughter, Anne. Tom Burnett died in 1938.

THE WOMEN OF THE FOUR SIXES

Anne, known around the ranch as "Miss Anne," was, like her dad, a top judge of horses and cattle. Together with her second husband, James Goodwin, she was one of the architects of the American Quarter Horse Association and she was a founder of the American Quarter Horse Hall of Fame. She was also the first woman to be named as honorary vice president of the Texas and Southwestern Cattle Raisers' Association and the AQHA. In 1969 she married Charles Tandy. "Miss Anne" had one child, a daughter also named Anne.

Anne Burnett Windfohr Marion, often called "Little Anne," has been running the ranch since her mother passed away in 1980. She is a hands-on manager; in fact, not since Burk Burnett himself has a family member taken as active an interest in the ranches as has his great-granddaughter.

CONTINUITY

But there has always been continuity at the Four Sixes. In the more than 125 years of the ranch's operation, there have only been five foremen at headquarters in Guthrie, a truly extraordinary record. George Humphrey was head man for forty years and the foreman today, Mike Gibson, took over from his dad, J. J. Gibson, in 1991. J. J. Gibson is now vice president of Burnett Ranches, overseeing the breeding and feedlot operations.

Cattle and horses each have their own place at the Four Sixes. The ranch is one of the largest commercial cattle outfits in Texas, and yet they are known worldwide for their horses. The commercial Hereford herd is the prime element in today's cattle operation, and championship crosses have been produced using Brangus bulls. The Brangus were brought on the ranch because they make such good use of the country. For one thing, they'll walk farther to water, which is not extremely plentiful in the central plains of Texas. The cow/calf operation manages the herds from birth through the feedlot, after which the cattle are sold to a meat processor. It's like other ranches, except larger—much larger. The Four Sixes runs about 10,000 mother cows.

Each spring, the cows and calves are rounded up and the calves are branded and vaccinated, the bull calves are castrated, and the dry cows are shipped to the packers. By summer, all the calves are sent to the Dixon Creek ranch, where they are put on grass. The ranchhands also examine the heifer calves, sending back about 900 to Guthrie as replacement cows. The rest, plus the steers, go to the feedlot, where they reach between 1,200 and 1,400 pounds before they are sold to the meat processor.

THE GREAT HORSE SIRES

Don't forget the horses. They also have a very important role in the operation of the Four Sixes. The horses all have the L brand in honor of Burk Burnett's father-in-law, Captain M. B. Loyd. The horses are raised primarily for ranch work, but surplus horses have been sold in Mexico, Brazil, Canada, and all over the United States. Quarter horse people have prized the sons and daughters of Joe Hancock, Hollywood Gold, and Gray Badger, three of their most famous stallions. Today the great stallion, Dash For Cash, bred by B. F. Phillips, Jr., of Frisco, Texas, stands at the ranch.

The horses raised at the Four Sixes are bred for cow sense, speed, gentleness, and confirmation. They are bred through artificial insemination by the resident veterinarian at a superb facility. And it's quite a sight to see such a band of fine horses in the green pastures just south of headquarters. The brood mare herd numbers about one hundred. All the males are gelded; they go into the remuda used by the cowboys. A few fillies are kept each year to replace older mares in the brood mare band.

It's so hard to summarize the story of a great establishment like the Four Sixes in a few pages. Certainly this only touches the surface, but this ranch is not an institution of the past. (Much of the early history was gathered from the

6666 barn with L horse brand.

ranch-produced booklet, *The Four Sixes*. This is a beautifully designed booklet and can be purchased at the 6666 Supply Store in Guthrie.) In fact, it is still a showplace, with tourists coming from all over the world to see how a big Texas spread operates. The Four Sixes has managed to keep its traditions alive. There is real longevity here, and cowboying at the Four Sixes is just about as good as it gets.

THE COWBOY AND THE WAGONS

One of the most important hands at the ranch is Joe Propps, the wagon cook. We met at his place just outside of Paducah, where he raises ostriches along with some cattle. Greeted with a hearty, "Take your boots off and come on in," we talk about cowboys and cooking. There are few people around who speak as forcefully about the cowboys and the cowboy way of life; Joe knows what he's talking about.

He was born and raised in the cowboy world. He was born on the Waggoner ranch at a cowcamp and grew up at a camp called "White Face." His dad worked on the ranch for thirty-six years, and as Joe says, "That's all I've ever known." He went off to college and has a degree in history from Texas A&M, just the background you need for a ranching career. "At that time, my folks wanted better for their kids and that meant trying to get a city job because back then a good ranch job only paid $100 a month and your house, lights, water, and gas . . . but eventually the kid has to go home. Instead of sirens or horns you have to hear cows bawling. It's just in your blood . . . "

In 1966, the Four Sixes needed a cook, and George Humphrey, the manager, hired Joe. He's been on the payroll ever since, nearly thirty years. In those days, cowboys made $100 a month, working seven days a week, 365 days a year. "The wagon boss and cook made three hundred a month . . . I was considered a pretty good cook so that got me the job and better money."

At the Waggoner ranch, his mother cooked at a horse camp for twelve to fourteen single cowboys, who were each assigned ten to twelve broncs to break. His mother fed three meals a day "and everyone helped. A lot of the cowboys even dried the dishes. I helped out a lot at the house because cooking was easy for me. I just plain like to cook. Even over here by myself, I sometimes get inspired and work all day cooking one thing."

THE WAGON—THEN AND NOW

Joe points out that you really don't find many ranches anymore that take the wagons out and you find fewer real chuck wagon cooks. "Now there are modern wagons with butane. There are more cooks for those than the kind that are wood only with no electricity, no running water, no anything. In the early days we moved every three or four days. Everything had to be mobile. We used a six-up hitch of mules. The hood wagon had two brown mules and it carried bed rolls and everything went on it. Sometimes we stayed a day, sometimes we'd be there ten or fifteen days." Remember, too, that when Joe talks about the "old days," he means the 1960s and 1970s, his first years at the Four Sixes. "In those days things were still pretty well like it had been done a hundred years ago. The ranch was totally self-sufficient. Even today, if they took all the electricity and all the gas away, this part of the country could function and function well. Anywhere there are western people and that kind of heritage, they can function without all the modern conveniences. In New York, if you close up Safeway, somebody's going to starve to death. We've still kept some of the old ways because they are the most efficient as far as work is concerned. It's kind of like a good working marriage. We took what old ways were good and took what new ways were good and matched them up to where it just made it easier for everyone." But even with the wagons the modern lifestyle has crept in. "Now maybe we camp at one place a lot longer because if it rains on one part of the ranch, by having our camp central, we can truck to another part of the ranch and have a drive while the other part is wet."

The wagons go out about March 15 and stay until about May 1 for the spring branding, then go out again around July 1 and stay out until September for the weaning and shipping to the Dixon Creek ranch. Every fall the owners have big hunting parties, bringing in people from the East and Europe, so the cowboys have to be finished with their work. "Hunting season is a big deal."

However, by no stretch of the imagination should you think that this huge ranch is a playground to the rich and famous. Joe makes sure you understand that "Miss Anne" runs this ranch for real. "If you cook for Miss Anne, you're going to have the best or she's just not going to do it. She's that kind of person. She's been over every bit of the ranch ahorseback herself. She's been out there working at daylight, she's been out there gathering the cattle. She knows what makes a cowboy hurt and she knows what makes him happy. She didn't inherit this job from a desk. She's had the other end of it. . . . She's a real astute cattlewoman. She wants to make the better changes as far as genetic engineering and different things ranchers do now if they've got the money to do it—that

A TASTE
OF
TEXAS RANCHING

6666

84

Joe Propps preparing a meal at his own kitchen. Joe is the wagon cook for the 6666 in Guthrie, Texas.

benefits everyone." That also helps to explain why there is so much loyalty at the ranch and so little turnover among the managers, cowboys, and cooks.

From Joe's long perspective in ranching, he believes that, "Nowadays you have to do everything in the world to make a place pay. There is not a lot of margin for error in the ranching business. You make too many mistakes and you're out. Everyone is pretty well working toward the same goals, like how to produce the quality and type of cattle that are wanted at the feedlots and wanted by the American consumer. And even how to handle those cattle so the animal rights people keep off your back." The Four Sixes is not in an area of abundant rainfall, but it is in very stable short-grass country. Joe says, "A ranch will tell you what to do, you don't tell a ranch what to do. If you start to tell it you won't be in business very long."

THE COOK WAGON AND THE HOODLUM

When the wagons go out to cover this extremely large ranch, they take the cook wagon and the hoodlum wagon. The Four Sixes chuck wagon was built around 1910 or 1911, and the tent and all the food are carried in it. The second wagon, or hoodlum wagon, carries the bedrolls and all the cowboy's belongings. "A man's bedroll was almost his living room, his dining room, his bedroom. Everything he had was eventually rolled up in that bedroll, protected with a tarp and thrown on the wagon. There wasn't any luggage to speak of or anything like that. They were stacked so high you couldn't hardly see the driver."

Back in the "old days," the land was thick with brush and mesquite, so you had to hire more cowboys. And you could afford to hire a lot of cowboys at $100 per month. "Now the land has been cleared, we don't use the mules, and we can park the wagon in one central location and go from there." In the nearly thirty years that Joe has been the wagon cook, he says that "they've modernized it, yet it's old enough so you'd still recognize things. Fifty percent change from the first year I came and 50 percent of it is still the same."

MORE VEGETABLES AND PLENTY OF BEANS

In the old days, the menu was different because they had to be so mobile that Joe couldn't carry the heavy canned goods that he has now. It used to be all the beef, red beans, potatoes, bread, and cobbler you could eat. They never had eggs for breakfast. It was just bacon, biscuits, gravy, and coffee. Now the menu is much more varied and includes more vegetables. In fact, Joe says that the meals are just "about the same as you could get in anybody's home."

Joe says that once the wagon boss, Bigun Bradley, was going to town, and asked if he could bring back anything for Joe. Joe asked him to bring some fresh vegetables. "He came back with a hundred pound block of ice . . . and brought me two bushels of bell peppers. And there's not a whole helluva lot you can do with two bushel baskets of bell peppers. But he did bring me vegetables. He didn't know one vegetable from another but he could look a mile off and tell you what kind of cow was out there and where she was going."

FEWER COWBOYS—THE SAME WORK

In the old days, there were twenty-five to thirty cowboys at the wagon. Now Joe feeds twelve to fifteen. Fewer cowboys can do the same work in less time because of some modernization. He also says that wages have really come up. Today the cowboys get their house, utilities, beef, and have both a good retirement plan and good medical insurance. "You have paid vacations. By doing that the ranch attracts a more stable individual that knows . . . in ranching he has an exceptional job. Someone has to die for you to get a job at the Four Sixes. . . . We have owners who actually care about us. We're all one family. If you're loyal, a decent employee, you've got a home from now on." The ranch encourages cowboys with families. "We're all proud of this ranch."

THE COUNTRY AND THE CITY

Although he is now approaching fifty, Joe's never been married. But he says he could have lived the same sort of life, "if he was married to the right kind of woman." Women, he stresses, have to understand that ranch work is often from daylight to dark. "Now at least there are days off, as modernization has made some things easier. If you were going to live in this country and maybe be as happy as possible in this country, you'd be better off marrying a country girl. Town people can't adapt. It's like putting a cowboy to work in a factory—probably he's not going to be very happy or stay very long. It's often turned out to be the same with city women. They can appreciate some things about the country but not all of it and it's made it difficult for them to adapt. Some did, some didn't."

A CAN OF SKOAL, A SADDLE, AND A BRIDLE

Nowadays, very often, guys and gals applying for a job buy themselves "a can of Skoal, and a saddle and a bridle, and they're a cowboy. But a real cowboy can set and watch a cow and tell you what she's gonna do because it's in his blood. He thinks like she does. The boy with just the Skoal can and a saddle doesn't know what she's gonna do. It takes time and experience. It takes wanting to be a cowboy. You have to dedicate yourself to get to be a good cowboy. It's the kind of job anybody can apply for but the first five minutes you're at work they know if you lied or told the truth because it's a job where you must produce and produce under all kinds of circumstances. Every minute of that day can be different. Every minute of that day you have to adapt to the situation, a lot of times to make your work easier or to get the cows or even just to save yourself from having a bad wreck. . . . You have to know what you're doing because there are a lot of unforgiving elements still out West."

HIRING YOUNG FAMILY MEN

When the Four Sixes hires, and that is rarely, they look for family men, under thirty, with kids. They prefer the younger men because they expect them to stay for a long time. Strong references are required; and they will be checked. "You don't have to know everything in the world but you do have to impress them with the fact that you'd be willing to learn. They do not expect to hire someone who is 100 percent to start with, but if a person will listen, within a year to five years you'll be 100 percent because you will have learned their way and you'll do things their way. That's what they want."

Joe summarizes it best when he says, "Basically, a good cowboy who understands horses, who understands cattle, and to a limited amount can put up with people, can find a job without a whole lot of problems."

ROPING AND RIDING

Cowboy skills are the same all over. You need to ride, rope a little, know a little animal medicine, and you really have to have the right attitude. At the Four Sixes, every cowboy is given a chance to rope calves in the corral as they drag them to the fire for branding. This is a ranch that definitely does not use chutes. "Chutes are for city people who buy ranches. We can brand five while you're putting one through the chutes. Everyone is given a chance to drag and patiently given it if he can't rope, because everyone has to learn. But the boy who can't rope may be out there in the pasture or the brush and be in the right hole when the right cow starts to run off. That's just as important because if you don't turn her then you don't bring her to the pens. The older people do the actual branding and vaccinating, and if you're stove up you get to do an easier job." Joe points out that on the ranch "age is very respected in our thinking, in our [cowboy] society."

When it comes to the horses, Joe sympathetically says, "Nobody really likes to brand a horse. It's hard to put a hot iron on your mount. They just didn't do more than they had to to a horse. That's your brother, your buddy, your best help. . . . A cowboy don't do much to his horse and nothing to his wife."

THE EASIEST JOB IN THE WORLD

When the talk finally got around to cooking and what it's like to cook for a bunch of good cowboys, Joe gave a resounding thumbs-up to the whole idea of cooking for a crew of hungry punchers out on the range. "It's about the easiest job in the world. A nutritionist would be hung the first damned day. But a cook they like. You fix meals that will stick to people's ribs. You fix meals that have enough grease in them that's gonna help keep 'em warm when it's cold. We don't count calories and we don't count cholesterol. People would look at our diet and say we're probably gonna die shortly, but on the other hand, the county gives free cholesterol tests and our cowboys are always setting there right on the money. They burn it up, they work it off. . . . But it's a heavy diet. I always figure at breakfast, around eight to ten slices of bacon per person. At noon, at least a pound of meat per person. There'll be all the potatoes and all the beans and all the bread they want to eat. There will usually be two vegetables every meal. It makes no difference if it's corn or green beans—any kind of canned vegetable."

Joe added an interesting insight about how they sometimes get fresh vegetables out at the wagon. He said that if any of the cowboys' wives have gardens and they have any extra produce, they usually send it out to the wagon. "We can get cucumbers from one, cantaloupe from another. We beg, borrow, or steal all the fresh vegetables we can get because everybody likes them and they are considered good for you. But basically, every day, you know you are going to have red beans. They don't want any black-eyed peas, they don't want any navy beans, they don't want any lima beans. They want red beans . . . "A cowboy has no use for a casserole of any kind. They just haven't made a good casserole as far as they're concerned. Meat was meant to be chewed, not ground." At the wagon, the favorite meal is fried steak, fried potatoes, gravy, red beans, and lots of cobbler. And those hungry cowpunchers seem to thrive on any kind of dessert.

JOE AND HIS STOVE

For Joe Propps, cooking at his wood stove out on the range is really an art form. "I have a real primitive setup as far as cooking goes. It's all definitely wood. There are no thermostats, there are no indicators of how hot the oven is. You tell by sticking a hand in the oven—whether it's a medium, or it's a hot, or a low heat. I know my old stove. . . . I know what it can do. That stove and I have been together twenty-eight years so we know each other and we can cook anything at the wagon you would want. And that's from an angel food cake to whatever. You just have to know how to do it. If I brought in the best chef from New York City, he couldn't do anything, whereas if I went to his place, I couldn't either . . . " Joe sort of summarizes the wagon meals by emphasizing that "the food is rich and good and there's plenty of it."

ROMANTIC JOE PROPPS

Joe Propps is a romantic, plain and simple. But in every way he is in touch with the everyday world of ranching. He knows the old ways, has adapted to the new, but still believes in things like loyalty and friendship. He talks about cowboys "riding for the brand," and how loyalty makes the whole group loyal to each other. He adds that "bad manners is never tolerated anywhere in the West." You've got to understand that to Joe, the West is not so much a geographical location as it is another name for the cowboy culture that he cherishes.

He believes that "you can see one fellow walking by the road and have another guy beside him and you can tell which one's a cowboy and which one's not. "If you don't have that gait. . . . I can look over in the pasture and from the way they sit their saddle or by their silhouette, I can tell which cowboy it is. Everybody has their own way, but they all look better ahorseback. They just don't care for the ground."

CARING FOR THE LAND

Joe is, if nothing else, an optimist. He says what's important is the land and the things that God gave us that we have to take care of. "We take care of the land. We don't abuse it in any way. The land is like a horse. It's there to use, but you pet him every chance you can."

To this romantic wagon cook, the glass is always half full, and at the end of every drought there is rain. Just have some patience.

THE GILLETTE RANCH

CROCKETT, TEXAS
PIPP, GUY, AND CATHI GILLETTE

HOME OF HORSES, CATTLE, WESTERN MUSIC, AND COWBOY COOKING

We first learned of the Gillette Ranch through a write-up in *Western Horseman Magazine*. Arizona author and camp cook, Stella Hughes, reviewed a new western music album by the Gillette Brothers titled *Home Ranch*, produced by Big Daddy Records, Crockett, Texas. Hughes stated: "While driving down the road in your pickup, the miles slip effortlessly by when listening to this tape. These boys are good."

Since we were writing for a regional magazine titled *Rocky Mountain Rider*, we sent for a review copy of *Home Ranch*. Stella was right. These boys are good. Just how good are they? We really didn't begin to understand that until we met them in person. Guy and Pipp Gillette, and Guy's wife, Cathi, proved to be some of the nicest, friendliest, most congenial and interesting people we met in Texas. And the most interesting thing about the Gillette brothers is—and please don't tell anyone—they're from New York.

Now before you get your rope ready, hear us out. The Gillette brothers have long family ties to Texas, and they've made Texas their home. Besides, they are hard working ranchers, as well as great musicians and excellent cooks. And they're working very hard to preserve the history and tradition of ranching, western music, and cowboy cooking. They are a welcome addition to Texas and they're doing their part to keep alive the ranch their maternal grandfather started in 1912 in East Texas. This is not normally thought of as prime cattle country but, in fact, has the highest concentration of cow/calf production in the state. A visit with the Gillette brothers is a mini course in Texas history, culture, work, music, and food.

"Back Porch Blues"—Pipp, Cathi, and Guy Gillette rest on the steps of the "Little Board Shack" that provided inspiration for songs on the "Home Ranch" album. Gillette Ranch, Crockett, Texas.

CROCKETT HERE, CROCKETT THERE, CROCKETT EVERYWHERE

Unless you've been living in a cave on Mars for the last century, you probably know who Davy Crockett was. If you have any doubt, just visit Texas. You'll quickly be educated on the history of this now famous frontiersman. David

Crockett was born in Tennessee in 1786, fought Indians in Florida, dabbled in politics, and died at the Alamo. In the process, he became one of the most famous names in Texas. There are Crockett schools, highways, buildings, and numerous statues and markers, and even a Crockett County, though old Davy never went anywhere near the place. The people in that area just liked him, so they named their county after him. Davy Crockett is big in Texas.

The town of Crockett was, of course, named after Davy and is the county seat of Houston, the oldest county in Texas. Davy is said to have camped at—where else—Davy Crockett Springs, with his men, on their way to that fateful rendezvous in San Antonio in 1836. At that time, Houston County was part of Nacogdoches territory, and in 1837, local leaders petitioned to become a county. That bill was passed May 17, 1837 and in January, 1845, Texas became the twenty-eighth state in the United States.

THE NEW YORK CONNECTION

According to local records, one Augustus Lundy of Georgia settled in Polk County, Texas, and her second daughter, Francis, married Jonathan Jenkins Porter. Four children were born to this union, one of whom was Virgil Hoyt Porter. Virgil Hoyt married Lucy Thornton, who lived near Lovelady, a half day's horse ride southwest of Crockett.

The town of Lovelady, with a population of less than 600, was founded by Houston and Great Northern Railroad investors as the line was built through a grant of Cyrus Lovelady, and is located near the communities of Nevil's Prairie, Pennington, and Weldon. The Lovelady post office opened on November 8, 1872. The town soon had livery stables, stores, a blacksmith shop, and hotels, prospering as a market and shipping point. By 1876, day school and Sunday school were held in a log house. The town incorporated in 1927 and is now a center for ranching and pulpwood production.

When we were looking for the Gillette Ranch, we zipped right by Lovelady. In Crockett we stopped at a local music store, figuring they'd know about the Gillette Brothers. They did. "Oh, yeah," the proprietor mused from behind a magazine, "them New York boys." We almost croaked. "New York City—Get a rope." It was too much. We retired back to the edge of town to a roadside park and took a nap to clear the brain.

Presently, there was a knock on the motor home and two weathered cowboys stood at the door. Guy: tall, slim, elegant; and Pipp: stocky, shy we thought at the time, but sharp, and witty. Just how witty we would find out later. The boys were on their way into town to swap trucks, saw the RV, and stopped by to invite us out to the ranch. That's pure quill Texas hospitality, something they surely didn't learn in New York. Fact is, the Gillette brothers have spent a lot of time in Texas, and Texas *is* their home.

Guy was born in Crockett, in the hospital, in 1945, one hundred years after Texas was admitted to the Union. Pipp, on the other hand, was born on Staten Island, New York, and has that quick New York City street-smartness about him. He reminds us of the New York comic/movie actor/movie producer Billy

Crystal, always making with the jokes and one-liners. He also makes excellent music and does the lead vocals on most of their songs. And he does most of the talking. In reviewing tapes of our conservation, it's difficult to pick out the facts from the fiction. It's difficult to pick out much of anything because everything is garbled with laughter.

BIG DADDY MARRIES BIG MOMMY

This is Pipp on his background: "Our grandfather [Virgil Hoyt Porter], who we called Big Daddy, was born in 1891 west of Lovelady in the Antioch community. He was my mother's father. My grandmother [Lucy Thornton Porter] was from the same area. Apparently grandfather would ride by her house and apparently ride by quite often and apparently cut a pretty handsome figure . . ."

Both Guy and Pipp say they are amazed how Hoyt married Lucy. "Big Mommy's best friend was home one evening when Big Mommy appeared. A few minutes later Big Daddy appeared. And a few minutes later a minister appeared. And they got married, right then, then both went back to their respective homes for a few days until they moved out to the ranch. This was in 1919."

In 1921, they had a daughter, Doris. After high school, she studied in Denton, Texas, for two years and then went to New York to study fashion design. So, the young lady from Lovelady went to the Big Apple. She took a job as a waitress in a restaurant to supplement her allowance, and there she met and married Guy Gillette, a budding actor, student, and photographer who was bussing tables. After marriage, the young couple came to Texas. "They were thinking of getting involved in ranching, but ultimately moved back to New York where my father was involved in acting in the theater," Pipp says. "He acted on and off Broadway. His first love being photography, he became a great photojournalist and worked for all the leading magazines of that period."

THOSE CRAZY YANKEES WHO RODE EVERYWHERE

Pipp was born in 1950 and speaks fondly of his earliest memories of coming to Texas—on the train. "We'd come down here every summer. We'd get on the train at Penn Station and get off at the depot in Lovelady. It was wonderful. We'd be wearing our jeans and boots and carrying our chaps and saddles. One time a lady told us, 'You know, they really don't dress like that out there anymore.' We knew they didn't in the city where she lived, but they did where we were going. We came to Texas to ride horses and work cattle."

Years later, when the Gillette brothers returned to Texas to take up ranching, they said they were remembered mostly by one fact: "Oh yeah, you're those crazy Yankees who rode horses everywhere."

"We did," Guy says, "everywhere. Everywhere we went we rode horses. I even rode my horse into a store one time. It was fun, but I got in a lot of trouble. Mother didn't think it was very funny."

A teen-age Guy Gillette checks the quality of his coffee with brother Pipp and their maternal grandfather, Virgil Hoyt Porter on the Gillette Ranch, Crockett, Texas (photo by Guy Gillette, Sr.).

"He'd seen too many Charlie Russell paintings," Pipp quips. "But mainly we rode to help with the cattle. We had to do a lot of spraying back in those days. So we'd have to gather the cattle and put 'em in a a little pen and spray 'em for ticks and flies. The ticks were terrible here then, and we had to spray two or three times a summer." Ah, the good old days, when there were plenty of ticks. The good news is that the ticks in East Texas are no more. The bad news is they've been eaten by fire ants.

GETTING DOWN AND FUNKY

"Now we have trouble with the fire ants," Pipp states. "They're very aggressive. They'll kill a young calf if a mother doesn't clean it up and get it moving. And they're everywhere. Not as bad as the ticks once were. But they're bad. When we were young we'd walk through the woods and just get covered with ticks. Thousands and thousands of tiny seed ticks. Every night it was standard procedure to de-tick.

"But as bad as the ants are, you can avoid them. They don't build big mounds. Just lots of little mounds. Everywhere. They'll come right after you, too. They make you take your pants off. I mean you'll just get down and get funky."

Getting down and getting funky is something the Gillette brothers know something of. After high school, Guy tried his hand at cowboying on a big West Texas ranch, then returned to New York where he and Pipp formed the Guy and Pipp Gillette Band about the time the Beatles became popular. "We saw them on the Ed Sullivan show with all those screaming girls and said, 'That looks like a good job.'" For almost two decades, they played country and western music, R&B, Blues, and fifties rock-'n'-roll up and down the East Coast.

MEANWHILE, BACK AT THE RANCH

The Gillette brothers were doing real well in that "good job" when their grandfather Porter died in 1974; then their grandmother died two years later. The ranch was leased out, and as the boys made music, the brush made a comeback on the pastures. A crisis arose in the early 1980s when the lease came up for renewal. A cousin wanted a ten-year lease to compensate for all the work that needed to be done. In New York, the Gillette brothers did some serious thinking. It was time to relocate. "Our original music had evolved into an almost exclusively Texas/Louisiana influence. We were a Texas band playing in New York and here was the perfect opportunity to play Texas music at the source and finally start ranching."

"We'd always had this plan to some day return to the ranch," Guy says. "In 1982, that some day became today."

"You know some people in music have this great plan," Pipp chips in. "'If I don't make it in the music business in five years, I'll become a brain surgeon.' We never put a time table on it, we just wanted to play music and ranch. We still visited the ranch occasionally, but we really weren't aware of what was going on there."

What was going on was benign neglect. When the brothers made their decision to return to their first love, they found out what many lovers find out—absence may make the heart grow fonder, but it also makes the weeds and brush grow, the pastures deteriorate, fences collapse, and buildings fall into disrepair.

GTT

Pipp on returning to the ranch in 1983: "The pastures had deteriorated to the point where there was very little open ground. What once was waving fields of grass was grown up in brush. The fences were like, sorta, gone. We thought we'd live in the foreman's old house as we fixed the place up. He hadn't lived there in five years and he shouldn't have lived there for the five years before that, maybe twenty years; it was a mess. The porch was falling down, the building was sinking, and the doors wouldn't open. They'd been sawed off at the bottoms to compensate for the lean. When we jacked up the house and leveled it, suddenly all the doors started swinging. 'We're free!'

"That's the way it all went. We just started cleaning up and fixing up. We started with a brush eradication program. We had to hire a cat [bulldozer] to clear the pastures. You give that brush five years and you gotta use a chain saw on it. We worked just like our forefathers, cutting down trees with a saw and grubbing stumps with mules."

They began stocking the place with cattle as soon as possible. Even though they'd spent many summers working on their grandfather's ranch, they had lots to learn about the ranching business. "We asked around," Guy says, "and everybody we asked had a different story. Finally we went to the Lambshead Ranch [near Albany, Texas] and bought some Herefords from Watt Matthews

[whom Guy cowboyed for out of high school and still admires and respects].
We thought we'd cross them with gray Brahmans and raise F-1s, that fabulous
hybrid that everyone talks about."

But the boys hadn't figured on how those English (Hereford) cattle, born
and raised in arid West Texas, would adjust to the heat and humidity of East
Texas. Pipp recalls, "What happened was the Herefords kept calving later and
later. First we'd get calves in March and April, and then it was June and July,
then August and September. We couldn't figure out what was the matter."
What was the matter was the cows couldn't take the weather. "You'd see 'em
standing under a tree, going, 'Gads, can you believe how humid it is here?' in
their English accent of course. 'Can you believe this humidity?'"

LEARNING THE CATTLE BUSINESS FROM START TO FINISH

Long-time cattleman Watt Matthews was concerned when he learned that
the Gillettes were going to put Brahman bulls on his first-calf heifers. "He gave
us a Longhorn bull. That's the kind of man Watt Matthews is. He was so
concerned about our ranching and his heifers, he gave us a bull. You don't find
many men like Watt Matthews."

And you won't find two young ranchers who learned the cattle business faster
than the Gillette brothers. "That first year, with the Longhorns, we did fine,"
Guy says. "Then we put them Brahmans out and our troubles began. That next
spring, we pulled almost every calf that was born on this place."

"I didn't know a cow could have a calf on it's own," Pipp says. "We got a
hands-on learning experience. We learned how to pull calves right from the
start. Now the F-1 offspring are eight years old and are doing great. We're using
Hereford bulls on those offspring and get what you call the terminal cross. We
end up with a quarter Brahman and three-quarters Hereford."

"The calves are all uniform and look great," Guy states. "We contract the
majority of our calves to a buyer, and we work with a couple of neighbors who
do the same thing. The market has been good for a longer period of time than
most folks can remember—let's hope it stays that way."

BRINGING TEXAS MUSIC BACK TO TEXAS

As for the music business, what the Gillette Brothers do now is western
music. Songs about cattle and horses and cowboys and coyotes, about the land
and the weather and the work, and about the cooks and the cooking. Western
music. Six years ago, the boys traveled to Abilene to the Western Heritage
Classic and heard Don Edwards and Riders in the Sky singing western music.
"They were doing great old songs," Guy says, but "we kept saying, 'Nobody's
doing the stuff we remembered from our childhood with the emphasis on
working cowboy songs.' So we recorded some of the songs we love on the *Home
Ranch* tape."

The tape has two original songs, one written by Guy and one written by Pipp,
and they are western songs about the West. "We've got quite an extensive

western library," Guy says. "We've read about every book there is on cowboying and the West. We've got almost every one of Will James' books except a couple from his 'Uncle Bill' series, and he wrote some twenty-three books." A friend gave the boys a book of western songs, and they discovered that the old cowboy standard "Cowboy Jack," which they recorded on *Home Ranch,* was recorded right in beautiful downtown Lovelady in 1936. "The fellow who recorded that song is our insurance man's father," Guy says. "Since we recorded it, people come up to us and say, 'I haven't heard that song in years. My grandfather used to sing it.' It's been a lot of fun for us. It's a wonderful feeling to get back into these old songs. It's like a breath of fresh air. It's real cowboy stuff. We love it."

The boys are in the process of putting together another album. This one will be titled *Cinch Up Your Riggin.* We got a sneak preview while we were with them. Guy has put a Jim Davis poem called "The Bogus Brown" to music. Pipp has added music to a Fran Hendrick poem called "The Cocinero." The rest are old— mostly unknown—cowboy songs.

PICKING AND GRINNING—AND COOKING

Visiting the Gillettes was pure pleasure. They've spent so much time rebuilding the ranch that their love for the place is evident. One of the most recently completed projects is a cook shack, modeled after the one on the Lambshead Ranch. The rectangular building is well lit, with plenty of windows. A modern gas range, and a woodburning range that belonged to their father's mother, provide plenty of cooking space. The ranch's number one cook, Guy's wife, Cathi, also does some open hearth cooking in Dutch ovens in the large brick fireplace.

The Christmas decorations were still up when we visited, making us privy to one of the most unique decorations of any Christmas anywhere—a collection of Dutch ovens stacked by the fireplace, with a tiny string of lights to attract attention to the little cast iron "tree." It doesn't get any more western than that.

While the boys filled a couple of tapes with ranch history for us, Cathi prepared one of the best meals we would enjoy on any of our visits. Everyone at the Gillette Ranch can cook, but Cathi is the real cook. Guy says his specialty is biscuits, Pipp's is maintaining fires, and Cathi's specialty is—well, everything else.

"We've always had an interest in Dutch oven cooking," Guy says. "That pot over there, my mother had for over thirty years. But it took us to get here [back to Texas] to get to where we're trying to perfect it [Dutch oven cooking]. We've got a wagon and we've built a chuck box. We studied the old XIT [Ranch] wagon and got the measurements. We weren't quite as authentic as we should have been and had to go back and change things." Authenticity is all-important, down to the last square nut and slotted screw.

They have become some of the top chuck wagon cooks in the state. Pretty bold language even in Texas. But, it's probably true. Trust us. They are good. In 1993, they participated in seven cook-offs. They won first place at four, second place at one, and third place at two.

Cook, cowgirl, and Dutch oven jockey, Cathi Gillette. Gillette Ranch, Crockett, Texas.

COOKING FROM THE ROOTS OF COWBOY COUNTRY

"I grew up in the Panhandle," Cathi explains, "near Clarendon, where Goodnight invented the chuck wagon. I didn't grow up on a ranch and I didn't grow up cooking very much. Then I met Guy and I started experimenting with gourmet cooking indoors and out. Cooking at a chuck wagon is challenging. After you get used to it, though, it's easier than cooking in an oven [in a house].

"If you've got one spot that needs browning, you just put some coals there. You can't do that with a gas or electric oven. It's just easier to cook some things over an open fire, however it's physically demanding. Especially when it's 103 degrees and the wind's blowing. But, I really enjoy it."

"We've been doing chuck wagon cooking competitions for about five years now," Guy says. "Our first cook-off was at the Western Heritage Classic in Abilene. Cliff Teinert was cooking there. I'd met Cliff at the Lambshead when I was cowboying for Watt in '64. He was a big influence on us. He's cooked in the White House; Reagan invited him. He took a bunch of calf fries along as part of the meal, but they wouldn't let him serve 'em, so the kitchen crew got to eat 'em and the guests missed out."

The Gillettes aren't missing out on much these days. They've got the ranch under control. They've figured out what bulls to put on which cows, and they contract their calves so selling them is no problem. They work part-time at the livestock auction barn in Crockett, and they read western history and write and record western songs. During their free time, they travel and cook and perform and say they just have one helluva good time.

Cathi has sent us one of her favorite recipes. She prepared this in a Dutch oven over an open fire in the fireplace and it is *delicious*. For a real taste of Texas, with just a sprinkling of Louisiana, try Cathi, Guy, and Pipp Gillette's Box Creek Etoufee.

BOX CREEK ETOUFFEE

3 pounds sirloin, cut into one-inch squares

2 cups water

2 cubes beef bouillon

2 large cloves garlic

1½ sticks butter

2 onions

2 bell peppers

2 stalks celery

2 cans cream of mushroom soup

1 can tomatoes with green chilies

2 ounces sharp cheddar cheese

4 ounces fresh mushrooms, quartered

½ teaspoon coarsely ground black pepper

½ teaspoon hot pepper sauce

¼ teaspoon cayenne pepper

⅛ teaspoon seasoned salt

1 tablespoon browning and seasoning sauce

Fresh cilantro, finely chopped

Rice, prepared according to package directions

Brown the beef pieces in a Dutch oven. Add water, bouillon, and garlic to meat. Bring this mixture to a boil, cover, reduce heat, and simmer for two hours.

After beef has been simmering for one hour, chop onions, bell peppers, and celery, and place in Dutch oven with butter. Cover and simmer for one hour.

Add vegetables and all remaining ingredients to beef except cilantro and rice.

Spoon etouffee over rice and sprinkle lightly with cilantro.

Serves six, generously.

HAPPY HEREFORD RANCH

HAPPY, TEXAS
NOLON AND BOBBY HENSON

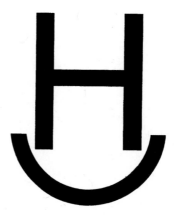

LONG TRADITIONS ON THE LAND

Heading south from Umbarger to the Happy Hereford Ranch, named not so much for the mental outlook of Nolon and Bobby Henson, as much as for the town of Happy, Texas, you're almost taken off guard as you drive around the beautiful Buffalo Lake National Wildlife Refuge, 7,664 acres of short-grass prairie, water, marsh, and croplands. It's all part of the Central Flyway and provides a valuable wintering area for waterfowl using this migration route from Canada to the south. Thousands of ducks and geese winter-over on the refuge each year.

But once past the refuge you are back on the flat range land, the kind that has sustained a long ranching tradition in Randall and the adjoining counties.

Bobby Henson is a third-generation Texan and was born right there on the ranch. Her maternal grandfather, William Graham, who bought the land in 1917, was a windmiller for the old XIT and took the job because it paid twenty-five dollars instead of cowboy wages of twenty dollars. He also had the first registered brand in Armstrong County, the "S," in 1893, that was eventually changed to the "$."

Nolon grew up in Oklahoma and Texas, and he's been in the Happy area since 1947. He met his future wife in church while they were both college students at West Texas State University in Canyon, just up the road from the ranch. They were married in December 1950 and they have three children: Jan, Walter Lee (known to everyone as "Rusty"), and Luan. Jan and Luan and their families still live on the ranch, and Rusty has his own operation, which belonged to Bobby's grandfather, near Quitaque, Texas, north of Matador.

Today the Hensons farm and ranch all on dry land. As they explain, "You'd have to go 400 feet for water, and even at 400 feet there isn't enough water except for stock water." On their 1,000 acres of cultivated land, they grow winter wheat, milo, and some feed for baling so that they have winter feed for the cattle.

CATTLE ALL OVER

Sitting around the kitchen table with these two experienced and articulate ranchers, you can't resist the urge to nudge them, periodically, to talk about the way things were years ago—when life was supposed to be slower and things "were better." But was it like that?

The Hensons are known for their Hereford cattle. Right now they have 100 mother cows, but twenty-five years ago there were 3,000 mother cows on the ranch. At that time they hauled heifers to South Dakota and New Mexico for summer pasture; they used the home ranch for the mother cows and they put all the weaned calves on the various leased grasslands. They had, and still have, superior breeding stock. They've sold cattle to thirty-seven states and more than five foreign countries, including Spain, Mexico, Portugal, Canada, Korea, and even Africa. At one time they were selling 100 bulls a year to the Four Sixes.

In those days, the "good old days," they had nine cowboys, full-time. At the end of World War II the ranch stopped cooking for the cowboys. They started to hire married men and let the wives do the cooking and the ranch provided good housing. Today, both their daughters and their families live in two of those houses, five others are unused, and several have been razed.

Bobby says, "We have hired single fellows to cook for themselves, but they run out of feed for themselves and they come in tired and open a can of soup for noon. And you can't work all afternoon on a can of soup." Nolon remembers, "One fella . . . he just got weak. He wasn't eating enough so that he could even function."

THE RANCH CHANGES

When asked how ranching has changed over the years, there is a really long pause and then Bobby says "I hardly know where to begin. It has changed in two ways. First, the home place was fundamentally a summer pasture for the cattle from the Quitaque ranch." Nolon adds, "It's always ten degrees cooler up here." The cattle were trailed on a three-day drive of about seventy-five miles, summered, and then driven back.

In 1937, they started to run registered cattle full-time, so they had to fence for smaller pastures. This was the second fundamental change. They needed the smaller pastures so a bull could service all the cows in with him. They had had pastures that were five miles north to south and three miles east to west. That was cut up into seven smaller pastures.

Nolon and Bobby Henson in the kitchen at their ranch in Happy, Texas.

And they add, after giving it some more thought, the registered cattle business is more dependent "on a show string. We've never showed cattle," and the expenses of show cattle are "tremendous."

There have been other changes. Some are anecdotal—you know, all those stories about the weather. And others are very specific.

Bobby and Nolon both agree that the weather seems to have changed. They claim that the rainfall period has moved—it's backed itself up by three or four months. Other ranchers tend to agree. "You could never get a decent milo crop," Nolon explains, "but now you can get a good crop on dry land . . . but it's hard to get in a wheat crop . . . the rain patterns have just changed."

The mechanical side of ranching has also undergone a great upheaval. Nolon says, "It's more mechanized so it is easier. The big round bales last two or three days rather than having to load up each day and feed the small bales. You can do in thirty minutes what it used to take all day to do."

TRACTORS, TRACTORS

At one time, the Happy Hereford Ranch ran twenty-three tractors and farmed 13,000 acres. Now, with less land, they're down to three tractors. But today, you can use one tractor for 1,000 acres, about what five of those older, smaller tractors used to do, and the new ones do it cheaper. "The old tractors weren't efficient and they were terribly uncomfortable. They were hard to start—sometimes you had to crank them by hand." So much for romanticizing about the old days and the wonderful equipment. Nolon says that today the new hands "won't hardly get into a tractor unless it's got a cab, air-conditioning, a heater, radio, and what have you."

Nolon jokes about how he used to hate to plow. "You look back at the end of the day and you might have done seventy-five acres. Now with these big tractors you look back and you might have done half a section [320 acres]. It looks like you've accomplished something."

THE COWBOYS AND TV

The Hensons seem to think that television has ruined the cowboys. "Nowadays, when it gets dark, they want to watch TV. Before, they went home and listened to their wife—so they stayed out and worked!" They really laugh when they tell the story of the cowboy who grew up and cowboyed all his life. "He was a real good cowboy—but you'd bet at 12:30 he was going to be at the house to see his soap opera, no matter what."

It's hard to get good cowboys today. Nolon says that the feedlots have some good hands. "The young people like to romanticize that being a cowboy is working for the Matador, Pitchfork, or Four Sixes, or those types of ranches, where they go out on horses and ride a horse all day long." The feedlot cowboys, he explains, are used to working an eight-hour day and then maybe rodeoing on the weekend or roping steers or calves for enjoyment. And the feedlots pay better.

Anyone who has been around ranchers knows that cowboys have their own image of themselves, and as Nolon explains, "Cowboys don't like to farm . . . they feel that if they can't do it on a horse they don't want to do it." And in a hare's breath, Bobby adds, "Period!"

Some of the men like camp jobs where they are not under the immediate supervision of the owner, manager, or foreman. They can, at the camps, pretty well do as they please—getting up when they want and going out and coming in when they want—as long as they get the job done. But they don't have camps on the Happy Hereford any more, so that no longer poses a problem for Bobby and Nolon.

NO MORE HORSES

At one time the Happy Hereford had between twenty-five and fifty brood mares. In fact, John Wayne's ranch in Arizona used to buy some of its horses from the Hensons, who raised all registered American quarter horses. Today, however, there are no horses on the ranch, because "this ranch is very flat . . . and there is virtually no place where you can't get around in a pickup—you don't even need four-wheel drive." They even move their cattle with trucks. "Just put some feed on the truck and they'll follow you anywhere," explains Nolon. And since they brand in the chutes, they don't need horses for that work, either. They calve starting in late February, but essentially the ranch produces only breeding stock, so other ranches that want to upgrade their own herds buy from the Hensons. They sell a tremendous number of their bulls to Old Mexico, though they also sell to Tennessee, Florida, and South Texas.

What is it that makes ranchers stay in a business that provides modest returns at best? Bobby says that she really doesn't "know of anything I don't like about ranching." Both Bobby and Nolon could have had other careers, and certainly could have made more money. Nolon, for example, has taught physics at Texas Tech in Lubbock and Bobby has taught elementary and junior high school. Yet, they never want to give up "that sense of freedom and independence and the love of the land that you don't get anywhere else." Bobby says, "I really like the country. I like living in the country and in this area in particular." And then Nolon interjects, with a big smile, "When the windchill factor is fifteen below zero, it would be nice to have an office job."

To show that she, too, is fully aware of the weather, Bobby adds, "or when the temperature is 100 degrees and the wind is blowing and the dirt is blowing, you wish to heaven you didn't even have to stick your head outside."

The Hensons never have considered ranching anywhere else. Nolon explains that where they are, "is one of the best ranch countries in the United States." It's what is called short-grass country but they get enough rain, around eighteen inches a year, to sustain their cattle. And it's good grass country in the winter.

But they sure do remember the winter of 1957, as do so many of the Panhandle ranchers. That was the year the snow got up to the eaves on the houses and "we were snowed in for three days until we finally got out the back window." Thousands of head of cattle, all over the Panhandle, froze to death in that storm. But Bobby explains, "That was in the last week in March and it wasn't extremely cold. The cattle actually drowned, they didn't freeze to death. The snow whipped around and got into their nostrils and then their lungs and they literally drowned."

Despite all the adversity, they enjoy "a happy-go-lucky lifestyle" on the ranch. "There's always plenty to do—we never get everything done. And there's always something that needs desperately to be done . . . "

Raising children on the ranch seems to have worked out all right. There were things that their three children did not do that town kids did; for example, they weren't in the band or many school sports—it's twenty-seven miles to school in Canyon—but they were active in the Future Farmers of America (FFA). Nolon sums it up proudly, "We have three real good kids who grew up working and helping on the ranch."

Bobby points out that their children "haven't much patience with people their own age [they are in their thirties] that expect the world to give them a living. It's these values that ranch life instills in people. I think they realize that you have to work for what you get."

But no matter how hard you work, the Hensons think that it's difficult to get into ranching these days because "it isn't a good paying thing. It's difficult to buy a ranch unless you can pay for it." And Bobby points out that the land of the Happy Hereford Ranch cost about two dollars an acre when they first bought it, where today it's apt to go for $150 per acre, "and frankly, it won't produce a bit more now. It may not produce as much. It's very hard for a young person to get into ranching."

Bobby and Nolon have done what they can to help young ranchers. They have hosted the Texas Christian University ranch management program since its inception in 1957. This prestigious program is open to people with ranch connections, and it teaches all aspects of ranching. They came to the Happy

Hereford because they had 1,700 acres of irrigated and dry land, registered and commercial cattle, and a solid operation. They even had a feedlot on the ranch.

Two of Bobby's favorite recipes are her potatoes with cream sauce and her Depression Pie or Fudge Pie. The potato dish "is so easy and our youngest daughter thinks it's the only way to have potatoes." The pie is fascinating because it has no eggs or milk, only ingredients that could be found in a camp wagon or maybe your own kitchen.

POTATOES WITH CREAM SAUCE

6 large potatoes (best are new red potatoes)
½ cup flour
1 cup milk
1 teaspoon dried chives
½ teaspoon garlic salt
1 teaspoon onion salt
1 cup cubed Velveta cheese

Cut peeled potatoes into large wedges (1½" to 2"). Boil until done—NOT SOFT.

Mix the flour and milk. Add the dried chives, garlic salt, and onion salt. Then add the cubed Velveta and all the water from the cooked potatoes. Cook until the mixture is thick, stirring often. Pour the mixture over the potatoes and serve.

FUDGE PIE

2 cups sugar
½ cup flour
3 tablespoons cocoa
2½ cups water
1 tablespoon butter
1 teaspoon vanilla

Combine the sugar, flour, cocoa and water. Cook them until the mixture is thick. Add the butter and vanilla. Cool and pour into a baked nine-inch pie crust.

KING RANCH

KINGSVILLE, TEXAS
TIO KLEBERG

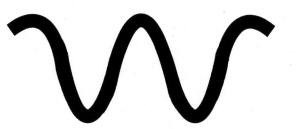

MANAGING A RANCHING DYNASTY

It is nearly impossible to write a book about Texas, and especially about ranching in Texas, without including a chapter on the King Ranch. Much has been written about King Ranch; at least a half dozen books and uncounted magazine and newspaper articles. Probably the most definitive book is *The King Ranch*, written by Tom Lea, published by Little, Brown, 1957. More recently King Ranch has published its own books, *Stewards of a Vision*, by Jay Nixon, ©King Ranch, Inc., 1986, and the *King Ranch Cook Book*, also ©King Ranch, Inc., 1992.

It is also nearly impossible to write about King Ranch without duplicating some of what has already been written. What is it about King Ranch that produces so much hyperbole, so many photographs, and so much print ink? King Ranch was one of the first ranches in Texas—actually, it was one of the first in the United States. It has been an innovator in breeding cattle and horses, in clearing and maintaining pastures, in developing water, and in marketing cattle and horses. King Ranch has been a leading force for over a century.

For us, cowboys and horsemen first before becoming writers, King Ranch and King Ranch horses and cattle were something we had heard of all our lives. A cowboy's visit to King Ranch was something akin to a Muslim going to Mecca. King Ranch is the epitome of ranching, of cattle and horses in America. King Ranch was a must-see on our visit to Texas. The awe-inspiring ranch that spawned a town, that was wrested out of a desert wilderness, that repelled repeated attacks by marauding Indians and rustling bandits, that not only survived, but prospered and grew to become the biggest ranch in the world.

King Ranch is a National Historic Landmark. And it is popular not only with Texans, but with tourists from all over the world. In fact, so many people want to see the famous old ranch, King Ranch, Inc., established a visitor program in 1989. Just off the entry road to the Headquarters Ranch, the King Ranch Visitor's Center was built and now offers guided tours, from 10:00 A.M. to 3:00 P.M., Monday through Saturday, and from 1:00 P.M. to 4:00 P.M. on Sunday.

In 1992, some 45,000 visitors toured King Ranch. Today there is the King Ranch Saddle Shop in downtown Kingsville and the King Ranch Museum, which has a full-time archivist and is open seven days a week. The ranch itself generally is not open to the public, because the large number of visitors would interrupt not only ranch work, but the private lives of the owners and employees who live there.

Once a year, in November, the ranch, in partnership with the Kingsville Chamber of Commerce Volunteers, sponsors a Ranch Hand Breakfast as part of the La Posada de Kingsville—a Celebration of Lights—the town and ranch's annual Christmas festival. At that time, the iron gates to the ranch are opened, the guard stands back and waves visitors through, and citizens get to enjoy the beauty of the King Ranch Headquarters and a King Ranch cowboy breakfast, cooked off the back of chuck wagons. King Ranch is a fun place to visit even if you know little or nothing about horses, cows, or cowboys, all of which are in abundance here in this oasis in the desert. As you ride past the well-manicured headquarters, stables, paddocks, and pastures, it is easy to let your mind drift back to a time when this dynasty began.

A COW CAMP ON SANTA GERTRUDIS CREEK

The story has been told thousands of times in as many ways. In the early 1800s, what is now King Ranch and the town of Kingsville were part of what was known as the Nueces Strip—a humid, barren desert in South Texas between the Nueces River and Rio Grande. The inhabitants of the Nueces Strip were mostly wild cattle, wild horses, and wild bandits and Indians. Few settlers or honest citizens dared cross this "Wild Horse Desert," as it was often called. Many Mexicans called the area, "El Desierto de los Muertos." Most reasonable and prudent men stayed out of this "Desert of the Dead."

But Richard King was not most men. He came from a poor Irish New York family and made his own way in the world, primarily ferrying goods and supplies on steamboats. In 1847, he came to Texas and partnered with Mifflin Kenedy, making a small fortune shipping supplies up the Rio Grande for General Zachary Taylor's army, at war with Mexico. King had modified his boats with a shallow hull and could easily navigate the treacherous Rio Grande. Richard King was an innovative man.

And he was a sharp businessman. In 1852, he was invited to Corpus Christi to the Lone Star State Fair. King, who loved horses, decided to make the 150-mile trip from Brownsville by horseback, a trip that took him directly through the dreaded Nueces Strip. His party traveled 124 miles through Wild

Good cooking, good cattle, and good horses have long been a tradition on the King Ranch, photo circa 1950 (photo courtesy King Ranch Archives).

Horse Desert in the hot sun. They were pretty dry and weary when they came upon a small creek they later learned was called Santa Gertrudis. It was surrounded by tall mesquite trees that provided cool shade. An oasis to be sure. King, a sea-going man, was dutifully impressed with the land and this stream, and when he got to Corpus, he inquired about ownership of the area.

Ownership of anything in the Nueces Strip had always been questionable at best, but King persisted, and after much discussion with Captain Gideon "Legs" Lewis of the Texas Rangers, King decided to purchase the "Rincon de Santa Gertrudis," a 15,500-acre Spanish land grant owned by the heirs of Juan Mendiola of Carmago, Mexico. King formed a partnership with Lewis and started the Rancho Santa Gertrudis, named for the small creek which provided the life-giving water as well as for Saint Gertrude.

Legs Lewis set up a cow camp on Santa Gertrudis Creek and began going about the business of establishing a working ranch. Gathering up wild horses and cattle and providing protection from marauding Apaches and Mexican bandits, Rancho Santa Gertrudis began to prosper and grow. The ranch was doing well when Legs got killed in Corpus Christi by a jealous husband. The year was 1855.

FROM COW CAMP TO CATTLE BARON

Another foreman was hired and ranching activities continued unabated. King and Kenedy's shipping business was hauling cotton to foreign markets. During the Civil War, King kept the Confederacy supplied and took time off to serve as a private in the Confederate cavalry. He was close friends with Robert E. Lee even before the war, and the famous general was frequently a guest at Santa Gertrudis. Lee wrote often of the pleasures of visiting the ranch; it was he who selected the site of the present mansion, which is known as the King Ranch Main House.

In 1854, just a year after starting the ranch, King married Henrietta Chamberlain, who had been educated at the Holly Springs Female Institute in Mississippi and taught at the Rio Grande Female Institute. Henrietta King inherited the ranch after Richard's death, and for some seventy years was the matriarch of King Ranch. Her graciousness, her morality. and her dedication to helping others is legendary in Kingsville.

Early on, King sold cattle primarily to Mexico. Later, he had cattle driven to markets in New Orleans, and after the Civil War, took advantage of the markets in the North. He drove his first cattle from Texas in 1869, a tradition that lasted for decades; he helped feed miners, railroad workers, soldiers, and settlers, and set the stage upon which the American cowboy became famous.

During the time that King was building up his ranch, he traveled into Mexico, found a herd of cattle he liked, and bought it. As he was leaving the village, it dawned on him that he was taking the livelihood of the people who cared for the cattle, so he took them—men, women and children—back to Rancho Santa Gertrudis. Many of these Mexican cowboys—these vaqueros—and their families have been with King Ranch ever since. They became known as Los Kinenos, the people of King Ranch.

As the cattle business prospered, King hired a lawyer to start buying up contiguous lands, so that by the end of the Civil War, the ranch encompassed over 146,000 acres. And he was just getting warmed up. King owned so much land and so many cattle that he began to brand his livestock to keep track of them. He developed the now famous "Running W," which some say represents water, or a wave of water. Regardless of the origin of the brand, developing a water supply still is a daily activity at the King Ranch empire.

After the Confederacy was defeated, the Texas Rangers, whom King had depended on to protect the ranch, were disbanded. Rustlers and bandits immediately moved back into their old haunts in the Wild Horse Desert, and the fight was on. King claimed he lost over 30,000 head of cattle to Mexican bandits. King himself was ambushed, but escaped. All hands and the cook wore sidearms everywhere they went, and King carried a sawed-off shotgun in addition to his pistol.

Pressure from ranchers and settlers across Texas resulted in reactivation of the Rangers in 1874; the now famous Captain L. H. McNelly recruited a company of Rangers to set about reestablishing law and order in the Lone Star State. In the book *The Texas Rangers,* author Walter Webb stated that, when McNelly's Rangers arrived in the Nueces Strip, there was a full-fledged guerrilla war going on. After some 300 cattle were reported stolen, McNelly took thirty-five Rangers into Mexico, killed a bandit chief, and returned the cattle to their rightful owners.

Later, McNelly and some of his men visited King Ranch and were invited to stay the night. At first they declined because they said they were too dirty— "hadn't changed clothes in ten days and there were ladies present." But King insisted, and the Rangers were given the opportunity to bathe, change clothes, and eat from the well-laden King Ranch table. More on that later.

THE KLEBERGS'S STEWARDSHIP

Richard and Henrietta King gave birth to five children: three girls—Henrietta, Ella, and Alice—and two boys—Richard and Robert. Richard King, the steamboat captain who started the King Ranch dynasty, died of stomach cancer April 14, 1885. His youngest daughter, Alice, was betrothed to King's attorney, Robert Kleberg, "El Abogado" (the lawyer). Mrs. King turned the management of the ranch over to Kleberg, who married Alice the next year. The Klebergs have been actively involved in managing the King Ranch ever since.

When King died, the ranch held more than 600,000 acres and ran over 40,000 head of cattle, 12,000 sheep, 500 mules, and 6,000 horses. Horses were always a big part of the King Ranch. Shortly after King started Rancho Santa Gertrudis, he paid more than $600 for a thoroughbred stallion out of Kentucky running stock. At the time, that was about twice the price he had paid for the entire ranch.

Under the stewardship of the Klebergs, the ranch continued to grow; more land was purchased, and better cattle and horses were bred and developed. The King Ranch contribution to ranching in Texas is nothing short of legendary.

Kleberg was active in establishing the towns of Kingsville, Raymondville, Robstown, Bishop, Corpus Christi, and the port of Corpus Christi. Kleberg introduced the farming of cotton and truck crops to the ranch. He worked to rid Texas of the scourge of cattlemen: the tick and the dreaded tick fever. Because the King Ranch sits on the edge of the brush country, Kleberg began a brush eradication program to provide more pasture.

Once away from the Rio Grande and the Gulf of Mexico, water is hard to find. After the drought of the early 1890s, when the ranch lost thousands of cattle, Kleberg began experimenting with drilling wells and brought in the first artesian well in South Texas, a far-reaching development that opened up thousands of acres of arid desert to grazing.

Kleberg was even more of an innovator than King, if that's possible. If so, it was only because Kleberg lived at a time when the country was more settled than in King's days. More time could be devoted to actually running the ranch, than spent in scratching it out of the wilderness and defending it from bandits and thieves.

Kleberg saw that better cattle and horses would increase profits, so he began to cross-breed shorthorned Herefords with the Longhorns to get more body mass. He rounded up thousands of wild horses and jacks and jennets from the desert and began a controlled breeding program. He brought in some of the finest blooded thoroughbred horses he could find in Kentucky, and soon King

On the King Ranch, as on most ranches, meal time gathers cowboys and cowbosses from all parts of the ranch (photo courtesy King Ranch Archives).

Ranch became known as a place to buy a good horse—a tradition that continues.

The union of "El Abogado" Robert Kleberg and Alice King also produced five children: Richard "Dick" Mifflin, Henrietta Rosa, Alice Gertrudis, Robert "Bob" Justus, and Sarah Spohn. Dick received a law degree from the University of Texas, and Bob studied agriculture in Wisconsin for two years before returning to the ranch in 1916; his father was not well and bandits were again raiding the Nueces Strip.

Once again, King Ranch had to defend itself against marauders and thieves. In August, 1915, some fifty-eight bandits attacked the headquarters of the Norias division and kept the entire crew of fifteen penned down in the main ranch house until dark. King Ranch suffered some twenty-six raids over the next six months. Shortly afterward, the United States Army and a company of Texas Rangers showed up in force, and the raiding gradually subsided.

But the problems at King Ranch remained. Another drought was wracking the country and an aging Robert Kleberg was suffering from palsy. Dick and Bob shuffled cattle from one division, one pasture to another, until 1919 when rains brought new grass and new hope for the future.

Henrietta King died March 31, 1925. Her son-in-law and ranch manager, Robert Kleberg, died October 10, 1932. Kleberg had run the ranch for forty-seven years. He had made many improvements, and had established King Ranch as a formidable force in agriculture in Texas, and around the world. At the time of his death, King Ranch encompassed more than 1,175,000 acres, and ran almost 100,000 head of cattle and 4,500 horses and mules.

The ranch then passed into the hands of Mrs. King's heirs. Inheritance taxes took a whopping toll, and in 1935, when the country was in the throes of the Great Depression, cattle prices were at a thirty-year low. The heirs established King Ranch, Inc., and the ranch was whittled to its present-day size of 825,000 acres; the fight to save the ranch began all over again. Bob and Dick Kleberg were faced with just as monumental a task of ranching as had the founder Richard King and his successor, Robert Kleberg. Only this time it was not just bandits and rustlers threatening the ranch—it was depressed cattle prices and a heavy debt load.

But like the founder and like their father, this new generation of Klebergs rose to the task. Bob and Dick established ranches in Cuba, Australia, Brazil, Argentina, Venezuela, Spain, and Morocco. Bob negotiated oil leases on the ranch with Humble Oil, and that helped finance expanding ranching operations. The Kleberg brothers helped develop the root plow, which was more efficient in brush control, and they carved ranches out of jungles where natives said ranches would never work.

Cattle and horses and ranching were the Klebergs's life, and they made the most of that life. Dick passed away in 1955, and Bob managed the ranch until his death in 1974. These two men had inherited a ranch riddled with debt and turned it into a ranching world power. They developed a new breed of cattle, as well as a new breed of horses. It is almost impossible to overstate the influence Dick and Bob Kleberg had on ranching in America.

MONKEY BUILDS AN EMPIRE

Caesar Kleberg, a cousin of Dick and Bob's, became part of the management team in 1901, and, in his travels across the state, noticed the influx of Brahman cattle from India. This animal seemed to do well in the heat and humidity of South Texas. In 1910, the Klebergs were given a Brahman-Shorthorn-cross bull by a friend, Tom O'Conner. By 1920, the King Ranch had a good crop of these distinctively colored red cattle on the ground on the Laureles Division; Dick picked a bull calf he particularly liked, named him Monkey, and selected him for the herd sire.

Monkey was bred to a select herd of first-cross heifers; those offspring were used in a line-breeding program and a new breed of cattle, the Santa Gertrudis, was produced. Today, just across the highway from King Ranch, is the modern, sprawling headquarters of the Santa Gertrudis Breeders, International, a living tribute to the men and the foresight of King Ranch management.

HORSES TO WORK AND PLAY

The original horses on King Ranch were mustangs, descendants of horses that had escaped from the early Spanish explorers. These were hardy horses, but small and inbred, and the ranch needed a better breed, something that could outrun and outthink a cow, and stand up to hard riding and roping in the Wild Horse Desert. King loved fine horses and began importing thoroughbreds to the ranch, crossing them with the mustang mares.

Once again it was cousin Caesar who saw a chance to improve a breed. In 1915, when the quarter horse breeder, George Cleeg, visited, Caesar talked him into selling the ranch a colt. This colt, named Old Sorrel, became the foundation sire of King Ranch Quarter Horses, now world-famous. When the American Quarter Horse Association was formed at the Fort Worth Fat Stock Show in 1940, a grandson of Old Sorrel, Wimpy, was grand champion and bequeathed the coveted registration number One in the AQHA, now the most popular horse registry in the world.

King Ranch also bred up and improved their thoroughbred horses, purchasing Kentucky Derby winner Bold Venture in 1936, and in 1946, one of Bold Ventures sons, a colt named Assault, won the Triple Crown for the ranch. But the cutting horse is what the ranch is most famous for, and in 1975 King Ranch bought Mr. San Peppy, a sorrel stallion that was eating up cows across the country in cutting competition.

Today Mr. San Peppy still stands at King Ranch, along with Peppy San Badger, but the ranch, now under the direction of a fourth-generation Kleberg—Steven J. "Tio"—does not hold the big cutting competitions as it once did. Tio, a Texas Tech graduate married to Jannell Gerald, says even though the ranch is world famous and runs many horses and cattle, it still has to be managed just like any other major corporation.

RAISING GOOD HORSES AND GOOD CATTLE, EFFICIENTLY

"There's always room for improvement," Tio says. "Like anyone else in business, we constantly try to cut costs and improve production. We work to improve our pastures, improve our nutrition, and our medication programs. We still do about 50 to 60 percent of our work ahorseback, but we use helicopters about 35 percent of the time, mostly for gathering. It's just more efficient. We still rope and drag to the fire to brand, but if it gets late in the season and the calves are weighing over 400 pounds, we'll run 'em through a chute. There's no use trying to flank a 400-pound calf and I don't think I can do it anymore."

Tio also says they don't send out the wagons on the King Ranch anymore. "We're more mechanized. Like most ranches, using vehicles just allows us to be more efficient. We can do more work with less men. We don't have the number of men working here we once did. Used to we'd use twelve to fifteen men during branding. There'd be six or seven [cowboys] holding the herd and six or seven roping and dragging to the fire. Now we get the same amount done with six or seven, total. We've had to make some changes. We're trying to keep up with the changing times. We want to continue to turn out good horses and good cattle, efficiently."

According to Kleberg, the ranch runs two breeding and calving seasons. "We put bulls out in November and December, and in May and June. That gives us a backup in case of a bad drought year. I'm not smart enough to figure out the weather or the market a year in advance, so we have two sets of calves to sell and none of our pastures are overstocked. Each ranch [division] is different and unique in its own way. The black land gets hot and the sandy land gets full of weeds, but it's hot and dry everywhere in August."

Tio says there are two things he remembers about growing up on the famous old ranch: cowboying and cooking. "I remember summers because we got to cowboy. It was hard work but it was outside and I loved it. I worked on the ranch every summer. Right up through college until I went into the Army." He served two years, then it was back to Texas, and cowboying, and cooking. Tio says he can cook anything as long as it's red meat.

"Just give me a big piece of steak and stand back. Only one way to cook a steak. Over an open fire with mesquite wood. Cook it rare and add a little sauce. Best in the world."

Tio has developed his own sauce and gave us permission to excerpt the recipe along with one for his beef and gravy, from the *King Ranch Cook Book*. Enjoy some fine Texas cuisine and a taste of Texas history.

BEEF AND GRAVY

1 onion, sliced

2 pounds lean ground beef or sirloin

Dash of garlic salt

Dash of black pepper

Dash of comino peppers

Dash of Tabasco sauce

2 cans cream of mushroom soup mixed with 1 or 2 cans skim or low-fat milk

1 package fresh mushrooms, sliced

In an iron skillet, brown the sliced onion, add beef and spices, and brown thoroughly. Pour in one can of soup and stir, then add milk to reach the consistency of cream gravy. If you like thicker gravy, add a second can of soup and less milk. The gravy will thicken as you simmer it over low heat. Sauté the sliced mushrooms in a second skillet and add before serving. Make instant rice in the microwave and pour beef and gravy over rice. Garnish with a sprig of chilitipiquins and serve with hot sauce. Serve on toast for breakfast on cold mornings.

TIO'S HOT SAUCE

¼ to ½ onion, chopped

¼ cup chilitipiquins, fresh off the bush

¼ teaspoon salt and pepper

¼ cup water

1 tablespoon vinegar

1 tablespoon olive oil

1 10-ounce can of Rotel chopped tomatoes

Grind all ingredients in blender except tomatoes, which are added last. Blend to the consistency that you like, chunky or pureed. Chilitipiquins vary in heat, according to the weather—generally the dryer the year, the hotter the chili. Adjust accordingly; add more tomato sauce in dry years.

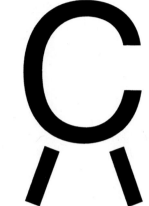

LEGGED C RANCH

ROUND ROCK, TEXAS

WAYNE MCMINN, AKA DOCTOR SEBASTIAN GOMEZ

HISTORIAN, AUTHOR, CAMP COOK, DOCTOR OF CRYPTO PHENOMENOLOGY

Out in the brushy plains north and east of the capital city of Austin, ranches tend to run small because water is plentiful, grass is strong, and people are versatile. This part of Texas is most interesting because of the history and because of the people who live here. You want history? You want cowboy cooking? Then you want to meet Wayne McMinn, a Texas original who bills himself as Dr. Sebastian Gomez, historian, author, camp cook, and Doctor of Crypto Phenomenology.

We were poking around the Texas Ranger Museum in Waco and stumbled into the Governor Bill and Vara Daniel Historical Village. We told the people there we were looking to interview someone in the area who knew some history, ranching, cowboying, and cooking, and they pointed us in the direction of Wayne McMinn. Wayne had helped build the Governor Bill and Vara Daniel Village, had a chuck wagon there, held seminars on camp cooking, and was an expert on chuck wagon history. Wayne was our man.

On a rainy December morning, we headed south down I-35 out of Waco, along the approximate route of the old Chisholm Trail, where cattle from south Texas were pushed to markets in the north. Just east of the bustling burg of Georgetown, the Chisholm Trail crossed Brushy Creek near a rotund rock. We're talking huge. The settlers once held dances on the rock and later changed the name of the settlement from Brushy Creek to Round Rock. That's how it stands today.

The country around Round Rock is mostly flat, with a few rolling hills interspersed with small streams. As more and more people move into Austin seeking jobs and security, other people continue to move out of Austin seeking privacy, solitude, and perhaps raise a few cattle and keep a horse or two. Wayne McMinn's outfit is typical of east Texas spreads; Wayne, however, is not your quintessential rancher. Even in Texas, where individualism is worn with pride, Wayne—Dr. Sebastian Gomez—is something of an enigma.

About four miles east of Round Rock on Highway 79, a small, one-lane road turns to the north. At the end of this lane you'll find the McMinn Ranch. It's obvious to visitors that this place has some history. Trees tower over wood-sided buildings that are weather-worn and nearly hidden with tall grass. Several models of Volkswagens are scattered about, partially obscured by grass. There is a new-looking shop and a very old-looking main building with a screened front porch. "Come on in," a voice says, "before you drown."

As we sprint for the porch, cats scatter in every direction. Wayne, standing about five-feet, two-inches tall and squinting through fogged eyeglasses, sticks out his hand. "Don't worry about this weather," he advises. "It won't last long. And don't worry about this kitchen. I'm batching and I ain't much of a housekeeper." But the people in Waco were right. Wayne is a historian, and more. Much more.

"This place was settled in 1845 by Andersons," he begins. "This house was built in about 1870. The last Anderson died in '78, he was going on ninety-two [years old]. Nine boys and one girl were raised in this house. Every room had an outside door. The kitchen had no shelves or counters; just a sink and a wood stove. [When I moved here] it was kinda like living in a tent. Really. I figured if I added up all the holes in the walls, there would be a three-foot opening in every room. You couldn't light a candle in here when the wind was blowing."

Wayne spent a lot of time and money fixing the place up; now that it is paid for, he can have his way about whatever he wants. What he wants nowadays is to restore chuck wagons, cook off chuck wagons, lecture and demonstrate on chuck wagons, and write about his experiences, which are numerous. He says he got interested in writing back in junior high school, along about the time he was christened Sebastian Gomez.

"I was dozing off, dreaming about Fords and girls, and the teacher asks me who did something way back in history. At the time I hated history and had no idea who she was talking about and really didn't care. My good friend, John Ogleby, was sitting right behind me and leaned forward and whispered in my ear, 'It was Sebastian Gomez.' So I jumped up and said, 'Sebastian Gomez.' 'Course the class cracked up and I been called Sebastian Gomez ever since. A few years ago, I was working at the museum in Waco and figured I needed a title. So I made Gomez a doctor."

A doctor of crypto phenomenology. "Webster defines crypto as something secret or hidden. And a phenomenon is a happening. So a crypto phenomenologist is someone who studies something so secret or hidden that no one knows what it is. Gives me a lot of time for doing unstructured work. That's what I do best. Mostly I just work when the spirit moves me, and lately it ain't moved me too often."

Wayne's whole world is kind of unstructured, but that's not to say he doesn't get things accomplished. For being born in the height of the Great Depression,

Historian, author, camp cook, Doctor of Crypto Phenomonology, Sebastian Gomez, aka Wayne McMinn, Legged C Ranch, Round Rock, Texas.

the son of a nursery laborer, Dr. Gomez has done pretty well for himself—and he's done most of it alone. Wayne's way. "I was born October 2, 1934, at home in Donna, Texas, in the Rio Grande Valley. Two more miles south and I'd been a Mexican. Daddy was a not-very-good farmer and rancher and later worked for a big nursery. He planted all those big old palm trees you see along the Rio Grande."

Mr. McMinn followed the nursery work to Houston and that's where Wayne was raised. "Went through the school system in Houston," he relates. "Was a terrible student. Only thing that interested me was Fords and girls. Along about the Korean War, I got scared I was gonna be drafted, so I decided to go to the University of Houston and get in the ROTC program." A good plan, and one that worked for many—but not Dr. Gomez.

"I was standing out on that parade ground in my little uniform and it was hot and the oil was dripping out of that M-1, and I could see my Ford coupe waiting for me and my mind snapped. I stuck that rifle down in the mud, put my helmet on the butt and climbed the fence, my lieutenant yelling at me all the time. I fired up that Ford and left 'em two big black streaks right down Cullen Avenue."

But that wasn't quite the end of Wayne's military experience. "A few weeks later, I got my draft notice in the mail. Well, they took me in and inspected, injected, and infected me, and set me in a little room and told me to read the top line on a chart. I said, 'What chart?' And they said, 'The one on the wall.' And I said, 'What wall?' And that was the end of that. I couldn't see, so they set me free."

But not for long. Wayne got married, and for the next few decades wandered from occupation to occupation, wherever the spirit moved him. "I been involved in a lot of things. Been a scuba diver, a racing boat driver, a mechanic, a carpenter, a farmer and rancher, and a marina owner." Wayne's wife bought a marina at an auction while Ol' Sebastian, ever the hustler, was scraping boat bottoms.

"My boss was a good friend and he came down one afternoon and told me I was fired. I said, 'What for? I'm doing a pretty good job here.' He said, 'Your wife just bought Highland Lake Marina and you can't afford to work here.' So I was in the marina business. We had the best floating dock on Lake Travis. Ran that for about three years. Kinda like hitting yourself in the head with a hammer. You don't know what it's like until you try it."

Over the next few years, Wayne and his wife tried many things. Some successful. Some not. "About '68 we decided we were pregnant and one of us was going to have to go straight and get a job. We'd been having a lot of fun. One time my wife was looking through the kitchen for something to eat and said there wasn't a thing there. We put all our money together and had thirty-six cents. We figured we could get a pretty good hamburger for thirty-five cents or we could go buy a can of worms and go fishing. We went for the worms and caught enough perch to last us a couple of days."

FROM CARPENTRY TO HISTORY

Wayne's world began to change when he signed on with the Texas Memorial Museum at the University of Texas in Austin. "I knew what a museum was," he states, "but I didn't have any idea of what they did there." They put Wayne to work as a carpenter, and that launched his career in museums and opened up the world of history for him. A world that had just been waiting for Wayne to discover it.

"In 1986, I went to work with the Governor Bill and Vara Daniel [Historical Village] as a Historical Restoration Consultant. A real good title that meant I got to put shingles on old buildings and drive nails all day. And it paid pretty good." Wayne worked as Historical Restoration Consultant until most of the major construction was completed in early 1990.

"Then I came back to the ranch and did what I do best—unstructured work and recreational research. Ran the ranch. Fixed the fence. Built a shop. Built a storage shed. Was doing pretty good until I ran out of money. Then it was beer can picking-up time again. Didn't even need a wallet. Only thing I carried was my driver's license. Basically, all I was doing was running up and down the road."

While running up and down the roads of east Texas, Wayne discovered antiques and that piqued his historical interest. "I got into the antique business. I got fascinated with chairs. Buying, fixing up, and selling old chairs. Found out that hardly no one canes old chairs anymore. It's so simple anyone can do it. So I ordered me some cane strips and went to caning chairs. I can pick up an old chair for seven or eight dollars, clean it up, put new cane on it, and sell it for over $125." Beats picking up beer cans.

But "the [Governor Bill and Vara Daniel] Village called again," and Wayne went back to work, this time as a weekend volunteer coordinator. At this writing, Wayne is enjoying that position. A doctor has to keep operating, and Wayne has too many talents to waste. It's good for the world that Wayne remains active. His lectures and demonstrations, like his cooking, are something to see and enjoy.

"I've always liked to cook," he explains. "I was a puny kid and didn't get out to run around much. Mamma was an excellent cook and a good friend. I started cooking with her when I was about seven-years-old. She stood about four-feet, eight-inches and was nearly as round as a washtub. She was a real character. She taught me how to cook. Taught me everything green wasn't bad for you. I even like spinach."

Wayne says the way his family was, if you didn't cook, you didn't eat. "I've always been a fisherman and a camper. I've spent a lot of time wandering around and camping and fishing. In about '86, I fell in with a guy who was building and repairing wagons and buggies and I got real interested in wagons. Especially chuck wagons." Which is good for the rest of us, but presents a problem for Wayne.

"The only problem with a wagon is, you gotta have horses." Or mules. And Wayne hasn't figured out how to bond with either. "I don't do horses. Mules? Maybe. But a horse will take one look at me and say, 'There's a stupid little critter we can bite or kick or run over—let's do it.' I got no problems with cows. I got one cow I really love. And I've been beat up by bulls. But horses and me don't mix."

But Dr. Gomez, being the creative individual he is, quickly figured that by working with only chuck wagons, he wouldn't have to do horses. He could concentrate on cooking. "I got interested in chuck wagons because it gave me an excuse to cook. I could play around with my recipes and not have to jack with horses. When I park something, I want it to be there when I come back. I don't want to have to chase the damn thing further than I was going to ride it."

Naturally curious about history since he graduated from Fords and girls, Wayne dove into the history of the chuck wagon, built his own wagon, then wrote, illustrated, and published a book about chuck wagons and chuck wagon cooking. "A friend gave me this old farm wagon. It was in fair shape. It'd only been sitting out in the pasture for twenty-five years. I started doing research on it and just thought I'd see what the cowboys cooked and how they ate. It'd give me a chance to camp out, cook, and sit around the fire telling lies."

So the good doctor built his own wagon from pictures taken by Irwin Smith, who traveled Texas in a wagon in the early 1900s and published *Life On The Texas Range,* a book which greatly inspired Wayne. "I built the box out of some old wood off one of these old sheds here. I built it along the lines of a chuck wagon you'd find in the 1880s. I like that time period. That was about the end of the big trail drives. By 1870, there were railroads in Kansas City, Wichita, Fort Worth, and Houston and the long drives were no longer necessary.

"My wagon fits that time period. My wagon is a farm wagon. It wouldn't be suitable to take on a trail drive. It's not big enough. Historically, the real chuck wagons were twelve, maybe fourteen feet long, about forty-one inches wide in the bed and thirty inches deep. They had big wheels; almost five foot high in the back, and the wheels were narrow. My wagon is twelve foot long; has smaller wheels, and could be pulled by two horses or mules. The trail-drive wagons had to be pulled by four—normally mules—because they were tougher over the long haul."

CHUCK WAGON AND CAMP COOKING

Wayne says he had to write a cookbook to travel with his wagon. "I had to justify to my wife why I was running up and down the road pulling a wagon. So I wrote this little book [*Chuck Wagon Lore, Camp Cookin' and Recipes from the Doctor's Outfit*]." He signed it Dr. Sebastian Gomez. It includes the doctor's favorite foods.

"Everything in the book I've tried and tested. I've cooked for a lot of people in a lot of different circumstances. You gotta stay pretty organized and you gotta stay pretty sober. Especially at Baylor [a Baptist college]. I've cooked in competition and I've judged competition cooking. I don't like cooking for competition. I'd rather just cook for fun." Or for people.

"You can't feed peppers to Yankees. They can't take it. You gotta be careful what you serve people. And you gotta be careful about the fire you use." The secret to camp cooking is to have an Indian fire. A small fire. Plains Indians mostly cooked over a fire in a hole so the wind wouldn't whip it all around. Wayne says his biggest problem in teaching camp cooking to newcomers is teaching them to control their fires.

"Summer-before-last, I had twelve kids in a seminar at Baylor and the first day we talked about history [of chuck wagon cooking], and the next four days we cooked. The first thing them kids did was set everything on the north side of Waco on fire. Man, they had enough heat to fire a steam engine. Took me all day to convince 'em we didn't need all that fire."

What you do need for camp cooking is a small fire and lots of coals to keep the heat steady. "I can cook all day," the doctor states, "and if the wind's not blowing, just use no more'n a tub of wood. Just get a good bed of coals and add your wood to it easy. But you gotta watch your fire all the time. It's all so simple, but you gotta pay attention to what you're doing. Chuck wagon cooking has always been simple. On the long drives they had to use simple, basic foods. Stuff that could be bought in bulk and would travel well. In my cooking and in my book, I've stuck to simple things. Anyone who can cook can enjoy these recipes." Doctor's orders: enjoy.

EGGS 'N' STUFF
(From *Chuck Wagon Lore, Camp Cookin'* and
Recipes from the Doctor's Outfit)

"If the cook was lucky enough to trade for some fresh eggs along the way, they were much appreciated. The secret to trail cooking is to stretch everything as far as possible. Scrambled eggs are good with almost anything else thrown in. Here are a few good ideas to stretch or liven up the eggs."

1 tablespoon lard (Crisco will do)

1 fair-sized onion, chopped fine

3 to 4 jalapeno peppers (omit if your cowhands are all Yankees)

1 tomato, cut into small pieces

Leftover bacon or sausage, chopped fine

Leftover beans or chili

5 to 8 eggs, depending on number to be fed

Put lard in large iron skillet and heat. Add onions, peppers and tomatoes. Stir until soft. Add any one—bacon, sausage, beans, or chili—or any combination. While this is heating, beat eggs in a bowl until smooth and foamy. When skillet and contents are fryin' hot, add eggs. Scramble until well mixed and eggs are not runny. Almost any combination of the above ingredients will do. Just throw in a little imagination and let 'er rip.

McANALLY CATTLE COMPANY

STINNETT, TEXAS
RONNIE AND KIM CHILDRESS

THE COWBOY LIFE—THE GOOD LIFE

Ranching in the upper Panhandle is quite a sight. As you drive along the wide open highways, you can't but wonder if the oil and gas pumpers don't outnumber the horses and cattle. Particularly on the stretch from Borger to Stinnett, home to the McAnally Cattle Company's historic Turkey Track division, a ranch started in the 1880s.

Arriving in Stinnett, a community of around 2,200 people, you know immediately that you are in small town America. Established in 1901 as a trade center and livestock shipping point at the northern edge of the Canadian River Valley, Stinnett seems to be content to remain as it has been for decades, built around a grassy town square. The ranch is located about six miles east of town, on a road that begins to reveal the rugged Canadian River Breaks country. The headquarters at the Turkey Track is home to Ronnie and Kim Childress and their four-year-old son, Joshua.

The young couple has been on the ranch since the spring of 1993, and being the only full-time hands, Kim says that, "Ronnie is the foreman and I am the chief cook." She laughs at this in the easy way that just seems to say that this couple enjoys their life.

Kim is originally from Pampa and Ronnie is from Wheeler, about forty-five miles east of Pampa. They met at a feedlot where Kim was the office manager. As she says, "I was a city girl, but since I've been on the ranches, I don't think that I could ever live in the city again."

Ronnie was ranch-raised on the old Alexander Ranch near Allison, Texas. He drove a truck for a while, but following a serious accident with a train, he returned to his cowboy roots.

Over the last few years, Kim and Ronnie, both in their mid-thirties, have worked on the Hayhook Ranch, a division of the Texas Beef Cattle Company, the Hansford Ranch, and, since 1993, the Turkey Track.

A NEW BREED

The Turkey Track is a good size operation, tending 360 mother cows on over 26,000 rugged acres. It is a cow/calf operation, with the calving taking place each spring. And because the terrain on the ranch is so rugged, the ranch must be worked on horseback. There is calving, branding, and shipping—all extremely intensive work seasons on a ranch. During the rest of the year, Ronnie and his day cowboy, Wayne, check cattle, winter feed (if necessary), do maintenance, and ride and fix fence, weather restrictions not withstanding—and in the Texas Panhandle, the weather can be a constant challenge.

One of the things that Kim and Ronnie find so stimulating on the ranch is the Chiford cattle, a new Hereford/Chianina cross that is just about to be accepted as a separate breed. The McAnally Cattle Company has been one of the pioneers in developing this breed, which aims at bigger cows that produce leaner beef. They also tend to grade out and yield very high. The full-blooded, registered Italian Chianina bull bred to a purebred registered Hereford cow produces an animal resembling a bigger and taller Hereford—although if you know anything about Hereford cattle, you just seem to know that they aren't Herefords. The McAnally Chifords have been winning Grand Champion ribbons at shows throughout the Texas/Oklahoma area for several years now.

Ronnie says he feels good about "being in on the start of a new breed." He quickly adds, "Hopefully this is our way of life forever. We'll stay here as long as they want us. . . . I'm like my granddad—he stayed at his job for forty years. He hated looking for a job and I can't stand looking for a job, either."

Kim joins right in, adding that they've been made to feel like part of the family by the McAnallys. If there is any one feeling you get as you drive around this sprawling ranch with this cowboy and his wife, it's a sense of their intense loyalty. This couple really does "ride for the brand."

RICH IN HISTORY

It seems only fitting that a new breed should be developed here. This spread was part of the great Panhandle Oil Field discovery in 1926. It also houses the sites of the famous Battles of Adobe Walls.

In 1864, in his last battle, Colonel Kit Carson, supported by 200 infantry- and cavalrymen plus seventy-five Indian scouts, just barely escaped defeat at the hands of the 3,000 Kiowa and Comanche warriors who had been attacking wagon trains as they crossed their homelands. Ten years later, in 1874, a raiding party of 300 warriors, led by the famous Quanah Parker (Comanche) and Lone Wolf (Kiowa), attacked some buffalo hunters' camp at the second Battle of Adobe Walls. A fierce dawn attack opened the battle, and though the hunters fought off the Indians, the twenty-eight men and one woman in the buffalo

Kim and Ronnie Childress with son Joshua on Turkey Track Ranch near Stinnett.

hunters' camp were surrounded. It didn't look good. On the second day, a group of Cheyenne warriors appeared on a mesa overlooking the camp. Inside the fort, Billy Dixon took aim and shot an Indian warrior right off his horse at a distance of about seven-eighths of a mile. The warriors were so shocked at the white man's shooting ability that they ceased attempts to mount a strong attack, and by the third day, they withdrew completely.

Ronnie bemoans that he "feels like an old man. . . . On the other side of the ranch all them cowboys are in their twenties." In reality, it doesn't look like the years have been too rough on him.

In addition to cooking, Kim does about 90 percent of the computer work for the ranch. They keep all the records for the Hereford Association, the Chianina Association, and the registered cattle on this newest piece of ranch equipment. But she says, "Every once in a while I talk Ronnie into sleeping in so I can ride out and check the cattle. . . . Let me out of here—let me drive the feed wagon or anything, just get me to the outdoors." And she says, the computer makes for more arguments because "the cowboys want to think that they're right with what they've got in their heads and we think the computer is right." The funny thing is "it's kind of fifty-fifty as to who is right . . . I've wanted to hang them and they've wanted to hang me."

Life on the ranch is demanding. In the past year, they've had to build at least six miles of fence—all built to very specific standards. On the ranch they use ten T-posts, then a cedar post with all pipe corners cemented and welded. So a cowboy can't just ride, although almost all of the cattle work is done with the nine horses in the remuda—three company horses and six belonging to Ronnie and Kim. He says that they don't do a whole lot of roping, and during the branding they have used chutes, though he wistfully adds, "I'd like to see us go back to dragging the calves to the fire. Nearly all the other ranches around here do it that way." And the cowboys have to make sure that the windmills are pumping and the natural springs aren't clogged up.

When the calves hit the ground they are all tagged on the right ear, tattooed in the left ear, weighed, a written description is made of each one, the sex is determined, and the heifers are dehorned with a dehorning paste. Registered Hereford bulls are the only ones that keep their horns. This activity all takes place on the first day.

The Childresses say they choose to be in ranching because it makes them happy. You can't much beat that. Kim then adds thoughtfully, "Money's not everything. If you're happy outdoors, and you like being around horses and cattle, you'll make it somehow."

Ronnie says that in addition to better paying jobs, there are surefire easier ones, though "a cowboy's life has its glamour and its drawbacks, such as cold, miserable nights calving out heifers. But it's also a rewarding job . . . there's nothing better than seeing a newborn calf get up and go to sucking. Pulling a calf . . . the adrenalin rush for me, is phenomenal. You never realize how hard you're working because you're trying to get that calf out safely. And after it's over you feel great. It's a great disappointment when you've worked that hard and you don't save the calf. But there's a lot of rewards in the work."

As for their young son, Joshua, Kim would prefer that he grow up to be a working cowboy than a rodeo cowboy—mainly because there is so much more security in ranch work, with not nearly the danger that a rodeo cowboy has to face every week.

With the Canadian River Breaks on the south boundary, the ranch terrain is particularly rugged. This is a ranch that you either work on foot or ahorseback—and no self-respecting cowboy works afoot. As you travel around the ranch, you're apt to run into a whitetail or mule deer, wild turkey, blue and bobwhite quail, and bobcats, often at the many natural springs or the tanks pumped full by the windmills that dot the pastures and wooded areas.

COOKING IS BASIC

When Kim and Ronnie first started at the Turkey Track, cooking was part of the job description. The McAnallys wanted the ranch to be more like an old home ranch, where the guys could come in for lunch and have a hot meal instead of having to run to town to grab a hot dog.

Kim gives her warm laugh as she remembers her early days as a cook. "I knew enough to get away with it. I just didn't like to do it." But now, since she isn't working out of the house and doesn't have to rush home from a nine-to-five job and get right into the kitchen, she says she really enjoys cooking. And, she says, she's learned that meat, potatoes, and gravy will satisfy any cowboy. "You don't have to cook pasta, you don't have to cook rice, and you don't have to cook vegetables." But she does make sure that the hands have a dessert at every meal.

Ronnie would be content with chicken-fried steak, mashed potatoes, gravy, and biscuits for nearly every meal, but that isn't Kim's favorite meal to cook. She'd prefer to cook a roast with potatoes, carrots, green beans, and hot rolls. She says that she can't bake bread to "save my life." When Ronnie interrupts to point out that she's never tried, she asks him if he remembers "those brick things I tried once. . . . They were like cannon balls." Ronnie—diplomatically—admits that he had forgotten that little misadventure. Jokingly, Kim says, "When the phrase dry yeast appears—well, forget it—I'm messed up right away."

Ronnie does want everyone to know that one of the best things that Kim ever cooked is her coconut cream pie. "Yes, that was one of the major accomplishments of my life. It turned out right the very first try and then I found out that none of the cowboys liked coconut."

Kim says that cooking on the Turkey Track or any other ranch is pretty basic. For example, neither Kim, Ronnie, nor Wayne eat onions or tomatoes. "We just don't like them."

Twice a month Kim heads to Pampa to buy groceries and visit her folks. If she needs some smaller items, she can always head the six miles into Stinnett and buy what she needs locally.

Kim's recipe for you good readers is Buttermilk Pie. She got the recipe "by finally nailing down Ronnie's grandmother's recipe from his mother who had written it down." This is one of Ronnie's favorites, but it took her some time before she could find the recipe that made it taste as good as he remembered it. He says that he "could easily eat one of them by myself." You're probably going to feel the same way.

KIM CHILDRESS'S BUTTERMILK PIE
(Makes three 9-inch pies)

3¼ cups sugar

½ cup flour

½ teaspoon salt

6 eggs

1 cup buttermilk

1 teaspoon vanilla

2 sticks oleo

3 unbaked pie shells

Blend together the sugar, flour, salt, and eggs. Stir just enough to blend the eggs and other ingredients together. Add the buttermilk and vanilla and stir until they are blended. DO NOT OVERBEAT. Melt the oleo and add to the mixture. Stir quickly and pour into the pie shells. Heat the oven to 350°F and bake for forty to sixty minutes or until the center of the pie sets. These are better if cooked a day ahead.

You can sprinkle nutmeg on top of the unbaked pies for a little different taste and look.

MATADOR CATTLE COMPANY

MATADOR, TEXAS
DALE AND JOETTA BUMGARDNER

THE SURPRISED RANCH WIFE

Few names are more well known in ranching history than that of the Matador. And the town of Matador, the county seat of Motley County, owes its very existence to the ranch and its cowboys.

Back in 1891, when the county was first organized, there wasn't a single settlement within its borders, not even a place to house the county government. There were only headquarters and line camps of the area's ranches, just like those of the then 400,000-acre Matador, which at that time was owned by a corporation based in Scotland. But in a turn of creative events typical of the budding ranch industry of Texas, the townsite was defined, and the necessary twenty businesses were set up and operated for one day by the willing cowboys of the Matador Ranch. As a result of their efforts, a patent could be granted by the General Land Office of Texas, and Motley County had its seat of government.

Today, the town still has less than 800 people and the Matador Ranch headquarters, sitting on a hill just south of town, continues to dominate the area.

This wonderful, historic old ranch was originally founded in 1879 by two Americans—Henry Campbell and Colonel Alfred Markham Britton—and some lessor investors. By 1882, they sold out to the Matador Land and Cattle Company, Limited, of Scotland, for $1,250,000, a pretty tidy profit. Control of the ranch shifted from Texas to Dundee, Scotland, where all the policy decisions were to be made.

The Scots appointed Murdo Mackenzie to oversee the ranch's huge holdings in Texas, Montana, and Dakota. As ranch manager, Mackenzie kept costs under control. In fact, one employee is quoted as saying, "We never buy a hobble rope on the Matador but they know about it in Dundee." Mackenzie himself lived pretty well, with mansions in Denver and Trinidad, and a son at Princeton University. He eventually left the Matador in 1911 to become manager of a ranch in Brazil that was even bigger than the Matador.

RANCH CAREER A SURPRISE

The ranch manager today is Dale Bumgardner, who, together with his wife JoEtta, is continuing the long and rich traditions of the ranch. They've been at the Matador since 1967, although they are both originally from Kansas. They were married in 1959 and have one son, Joe, now in his mid-thirties. The Bumgardners come to ranching from quite varied backgrounds. JoEtta grew up on a Kansas farm and is a registered nurse. Dale was born to an oil field family and even served as a Kansas Highway Patrolman before ranching came into the picture. Joe, who worked on the ranch as a youngster, now works in the oil business for Koch Industries, the present owners of the ranch. They've owned the Matador together with her sister ranches, the Beaverhead in Montana and the Spring Creek in Kansas, since 1951. As large as the ranching operation is—and it is a very large operation—it's really only a blip on the Koch Industries corporate chart.

When Dale and JoEtta married, they had no plans to become ranchers. But Dale went to work for Koch Industries and eventually got into the ranching end of the company in November 1971. He had always been interested in cattle and ranching, but this was his first taste of it as a job. They both agree that, even though it wasn't planned, life on the ranch has been wonderful. As Dale says, "I wouldn't trade it for a good job."

Being on the Matador is something special. JoEtta lights up when she says, "I still get a good feeling when I'm pulling down the driveway and I think, 'Oh boy, I'm coming to the Matador,' . . . coming from Kansas I never, in my wildest dreams thought I'd live in Texas." Dale adds, "I'm very proud to be part of the Matador." The Matador has a long, rich history, and people frequently stop by because they had an uncle, or father, or grandfather who was once a Matador cowboy.

FAR FROM HEADQUARTERS

Today the ranch is still over 200,000 acres in deeded and leased land. It's a cow/calf operation, with the majority of the stock Brangus cattle, a Brahman/Angus cross. Traditionally, the ranch had run straight Herefords, but they changed to keep up with the demands of the cattle market. The ranch is still worked from the back of a horse and they "use plenty of them [horses]," although they do not breed their own horses anymore. Now they buy good "ranch" geldings and only geldings—no mares or stallions.

The Matador employs ten cowboys and cowgirls and they are scattered all over the large ranch. Three are at headquarters and the others are in various camps. The one cowgirl has a ranch-owned house in town, less than a mile from headquarters. One of the great changes in modern ranching is the closing of the traditional bunkhouse in favor of hiring married cowboys. The ranch supplies them with a house and they are pretty much on their own. There is only one single cowboy and a single cowgirl among today's crew. And the wives of the cowboys hold a variety of jobs—two are nurses, one is a teacher, one drives the Senior Citizens' bus, and one drives a school bus and is a teacher's aid. And this also allows the cowboys to work at jobs they love and have families at the same time. Quite a change from the old-time cowboys who were traveling fast and light and never seemed to be attached to anyone.

The camps are far from headquarters, and when you consider that the 206,000 acres is nearly 322 square miles, you get an idea of the distance someone can be from headquarters and still be on the ranch. One camp is twenty miles away, another is forty miles—well, you get the idea. Dale says he sees his cowboys "more often than I think I should. We have telephones so we talk to them every day." At one time the ranch had over 300 cowboys on its payroll.

Since there are about 5,000 mother cows, each cowboy at his camp is responsible for his own small herd. They start calving in late October, brand in February, and ship in September. "Here at the Matador we fight the heat more than the cold."

COOKING IS TIRING

JoEtta's mother taught her to cook. "We used to cook for the harvest hands on the farm . . . I just grew up cooking." She also cooked for the hands at the Spring Creek Ranch in Kansas, also owned by Koch Industries, where Dale and JoEtta started. Then she cooked at the Yellow House Ranch down by Levelland, Texas, but that outfit is no longer owned by the Matador. After that, they moved to part of the old Bell Ranch in eastern New Mexico, which had been leased by the Matador. Cooking, she says, "is hard work. You get up at three in the morning to cook breakfast, then haul dinner [lunch] to them." She had to "haul dinner" because the ranch was so big the cowboys couldn't come in for the noon meal and make it back to work without losing too much time—a seventy-mile mile round-trip. Dale says the rough road "sure blended the meals." JoEtta cooked for about twenty-two cowboys on a regular basis, although she says with a sigh, "One time, forty-three came in for lunch, and if the neighbors saw you, they came, too." Those cowboys liked chicken-fried steak, gravy, and beans. There really should be a monument to chicken-fried steak and gravy in every ranch museum in Texas. But JoEtta says that they don't like salads very much, "and you might get a few vegetables down but not many . . . and they sure do like homemade bread." She quickly repeats, "Cooking for cowboys is tiring," adding, "Cowboys aren't picky as long as they have meat, potatoes, and beans . . . that's about it . . . and most of them show respect and will always say thank you."

Dale and JoEtta both agree that cowboys show respect for women on the ranch as long as the women demand it. "But if she is nasty-mouthed, they will

be, too." Dale notes that if one of the boys is disrespectful, the other cowboys will jump all over him. He also explains that the ranch no longer provides a beef to each camp because the IRS classified it as income and started to tax the cowboys for its value. So the ranch owners stopped the practice, which is pretty traditional all over the country, and gave each of the hands a raise. Dale says proudly, "They treat us right." In fact, Koch Industries even paid all the back taxes. So the old saying that cowboss and corporation just seem to naturally collide might not always be true. It sure doesn't seem that way talking to Dale and JoEtta.

Dale says he was at the Montana ranch, the Beaverhead near Dillon, in January and "nearly froze to death." As we sat and talked in late January in Texas, there were nine or ten inches of new snow on the ground, but it still wasn't what you'd call cold—certainly not Montana cold. JoEtta smiles as she tells of the time she and Dale moved to Texas and were living at the Lucky Knob camp. She says they had about the same amount of snow as was on the ground when we visited—not much to worry about by Kansas standards—but when they came to town they saw fender-benders and the people were talking about how bad the weather was. "I just had a light jacket on and I didn't think it was that bad—but now I'm just as bad as they are."

The summers can get into the 100-degree range, but the Bumgardners don't seem to mind that, either.

Dale Bumgardner dragging a calf (left) and ropmg one at the Matador branding (photo courtesy Dale Bumgardner).

COWBOY ETIQUETTE

"Ranching is changing fast. It's a new breed coming up." And what particularly concerns Dale is that the new hands don't seem to know the cowboy etiquette. For example: "You never rode in front of the old-timers, you never rode between a man and the herd . . . they don't know that. It used to be considered disrespectful. You never rode into a man's herd to cut unless you were told to by the foreman or one of the top hands. Now they just ride in." JoEtta adds that the new hands all want to ride up front, not in the rear, or drag, as they did in the old days.

Dale sometimes thinks that he's "more of a baby-sitter than a ranch foreman" since so many of the newer cowboys come out of college ranch management programs rather than from ranching backgrounds. "But if they've got any memory, they can learn to do a pretty good job. We've been pretty lucky. It just takes time." Nearly half the cowhands at the ranch are college graduates.

There isn't a week that goes by that the Matador doesn't get at least five inquiries from people looking for jobs. Some have a little background, some have none. But they all want to work on the Matador. If you want to work there, you'd better be able to ride and rope a little, but be prepared to mend fences, maybe work on a windmill, and know something about cattle.

The only time on the ranch when all the cowboys and cowgirls are together is during the weaning and shipping in September and the branding in February. That's when they really have to help each other.

They still drag the calves to the fire for branding and with nine cowboys they can brand "300 calves a day, easy."

COMPUTERS AND GENES

At the Matador, computers have found their way into the barn and have taken over as the main source of record keeping. They keep track of all the heifers and all the other cattle. They know which bull has bred which heifer or cow. And they are also able to keep track of all the calves.

The Matador buys all its bulls, about 230 at any given time. All of the bulls are registered—more record keeping for the computer. They are kept until they have bred in their seventh year, then they are shipped to the packing houses. The Matador doesn't keep its own bulls because "we need the change in genetics. Hopefully we upgrade our herd, and I think we've done a good job of it."

The ranch ships its cattle to their own feedlots—they have three in Kansas and one in Texas. That way they can keep tabs on their cattle and be sure of the quantity and quality of the beef that they are producing. The ultimate in quality control.

JoEtta offers us some good eating from the ranch in Texas, including West Texas Chili and Hot Fudge Pudding.

WEST TEXAS CHILI

2 pounds meat, browned

1 tablespoon cumin

⅛ teaspoon oregano

2 teaspoons salt

½ teaspoon paprika

1 teaspoon onion powder

1 teaspoon garlic powder

½ cup chili powder

2 tablespoons masa

1 teaspoon red pepper

1 8-ounce can tomato sauce

2 8-ounce cans water

Cook all the ingredients together until the mixture is thick.

HOT FUDGE PUDDING

1 cup flour
¾ cup sugar
2 tablespoons baking powder
2 tablespoons cocoa
¼ teaspoon salt
Nuts if desired
½ cup milk
2 tablespoons melted shortening
¼ cup cocoa
1 cup brown sugar

Sift the flour, sugar, baking powder, two tablespoons cocoa, and salt. Add to this the milk and melted shortening. Then mix the quarter cup of cocoa and brown sugar and pour over the mixture. Pour one and three-quarters cups of hot water over all and bake for forty to forty-five minutes in preheated oven at 350°F.

MEANS RANCH

VALENTINE, TEXAS
ALFRED AND RUTH MEANS

A LIFELONG LOVE AFFAIR WITH A LIFESTYLE

Valentine, in the southwest corner of Jeff Davis County, boasts a population of 217, but that is swelled considerably every February 14, as lovers come here from across the country to mail Valentine's Day cards. The Valentine area always has been a popular place with lovers. The native Indians loved the area for a seeping spring that provided life-giving water—a commodity in short supply in this high, dry plateau nestled between the Apache and Sierra Vieja Mountains.

When the white settlers came to the wide open West Texas plains, they, too, fell in love with the area around the Van Horn Wells, and as might have been predicted, more than one dispute has developed over ownership of this valuable commodity. In 1878, General John Bullis was sent into the lower Trans-Pecos country to drive out the Indians who had been raiding white settlements. Near present-day Valentine, the Army captured a Mexican disguised as an Indian. In a clear case of rejection of an old lover, the captive led the troops to the springs and showed them the Indian trail that led to San Antonio.

In the following years, the Butterfield Stage Line built a stage station at the wells. It became a favorite rest spot for travelers, cowboys, ranchers, and, of course, lovers. An increasing number of pioneer families settled in the area. Among those early settlers were John and Exa Means who took up a homestead in 1884. According to their grandson, Valentine area rancher Alfred "Alf" Means, those lovers settled on Cherry Creek and lived in a tent for two years while putting together the makings of the Means Ranch.

A town for lovers, Valentine, Texas.

TRUSTING THE LORD FOR RAIN

"My granddad came out here to raise a family," says Alf, a third generation West Texas rancher. Alf is tanned and hardened by the sun and wind. "He homesteaded and was friendly to the other homesteaders. They called 'em nesters back in those days. Lots of ranchers would run 'em off. But Gramps hired 'em to work and he hauled 'em water and when they starved out, he bought their spreads and he got pretty big pretty quick."

Alfred and Ruth Means raised their two sons and their daughter in the same house that his grandfather raised his family in. Now, Alf's son, Bodie, is raising his family in that old Means homestead. The Means family goes way back in West Texas tradition and history. "In June 1984, eighty family members gathered on the original homestead site for a memorial service, right under the same trees where they had stretched their tent a hundred years before," Alf states. "It was a good feeling. And it was educational. The creek wasn't running. It had dried up. That's typical of this country. It can get beautiful, then it can get pretty tough. We just trust the Lord for rain."

Trusting in the Lord and working hard has been the Means's motto for over a century, and today his sons and grandsons carry on a west Texas tradition, carving a life for families and livestock in the Trans-Pecos Llano (Highland). "Where we lived," Alf recalls, "Gramps and Grandmother liked to have starved out for lack of water. Then he hired a steam-operated drill and they went down to 130 feet and hit 100 gallons a minute. Water just as clear as a crystal and so pure it's like distilled water. You can ranch with that."

COWBOYS AND COWMEN

And ranch they did. Alf's father, Cole, and uncle, Bug, ran the ranch for years after taking it over from Alf's grandfather. Then, in about 1937, the Means boys split the ranch; that's the way it stands today. "They had 250 sections of this old country," Alf says of the original ranch. "They ran a fence east to west and divided 'er right down the middle. My nephew, Jon, runs the north ranch and my son, Bodie, runs the south part—the old Y6. That was Gramps's brand. We still use it today."

Alf says that in the early days of the Means ranch, his grandfather branded EXA on his cattle's rib cages and his grandfather's brother-in-law, George Evans, branded KATE on the ribs. "They could see that [brand] a long way. There were no fences then. [It's] so very important to read brands from a distance. They branded lots of cattle. They ran about 2,500 head, and I'm sure they must have had a lot of dry cows. But there was plenty of grass then and they were just learning this country."

Alf started learning about the country and about ranching well before he started his formal education. "We learned to ride right after we learned to walk. And we worked. They got all the use out of us they could before we went to school. And when we started school, they planned all their works [roundups and brandings] around school holidays."

Alf attended school in Valentine and says at that time the town was a popular shipping point. "In those days we shipped everything by rail. We had a good setup. Our pastures ran right up against Valentine, so we'd just have these big drives and take the cattle right to the stockyards by the railroad. Bug was the 'Caporal' [foreman]. He ran the outfit. He'd lead a drive going one way and my dad would lead another. We'd meet at the back side and drive 'em to the stock yards. Those fellers were cowmen. Not just cowboys."

In the late 1930s, according to Alf, the Means got to running sheep to better utilize the land. "We have some rough old country here that cattle hardly ever use, and boy, the sheep did well up there. They built fences to hold 'em and we still have 100 miles of woven wire fence on the ranch. The sheep helped this ranch through some hard times. It was a delightful situation."

SHORE'NUFF HORSES

Another thing that helped the Means Ranch survive the dirty thirties was their horses. "We had awful good horses," Alf says. "Awful good horses. Nearly everybody made fun of us because we had thoroughbred horses. I've still got the papers on a horse named 'Frustrate.' He was born in 1910 and the ranch bought him off the race track in Juarez. They bred him to what we call Spanish mares. They were good horses. They could go all day but they couldn't run much faster than I can run. And in this country you need to be mounted on something that can turn a cow."

So the Means began crossing the English Thoroughbred with the Spanish Bard and came up with a Texas cow pony that was the envy of horsemen everywhere. No one was laughing anymore as buyers trekked to the Means ranch in search of a polo prospect. "They were shore'nuff horses," Alf remembers those tough offspring of their breeding program. "They could go all day. You couldn't hardly ride one down."

Word of the Means-bred horses reached all the way to the east coast; Alf says a Mr. Post, of Long Island, New York, began buying their cow ponies to convert to polo horses. "Really, that's what got us through the '30s," Alf recalls. "They sure helped us out. Boy, they were good cow ponies and good cutting horses. Nothing got away from 'em, I'll tell you that."

NO SPOILED KIDS—NO SPOILED CATTLE

Alf says that in the days of the Depression, there were also lots of good cowboys and nothing much got away from them, either. "We thought we were short-handed if we left the corrals with less than eighteen men. And every one a good man. They didn't miss many cattle. They were quiet around a roundup and they worked all day for little or no pay. They'd show up at the post office 'cause they knew Dad or Bug had to come in and get the mail. And they'd hire on for meals.

"They'd come out and ride anything you'd lead out. Anything. Lots of those horses would pitch. Bug's and Cole's horses would pitch, too. When the boss's horse starts pitching, you know you better be watching your horse. We learned to pay attention to their ears. If their ears got a little too stiff, you better reach down and get ready to ride."

From an early age, Alf not only learned to ride, but even more importantly, he says he learned to ranch. "We were taught to ranch as soon as we could ride. How to shape a herd up. Handle cattle. Go easy. Dad always said, 'Make up all your time before you get to the cattle.' When you start in on cattle, you go slow. You take care of cattle because the cattle take care of you. Dad and Bug would always say, 'No spoiled kids. No spoiled cattle.'"

Alf says as children, he, his brother, their cousin Coley, and their neighbors' boys did most of the roping during branding time. "When we were too little to hold a calf down, we had to do all the roping. We'd rope 'em around the neck and drag 'em to the fire. Those old cowboys on the ground would slap your horse when you went by and holler, 'More cattle.' They kept us going. When I was about fourteen, I thought I was a pretty good roper and daddy told me, 'You won't make a good roper until you get so tired you can't hardly stand to rope. Then you won't waste a single loop. That's what makes a roper.'"

Alf not only turned into a pretty good roper, he became a top hand, and today he is a successful rancher who says he has enjoyed every minute of it. "We had more fun than the law allows. We were working hard but we had fun. We thought we were rich people. We never had a clue that we were so near broke. But we were always trying to do better. Trying to improve our waterings. Trying to improve our pastures. Trying to improve our cattle. It's been a lot of hard work but it hasn't been all bad."

BEING FLEXIBLE IN A CHANGING WORLD

The Means Ranch runs a hybrid cow today, and Alf says they are happy with the results. "We put J.D. Hudgins Brahman bulls on Hereford cows and Angus cows. We keep those half-blood cows. She's the best momma cow we've ever found. You can breed her to anything and she'll let that calf express every bit of the genetic potential he has. She makes a good hustler out of the calf. We used to just strain to raise a calf weighing 440 [pounds]. Now our steer calves are weighing out around 750 pounds." The times certainly are a-changing.

"Things have really changed now. It's a different world. You need to be flexible. You got to keep up." The Means not only keep up, they are forging ahead in their cattle program. "Bodie is an A.I. technician. He'll start his twenty-fourth year now. He sells lots of our heifers around Fort Worth, Houston, and San Antonio, where people have smaller spreads and want tamer cattle. They'll pay a lot for those heifers, but they're buying F-1 cows, which will last fourteen to fifteen years. It's a good deal all around. We've gone from quantity to quality, and it's working well."

Craig Means, Bodie's younger brother, ranches near Fort Worth. He sells bred F-1 (half-blood) heifers, a business Alf says he is doing well in. That leaves Alf, Ruth, and Bodie at the home ranch with their two hired men. "We're very fortunate to have these two fellers," Alf says of his crew. "They're Latins. Both good men. The younger feller is an excellent horseman. He's thorough, he listens; just a top hand." Good men, it seems, are hard to find.

"I look for an honorable, reliable person who has a clean mouth and is loyal. You can put up with a lot if your people have those qualities. We shy from people who drink. We don't get up and get going as early as we once did, but we still do a good day's work. I'm getting old and stove up, so I let the boys take the lead and that's working well. It's been no big deal. They just seem to know that I expect it and they love it. They love this ranch. We all do. It's our life."

Alf says his father was fond of saying that the West Texas country was the best place in the world to live, if you can find some way to buy your groceries. Apparently, that's never been a problem on the Means Ranch.

A GROUCHY COOK IS A GOOD COOK

"We always had plenty to eat. And we always had good cooks. But I think old Claudio was the grouchiest cook I ever saw. I was just a kid, but I remember him being grouchy all the time. As I got older, I began to understand that he wanted to do as good a job at the [chuck] wagon as Dad and Bug were doing with the cattle. He wanted to run that thing right. He wanted good, hot, clean food, and he didn't want anybody getting in the way, messing with the chuck."

Alf says they'd butcher a heifer in the cool of the evening just before dark and hang the carcass on the north side of the house. The beef would be wrapped in a tarp and put in a shady spot during the day and the cook would just slice off what he needed for the next meal. "The first thing we'd have would be son-of-a-gun stew," Alf remembers. "Then, the next morning, Claudio would slice thin strips of liver and fry it in hot grease. He'd serve that with hot biscuits and lick and boy, that was good. We had that old 'Dixie's Best' lick and it was sorry stuff, but it shore tasted good to us kids. We fared good. I'll tell you that."

Of all the great cooks who have practiced their craft at the Means Ranch, the best of the bunch by far, is Alf's wife, Ruth—the one who almost got away. "I like not to have got married," he recalls. "I was twenty-nine and thought I had to get a ranch-raised girl who would marry a cowboy. Then it finally occurred to me the only girl I could get to live in the country was someone who didn't know any better."

Ruth was a city girl and had never been on a ranch, but she jumped in with both feet and hands, and according to Alf, she is one of the best cooks in the West. "You ask anybody anywhere [about ranch cooking] and her name is at the top of the list for cooks in this country. She's got lots of recipes, but she don't write 'em down. She's a hard worker. A wonderful cook and a wonderful wife. Raised three wonderful children. I'm a blessed man." It's a true love story from Valentine, in the heart of some beautiful country.

It took us a while, but we finally tracked Ruth down and convinced her to write down one of her favorite recipes. She says it's quick and easy, and will feed a hard working family or small roundup crew.

RUTH'S CHILE RELLENO CASSEROLE

1 pound lean ground beef

½ cup onion, chopped

½ teaspoon salt

¼ teaspoon pepper

2 4-ounce cans whole green chilies, sliced and halved

1½ cups shredded cheese

1½ cups milk

¼ cup flour

4 eggs

Dash of hot pepper sauce

Brown beef and onion in a little oil. Drain off excess fat and sprinkle meat with salt and pepper to taste. Place half of the meat mixture in a thirteen-inch x nine-inch casserole pan. Put half of the chilies on top of meat. Sprinkle with cheese. Put another layer of meat, chilies, and cheese in pan.

Combine milk, flour, eggs in separate bowl and beat until the mixture is smooth. Pour this over meat mixture and bake forty-five to fifty minutes in 350°F oven. When a knife will come out clean, the casserole is done. Cool it for five minutes then slice into squares and serve.

"The amount of ingredients can be doubled to serve more cowboys. Serve with French bread, green salad, and chocolate cake." And you have a real ranch meal. A Means Ranch Meal. Enjoy.

PITCHFORK LAND
AND CATTLE COMPANY

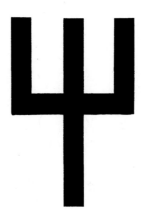

GUTHRIE, TEXAS
TOMMY AND PATRICIA TOSH

KEEPING THE OLD TRADITIONS ALIVE

Driving on Highway 82, between Dickens and Guthrie, you can't help but be impressed as you approach the headquarters of the Pitchfork Land and Cattle Company. From the stately entrance gate, down the tree-lined road to the modern complex of buildings, the ranch exudes history and tradition and its classic ranch environment. Nestled next to the easy-flowing South Wichita River, the headquarters is home to the ranch office, cookhouse, garages and shop, museum, bunkhouse, roping arena, and individual houses for some of the married cowboys. But the crown jewel of the complex is the magnificent colonial, two-storied manager's residence. This white colonnade building is reminiscent of George Washington's Mount Vernon. Surrounded by towering elm trees, this stately ranch home, a portion of which was built back in the 1890s, surely is the dominant feature of the Pitchfork Ranch headquarters.

Now well past its centennial (it celebrated its one hundredth birthday in 1983), the Pitchfork Land and Cattle Company exemplifies friendship, confidence, and vision. Its story begins in the days before the Civil War in Mississippi, where Eugene Flewellyn Williams and his distant cousin, Daniel Baldwin Gardner, were born in 1851. While they were growing up, the cousins spent a considerable amount of time together and formed a bond of mutual respect that lasted throughout their lives.

FROM THE RAVAGES OF THE CIVIL WAR

The Civil War left the Gardner and Williams families in shambles. Impoverished, with no real prospects, Eugene Williams and Dan Gardner left their respective plantations to search for their futures, each in his own way.

Williams eventually wound up in Saint Louis, working for the Hamilton and Brown Shoe Company. In 1876, after four years of hard work, he was made a partner in the firm.

Gardner remained in agriculture, but by 1871 he was headed West—headed for the Texas frontier, where opportunities seemed plentiful. At Fort Griffin, near present-day Albany just northeast of Abilene, he began to set his roots firmly into the Texas ranching life—first as a cowboy for local ranchers E. L. Walker and J. C. Lynch, then on a cattle drive headed for Colorado. It was the cattle drive that gave him the opportunity to see firsthand country that would eventually become some of the most productive and important cattle country in the West.

By 1875, after holding several jobs, he went back to cowboying, this time for Colonel J. S. Godwin and his son, D. W., who owned an outfit near present-day Seymour, Texas, southwest of Wichita Falls. Within six months Dan Gardner was made foreman.

INTO THE CATTLE BUSINESS

In 1877, the Godwins sold their ranch and Gardner was without a job. But in 1878, he rejoined the Godwins in buying twelve hundred head of cattle near Albany. Although he was a minor partner in the deal, he was manager of the herd and the partnership became very successful. In 1879, they branded their first calves—1,054 head—with the WOO brand. Shortly the Godwins again sold out for a profit, and once again Dan Gardner was without a ranch base.

In 1881, Gardner heard rumors that a fellow named Jerry Savage, who was grazing cattle on the South Wichita River using a Pitchfork brand, was willing to sell out. Dan, still with no real money of his own, asked Colonel Godwin to help finance his purchase of the Savage herd. Godwin agreed, however, a series of personal problems caused him to bow out at the last minute. With little time to spare before he'd lose the opportunity to buy the Savage cattle, Gardner turned to his old boyhood friend, Eugene Williams.

Williams had made a real go of it in the shoe business, and when he got Gardner's request, he hurried to Fort Worth to go over the deal. In December, 1881, meeting at Colonel Godwin's home, Williams agreed to go into the cattle business, without ever seeing the herd. Trusting in his friend, he wrote a check that night, entered the cattle business, and before taking the night train back to Saint Louis, had renewed a bond that would last as long as they lived.

THE PITCHFORK LAND AND CATTLE COMPANY

For something around $50,000 (Williams put up $40,000, Gardner $10,000), the new partnership bought twenty-six hundred longhorn cattle, seventy horses, and wagons and camp equipment, but almost no land. However, this was the beginning of the present-day Pitchfork Land and Cattle Company.

By May of 1882, they bought another 450 two-year-old steers for fourteen dollars a head, but money remained tight. The partners knew for their new ranch to grow, they needed more capital. So they added A. P. Bush, Jr., a young Saint Louis businessman. He bought one-half of Williams's interest for $50,000. With Bush's investment they bought 269 more cows, calves, and steers. And knowing that the open range days were fast coming to an end, they began to fence their own range.

By the end of 1883, the ranch had more than six thousand head of cattle and Williams and Gardner had more than doubled their original investments.

The Pitchfork back then was bordered on the north by the Matador Ranch and the Espuela (Spur) Ranch on the west. The land squeeze was on, and to make the picture even more difficult for the Pitchfork, Samuel Lazerus, a young merchant from Sherman, Texas, got title to 52,000 acres of land that was on what the partners considered the Pitchfork range. Lazerus also got control of some state land. All at once he had over 100,000 acres.

Lazerus had the land, the Pitchfork partners had cattle—a merger seemed to be in the cards. By December, 1883, they all agreed to a joint stock company combining the operations of the Pitchfork and Lazerus's FA Ranch into a new corporation: the Pitchfork Land and Cattle Company.

The ranch, as it was then formed, was home to several tributaries of the South Wichita River. Willow Creek, Davidson Canyon, Turkey Canyon, Brushy Creek, and T-41 Canyon provided lots of water in good years. During those times when there was above average rainfall, the ranch had enough water and grass to support some fifteen thousand cattle. The ranch's native short and gramma grasses provided excellent pasture.

By July, 1884, the ranch held its first cattle sale. They sold 288 three-year-old steers for thirty-five dollars a head, not bad money in those days.

FROM POLO PONIES TO COW PONIES

From these early investments and negotiations, one of the most enduring ranches of the Texas Panhandle—if not the entire West—came to life.

This was not just a cattle ranch, however. Horse always have played an important role on this spread. As the big sign on Highway 82 at headquarters announces: Pitchfork Land and Cattle Company, Hereford Cattle, Registered Quarter Horses.

The development of the fine horse herd is a relatively new thing in the ranch's history. For the first fifty or so years of the Pitchfork's existence, the cowboys relied on native, or Spanish ponies. But the Williams brothers, heirs of Eugene Williams, were fine horsemen and they loved polo. After Dan Gardner died in 1928 (Williams had died in 1900), the Williams brothers introduced thoroughbred mares and stallions to the ranch. Four of the mares were bought from beer tycoon August Busch, Jr. Although the Pitchfork cowboys were able to field a polo team, the thoroughbreds didn't do much to add "cow" to the horse herd, a quality all good cowboys want in their mounts.

In 1940, when Rudolph Swenson became ranch manager, he pushed for the owners to get some quarter horses on the ranch so that they would have better cow ponies. By 1941, Swensen was able to buy the first quarter horse stallion for the ranch, a stud named Seal Brown. He sired a good band of brood mares, and after his death in 1946, D. Burns (the new ranch manager—Swenson was killed in an automobile accident in 1942) traded with the Four Sixes for a young stallion. Burns, whose brother John was the manager at the Four Sixes, described the new stud, Joe Bailey's King, as "one of the best horses they [the Four Sixes] have produced."

Eventually, the horse herd grew in both size and quality, and the Pitchfork horses gained a reputation as excellent cow ponies with a good deal of stamina. Burns said, "We have no place on the Pitchfork for a horse that cannot take cowboys to the backside of the pasture and return, doing whatever cow work is necessary coming and going."

By 1963, the ranch held its first horse dispersal sale. Buyers came from far and wide. The sale was so successful that the ranch decided to hold other, similar sales periodically, though never yearly, and not on a regular basis. The sales are held when the horse herd outgrows the need the ranch has for a specific number of mounts.

THE CENTENNIAL

The Pitchfork, ever changing, maintains the integrity of the initial ranch, though the owners have kept up with the times. For example, around 1910 the ranch acquired its first motor vehicles. In 1935, they bought their first purebred Herefords, although they had been crossing Hereford bulls with their cows since the ranch was started. Later they added Simmental (1974), Limousin (1975), Beefmaster (1977), and Simbra (Simmental-Brahman cross, 1978). These new bulls were bred to crossbred cows who were the offspring of the Hereford-Angus heifers and the Hereford bulls. At no time, however, did the Pitchfork give up its purebred Hereford cattle herd.

They also increased their land base. In addition to the local land they had been acquiring, the Pitchfork bought the Flag Ranch, just south of Laramie, Wyoming, in 1952 (it was sold in 1993) and the Flint Hills Ranch near Eskridge, Kansas, in 1978.

By 1983, the owners of the Pitchfork Land and Cattle Company were able to proudly celebrate the first hundred years of the ranch's operation. (Much of the material on the early history of the ranch came from *The Pitchfork Land and Cattle Company: The First Century,* by David J. Murrah, ©Pitchfork Land and Cattle Company, 1983.)

CHANGES AND TRADITION

The more things change, the more they stay the same. The ranch, as modern and up-to-date as any ranch could possibly want to be, still speaks to a time gone by. The romantic traditions of ranching come to life as you watch wagon boss James Gholson or cowboys "Easy" Zamora or Chris Littlefield do their work

Wagon boss James Gholson ready to do some roping in an arena near ranch headquarters; Pitchfork Land and Cattle Co., Guthrie, Texas.

from the back of a horse. There is a reassuring feeling that ranching and cowboys really are here to stay.

Today, Bob Moorhouse is the manager, having taken over from his father, Tom, who in turn, had taken over from the legendary Jim Humphreys, who first assumed the job when D. Burns retired in 1965. Moorhouse was appointed assistant manager in 1973 and manager in 1983, when Humphreys retired. He is from an old Texas ranching family near Benjamin. He is also well-known as a very fine ranch photographer. He held a show in November, 1993, at the American Quarter Horse Association Museum in Amarillo, winning well-deserved critical acclaim.

At the ranch there are still more than 300 miles of fence that have to be maintained, there are 113 windmills that need the attention of a full-time windmill repairman, and the cowboys still have to shoe their own horses and tend more than 5,000 mother cows. The cycles at the ranch are constant.

In the early spring, the bulls are put with the cows. By July, the bulls are separated. The cows calve in the spring and fall. The cattle are branded in March and May, and weaned in the fall, usually from mid-September to Thanksgiving. The Pitchfork winters its yearlings, not shipping until May.

In late summer, the mares and colts are brought in from their pastures to be branded. The horses at the Pitchfork are branded on the left front shoulder. The colts are weaned from the mares and carefully assigned to the cowboys for the beginning of their training.

THE COOKHOUSE AND THE WAGON

And meanwhile, back at the cookhouse, Patricia Tosh is in charge of feeding a good part of the Pitchfork crew; her husband Tommy takes over when the wagon goes out. He also does some of the cooking at the ranch.

Tommy is from a ranching background. His dad still ranches about 130 miles east of Guthrie. Patricia is a city girl from Brownwood, Texas, about eighty miles south of Abilene. They were married in 1981 and have been on the Pitchfork since 1989.

We talked in the cookhouse, after a classic Texas ranch meal of chicken-fried steak, mashed potatoes, asparagus, beans, and bread, with cake for dessert. Eating with the wagon boss and cowboys, and listening to their easy banter, we realized quickly that these ranch hands enjoy their work and eat well, both in quantity and quality.

Tommy learned wagon cooking from Jimbo Humphreys, the son of the former ranch manager. Jimbo is known throughout the West as a champion chuck wagon cook.

Tommy and his crew have taken the chuck wagon to the Cowboy Hall of Fame in Oklahoma City, and they've been to Stamford for the Texas Cowboy Reunion, and to Abilene for the Western Heritage celebration. They've also journeyed to Wichita Falls.

Patricia learned to cook from Jo Sibert, the Pitchfork's previous cook. At the time that Patricia and Tommy first came to the Pitchfork, Tommy was actually a mechanic, but when Al and Jo Sibert retired, the Toshs took over. Since Patricia had helped some in the kitchen, she started cooking while the ranch sought Jo's replacement. When they had trouble in finding one, the ranch owners asked Patricia to take the job full time.

TEXAS COWBOY EATS

Patricia says that one of the most difficult aspects of cooking at the ranch is having to "second-guess them because you may have cooked for ten but maybe twenty show up. But you have to be sure to have enough no matter how many show up. . . . You have to overcook."

The ranch has five camps away from the headquarters where the cowboys live with their families. At the cookhouse, they have to feed all the cowboys in the bunkhouse, the manager, the secretaries, the mechanic, windmiller, yard-man, and guests. "And when the owners come in, we cook for them and maybe the owner's friends."

Range camp at the Pitchfork, 1950s (photo courtesy Pitchfork Ranch).

During the busy times there might be as many as seven or eight cowboys in the bunkhouse. "I have fed as many as thirty-seven hands when we were working cattle." She adds, "I love cooking for cowboys. . . . They're mostly easy to please." She says that you can't please everybody all the time, but mostly she's learned they stay pretty happy as long as she doesn't serve casseroles, vegetables, or beets. "They do like chicken-fried steak, mashed potatoes, gravy, and homemade bread . . . they will not eat beets." Tommy says, "They'll eat doughnuts any time we fix them." And they love cobbler and pie.

FOLLOW THE RULES—OR ELSE

Because you have to keep order in this large operation, there have to be rules, and the rules Patricia and Tommy have imposed are both traditional and they just make plain, common sense.

First, stay out of the cook's way. Don't ever walk between the cook and the stove. And don't tie your horse to the fence outside the cookhouse.

Patricia rings a bell fifteen minutes before lunch, and then again right at noon. So don't seat yourself at the table until the last bell has rung. At twelve o'clock sharp, the last bell resounds through the headquarters and then they eat. However, "If the cowboys are out working cattle, then we wait for them. I have waited until four o'clock."

There are to be no hats worn at the table and you can't "pass wind, no belching, and no cussing." For anyone who doesn't get the message, "we make sure they get informed quickly."

One final courtesy: after each meal, the diner's all wash their own dishes. "We try to have them all hold to normal courtesies," explains Tommy. "We try to hold on to the old traditions. It's not so much that we go out of our way to do it as much as it's some of the things that have been done down through the years." The cookhouse itself houses a treasure of old memories and traditions. It was built between 1900 and 1919 and "has changed very little in the course of time other than the fact that we got a propane cookstove now and we used to have a wood-burning one." The walls are covered with photographs from the past, and you can just about trace the history of the ranch as you enjoy your meal in this historic building.

THEY COME, THEY GO, THEY STAY

The cowboys at the Pitchfork, like cowboys from the days of the first ranches, are a pretty transient group. The punchers at the camps, usually family men, stay longer than the bunkhouse crew, who tend to be younger and single. The five camps at the ranch are all ten or more miles from headquarters, and in some ways are independent from the day-to-day goings on at the home base.

Tommy points out that "the cowboys are more permanent now than they have been in the past. When we first came here in '89, you might have three crews through the bunkhouse in the course of three months. They just come and go. Now we have some who have been here going on three years." Tommy and Patricia both agree that the married men are more settled and usually take a longer view of their work than do the single hands.

COOKING FROM SUNUP TO SUNDOWN

When there are busy times at the Pitchfork, like during the calving, branding, shipping, roundups—when there are big crews—Tommy cooks breakfast and Patricia takes care of lunch and supper. During the regular day-to-day operations, breakfast is at 6:30 A.M., lunch is at noon, and supper is at 6:00 P.M. Tommy has to be in the cookhouse getting ready at 4:30 A.M. "It takes two hours to fix homemade bread." Patricia adds, "You can't clean up after the last meal until they've all come in and are gone."

During the more active seasons, they start serving breakfast at 5:30 A.M., and the single cowboys from the bunkhouse have to be in for supper by 7:30 P.M. when they're working "or they'll straggle in 'til midnight." Tommy says, with a very broad smile, "They'll be drinking beer and telling tall stories. . . . If you don't set a time limit on when they can eat, supper it's impossible. We have to get all cleaned up and get ready to go to bed and then have breakfast at 5:30—and you have to start at 3:30." "And you can't stay up 'til midnight cleaning up," points out his wife.

One thing about the cookhouse—the dining area and the kitchen are both spotless.

There are occasional rough spots the two cooks must deal with. Patricia says, "I have to watch them on their drinking in the cookhouse. They try to bring it in and I have to tell them they can't. I have to watch their language. I have to tone it down." Tommy says the drinking is only in the evening when "they have started drinking beer," when the day's work is over.

WHERE HAVE ALL THE COWGIRLS GONE?

There are no cowgirls on the Pitchfork. Both cooks agree that "it's not so much improper as it would be hard to have a girl with the guys in the bunkhouse or out with the wagon." Tommy adds, "It's not that we feel that they are inferior, it's just that there's no place to house a woman—it would create problems because when we're out with the wagon day and night, there aren't any outdoor toilets." Some of the married cowboys have their wives ride and work with them and help feed and do some of the chores. But there are definitely no girls allowed in the bunkhouse at night.

Cowboy work was hard in the past and, despite mechanization, it remains hard. On the Pitchfork, for example, there is a large area called the "Croton Breaks," so rugged that years ago the pasture was home to hundreds of wild cattle. This part of the ranch was bought from the Matador in 1947, and the cowboys and locals still refer to it as "The Badlands." Even though the area is accessible by horseback—a tough, tough ride—the Pitchfork uses a helicopter to help gather the cattle. "It's almost impossible," says Tommy. They have another pasture called the "Devil's Playground"—a dark canyon where the sunlight rarely reaches the ground. Tommy and Patricia agree that this one is well named.

HORSES, HORSES, HORSES

The Pitchfork is still a ranch where the cowboys work ahorseback. Their quarter horses are well known and respected, and they continue to raise their own mounts. Nowadays the punchers transport their horses in trailers and trucks to wherever they have to work, maybe a pasture some fifteen or so miles from headquarters. "Once they unload, they may trot another six or seven miles to the backside of that pasture to start a drive, pushing the cattle toward the pens."

There are still about forty brood mares and five stallions at the ranch. Tommy points out the Pitchfork raises horses primarily for their own use, although they do on occasion sell the surplus. The Pitchfork is a charter member of the American Quarter Horse Association, and some of their foundation stock is highly revered in the horse world, especially among those who are interested in working cow horses.

Each cowboy, as in the past, has his own string of horses. He cares for and uses these in his daily work. That care includes shoeing, grooming—whatever must be done to keep a mount fit and ready for the work on a ranch, especially one as large as the Pitchfork.

TAKING OUT THE WAGON

For Tommy, the busiest times of the year are when the wagon goes out. They first go out late in April and stay about two weeks. Then they go again in the fall, usually the first two weeks in November—depending, of course, on the weather. They use the wagon down in the "Croton Breaks" country because it is so far from headquarters that it would make no sense to try and get there and back in one day, even using pickups and horse trailers.

While the wagon is out, the cowboys stay with the wagon. They sleep in their old-styled "tepee tents," or they can sleep under the wagon fly. It's pretty much the same as it was a hundred years ago. The wagon fly is forty by sixty and even has walls, so it provides the cowboys without tents more than adequate protection.

Patricia stays at the ranch when the wagon is out because she has to cook for those staying at headquarters. She also has to be able to provide the groceries for the wagon whenever Tommy sends someone in with a list.

If you're wondering, don't for a minute think of the meals at the wagon as some sort of picnic fare. Not for the hardworking and very, very hungry cowboys out on roundup.

Tommy usually has breakfast ready by 5:30 A.M., about a half hour before the sun comes up. The sleepy cowboys have scrambled eggs, pancakes, bacon and sausage, sourdough biscuits, and gravy.

For lunch they chow down on some sort of beef, potatoes, corn, pinto beans, homemade bread, and a cobbler or cake for dessert. "Dinner is pretty much the same as lunch, just a different variety." And as the sun sets, and the tired cowboys enjoy their last meal of the day, they eat just as you'd expect after a full day in the saddle chasing cows through rugged country—with a healthy appetite.

By the way, Tommy makes everything at the wagon from scratch and cooks all the food in a Dutch oven.

NO SPICES FOR THE COWBOYS

Wagon cooking, and even cookhouse food, has fewer spices than many people are used to. Patricia says, "It's too hard on the cowboys. It causes all kinds of problems." Tommy adds that too many spices either cause diarrhea, an upset stomach, or indigestion. Salt and pepper "is basically all we use. . . . During the busy work seasons we don't serve chili and no Mexican food—it's just too spicy. I can't hardly use onions. They have to carry a bottle of Tums." Patricia says since she's been cooking, she's noticed that "onions make the cowboys sleepy and they don't need to be sleepy." Tommy says they learned a lot about these dietary problems from an old cowboy on the ranch, Bobby Allen, who was a Pitchfork hand for thirty-seven years. His daddy and granddaddy had been Pitchfork cowboys before him. "Everybody in Texas knew him."

Cowboys having noon meal at Pitchfork Ranch.

WHERE'S THE CHOLESTEROL?

Patricia and Tommy say some reporters once came for a visit, and after a good solid meal in the cookhouse, they remarked they couldn't believe the cowboys "just didn't keel over from all the cholesterol." The two cooks think that the hands just work too hard to get fat or have a cholesterol problem. And it's true, you really don't see too many heavy cowboys.

Everything the people at the ranch eat is determined by Patricia. She makes out the grocery list once a week and the secretary does the shopping. They try to buy locally, usually in Spur, Texas. As Tommy says with some pride, "We put the money back into the local market."

Looking back over the years ranching, from his childhood to his present job on the Pitchfork, Tommy thinks that the biggest change, and maybe the only real change in ranching, has been the introduction of the pickup and horse trailer to replace the old wagons. Until that time—which wasn't until the 1960s and early 1970s on the Pitchfork—taking the wagons out to the far pastures was the only way to get the work done. Now the wagon is used rarely.

Tommy and Patricia have each given us a sampling of the kind of cooking that we could get at the wagon or the cookhouse. Tommy says that you can't eat good Texas ranch food without having a recipe for chicken-fried steak, and Patricia lets us have a recipe that satisfies the cowboy's sweet tooth: Cowboy Cookies.

COWBOY COOKIES
(Patricia Tosh)

2 cups flour

1 teaspoon soda

1½ teaspoons salt

1½ teaspoons baking powder

1 cup butter

1 cup sugar

1 cup brown sugar

2 eggs

2 cups quick cooking oats

1 teaspoon vanilla

1 package chocolate chips

Sift together and then set aside the flour, soda, salt, and baking powder. Blend together the butter and sugars. Add eggs and beat well until they are light. Add flour mixture plus the oats, vanilla, and chocolate chips. The dough should be crumbly. Drop the dough by teaspoonfuls onto a greased cookie sheet and bake at 350°F for fifteen minutes.

CHICKEN-FRIED STEAK
(Tommy Tosh)

4 pounds tenderized steak

2 eggs, beaten

2 tablespoons milk

2 12-ounce cans evaporated milk

Flour

Dash of garlic salt

Dash of pepper

Oil for frying

Cut the steak into two-inch x two-inch squares. Pound with the bottom of an old Coke bottle to tenderize. Combine the eggs and milk. Place the steaks in the mixture and let soak for thirty minutes. Combine flour, garlic salt, and pepper. Thoroughly coat the steaks with the mixture. Heat one-half inch of oil in a large skillet until it is very hot. Fry steaks until golden brown, about ten to twenty minutes. Drain on a paper towel.

3-

THE PRUDE RANCH

FORT DAVIS, TEXAS

"BIG JOHN" ROBERT AND CHIPPER PRUDE

LIVING HISTORY AT A GUEST RANCH

The sleepy little town of Fort Davis rests in the center of Big Bend country, a cradle of Texas history. Established in 1854 along the San Antonio-El Paso road to protect settlers from Comanche and Apache Indians who were defending their hunting grounds, Fort Davis was named for the Secretary of War, Jefferson Davis. Previously the county seat of Presidio County, Fort Davis now is county seat of Jeff Davis County. If it's living history combined with spectacular scenery you're looking for, a visit to the heart of Big Bend country is a must. And a visit to the Prude Ranch, one of the oldest guest ranches in America and one of the oldest cattle ranches in the area, is also a must.

Just six miles from Fort Davis, up oak tree-shaded Limpia Canyon in the Davis Mountains, the Prude Ranch was established in 1898 and has been taking in guests since the 1920s. The people of the Prude Ranch will fill you with history, horses, cattle, and cooking.

"I'm the fourth generation Prude to live here as owner-operator," "Big John" Robert Prude states between phone calls in his cluttered, open, busy office in the original 1910 ranch house. "I was born here in 1927 and have been here all my life, except for a few interruptions [while a teacher and principal in Odessa until retirement]. We're whittled down from hundreds of thousand acres to a little more than five thousand due to the crash of '29, the oil bust of '85, and other financial disasters we didn't have any part in but were caught anyway in a bad position."

John Robert's maternal grandparents were the P. H. Pruetts, who came to the Fort Davis area from Arkansas in 1879. The Prude family arrived from Alabama three years later. "They all drove cattle into this country," he says.

"The last drive was about 3,000 head and went up the McDonald Observatory area [ten miles north, atop of the 6,800-foot Mount Locke]. Both families were in the cattle business."

The Pruetts brought Durham cattle, which John Robert says were good milk producers as well as good beef cattle. "Grandfather [Pruett] found a market real quick 'cause the soldiers would pay fifteen cents for a glass of milk and a dollar for a pound for butter. He was smart enough to know every time he sold two glasses of sour buttermilk he could buy an acre of land. He kept up that process until he'd put together 253,000 acres. It's still the largest ranch in Jeff Davis County; we just don't own it anymore."

The original Pruetts had seven children, and when Mrs. Pruett died, Mr. Pruett married his housekeeper, who convinced him to sell the ranch. "So in 1910, Grandpa sold for six dollars an acre and made quite a profit. The Kokernot family from San Antonio bought it and still owns and operates it. It's called the 06 Ranch, because they gave six dollars an acre for it, I guess. They're nice people and take good care of the land, and it's nice to know if you have to sell something, someone will buy it who loves it and cares for it as much as you do."

The Prudes had put together a cattle ranch on Limpa Creek, near what is known as "picnic rocks," where John Robert says [Andrew] Prude courted [Ora Jane] Pruett. "They musta courted pretty good, because when they got married they decided this was where they wanted to live. They put this home up and built the ranch up to over 40,000 acres when the crash hit in '29. Things were pretty rough in those days, but Grama [Ora Jane, who lived to be 100] said she wasn't leaving, so they began to sell off acreage to survive. Today we're down to about 5,000 acres, 100 cows, and 100 horses, and we're still surviving.

DUDE WRANGLERS AND CATTLE RANCHERS

The primary reason the Prude Ranch survived the Depression and fluctuations of cattle prices over the years is that John Robert, like his grandmother and his father, "Big Spur," before him, believes in diversification. "Grandmother took in the first guest in 1921," he says. "We've been in the guest ranch business for over seventy-two years. Our guests have taken us through some hard times and we pay 'em back by running a quality operation. However, we are still a cattle and horse ranch. We still brand horses and cattle with the same brand they've used here since the early 1900s. We're just not branding as many cattle as we once did. We're dude ranchers and we're cattle ranchers. But there's not too many outfits our size doing two million dollars [business] a year."

The Prude is very diverse in it's guest operations. Their showcase is an environmental education program that takes in high school students form across the country for three to five days of intense, outdoor, hands-on studies. Another fast-growing facet of the ranch is the Elderhostel program, an adult spin-off of the environmental education curriculum. Then there's the "Junior Camper Program" for youth ages seven to nine; the "Senior Camper Program" for those aged ten to eleven; "City Slickers" for twelve-to-thirteen-year-olds;

Chip Prude, Prude Ranch cowboy cook and the somewhat modernized chuck wagon formerly owned by the famous old cocinero, Raymón Hartnett who retired from the 06 Ranch.

and for the "Old Timers" (fourteen years and above), there's the "Advanced Camper Program." Prude Ranch offers something for everyone, regardless of age. As John Robert's son Chip says, "Here you can be a kid as long as you want to be."

John Robert says his father, who at ninety is the oldest kid on the place, is also the number one horseman at the Prude ranch. "He still rides every day. He took a ride out this morning. He loves horses more than anything in the world. He keeps a bunch of brood mares and raises a lot of our own colts and knows the background and lineage of every horse on the place. We buy a lot of gentle ranch horses for our guests, but 'Big Spur' loves a hot horse. He's our horse expert."

BUSINESSMAN, RAMROD, AND COOK

The cooking expert on the Prude Ranch is Chipper. A fifth generation Prude rancher, Chip grew up following the tradition of his forefathers, and mothers. "Growing up, I had to milk cows every morning. I had twelve milk cows and sold milk and butter in town. I used grandmother's old five-gallon churn to make butter. I still have it. It'll make seven pounds of butter. She told me she'd get $1.50 for a gallon for skimmed milk in the '30s, $2.00 for milk with the cream on, and $2.00 for a pound of butter."

So, while still in elementary school, Chip was a budding businessman, ramrod, and cook. "Mother [and daddy] was teaching school," he says, "and my [two] brothers had 4-H cattle, so we'd all have to get up early and do chores. Since I was the oldest, I would cook breakfast. I got to where I was pretty good and got to enjoy it."

A self-described jack-of-all-trades, Chip can also repair about anything on the ranch, and his skills have always been in demand. "When I left to go to school [University of Texas, Texas Tech, Baylor, and M. Ed., Sol Ross], I'd find every time I'd come back I'd be six months behind on my work. One time I left and went to work for a farmer friend, and no matter how hard I spurred that tractor, it only went one way. Finally, I just gave up and come back for good."

And that's been good for the ranch. Chip has his hands in about every operation on the ranch, which is a considerable number. He doesn't run the kitchen; he cooks mostly for fun. And profit. "I got started cooking professionally when I was seventeen. A bunch of deer hunters had a camp in the hills north of here and hired me to go up there. They lived in tents and I lived in a hole in the ground." And cooked on the ground.

"It wasn't too bad, really. The dugout was about fifteen foot across and had a tin roof over the entrance and was pretty comfortable. I'd never cooked in Dutch ovens before, but they wanted something old-timey, so I tried it. I burned a few things at first, but then I began to get the hang of it. I had four [Dutch] ovens back then. Now I've got ninety-six. I collect 'em and I go to a lot of cookoffs with my partner. We enjoy it."

Chip's partner is Glenn Moreland, the maintenance supervisor at Prude Ranch, and it was he who got Chip into chuck wagon cooking competition. "Glenn got this flyer," Chip says, "about a cookoff in Ruidoso [New Mexico], so we went up there and we won it. We had a real good time and we've been to a lot [of cookoffs] since. You go more to see your friends than anything. We've won so much and it's gotten so big, I don't care to compete anymore. I've about dropped out."

Out of the competition. Not the cooking. Chip says he gets more fun out of cooking for the Elderhostel at the ranch than cooking for competition. "Those people really get a big kick out of cooking in a Dutch oven. We have about thirty people at a time and I'll show 'em how it's done. Then they get to try it. They love it. Cooking in a Dutch oven is a challenge. But it can be done anywhere and you can cook anything. It's just something I love to do."

Chip also loves to collect things and has the original chuck wagon that came from the old cook on the 06 Ranch, part of his heritage. Ramón Hartnett is legendary among chuck wagon cooks. Now retired and living in Fort Davis, Hartnett cooked at the 06 for fifty years. In his youth, Chip got a chance to be Ramón's helper and pot scrubber, and the old cocinero [chuck wagon cook] never forgot the young biscuit burner.

"He gave me his wagon when he retired," Chip says as he pulls back the tarp covering the cobbled-up cupboard on a pickup bed trailer. "And all his iron [Dutch ovens]. Every cowboy who ever worked on the 06 has his brand on the wagon. It ain't much to look at, but it's worth a million dollars to me. He knew I'd take care of it. I never trade anything off. I'm always collecting more stuff."

Like recipes. Even though Chip has almost thirty years standing over a lid, he still likes to experiment and develop new recipes. He and Glenn have collaborated on a cookbook they call *Camp Cookie Cook Book* and pass it out to the Elderhostel guests. "About everything in there is taken from somewhere else, except the recipes," he states. "The recipes are ours. We don't have to borrow recipes. We've got plenty of our own." And certainly enough to share. We picked Glenn's chili, which he and Chip swear is the best in the land. You be the judge.

[Note: Besides keeping the ranch running smoothly by fixing and repairing anything that's broken, and occasionally filling in in the kitchen, Glenn Moreland partnered up with Chip on their chuck wagon and they toured Texas, putting on cooking demonstrations. Since we visited the ranch, Glenn has fallen off a ladder, broken both ankles, and hasn't worked at the ranch since. Instead, he has gone into chuck wagon restoration and repair, blacksmithing and cowboy art, and can be reached at his home in Fort Davis at (915)426-3793, or at his Cow Camp Galleries at (800)887-9187. He sends his Davis Mountain Chili recipe, a favorite of his, and once you try it, a favorite of yours, as well. Enjoy.]

GLENN MORELAND'S DAVIS MOUNTAIN CHILI

6 lbs. boneless sirloin tip roast. Remove all fat and connecting tissue. Cut into ³/₈-inch cubes.

5 tablespoons cooking oil

2½ medium white onions, minced

1 12-ounce can of beer (I use Tecate, a Mexican beer)

1 8-ounce can tomato sauce

1 6-ounce can tomato paste

1 8-ounce can hot water

6 large garlic cloves, mash in oil until puree is formed

2 cups beef broth (two bouillon cubes)

3 tablespoons paprika

2½ teaspoons salt

2 teaspoons pepper

¾ cup commercial chili powder (hot or medium)

3 tablespoons cumin

In a big skillet with two tablespoons of vegetable oil, brown the meat until it turns grey in color, then pour into a cast iron pot. Sauté onions in one tablespoon of oil until clear, then pour into pot. Add beer, tomato sauce, tomato paste, hot water, beer broth, one-half of garlic mixture, two tablespoons paprika, one teaspoon salt, one teaspoon black pepper. Simmer over low heat for two hours with lid on pot. Stir occasionally.

When meat is tender, add remaining garlic, chili powder, cumin, 1½ teaspoon salt, one teaspoon pepper. Simmer for one hour or longer.

If you like it hot, add ¼ teaspoon ground chili japones.

If chili cooks down too much and gets too thick, add more hot water.

"Eating this cobbler is just like kissing your sweetheart—it takes oh so long to get enough and you'll always go back for more."

1 cup all-purpose flour

½ cup brown sugar

2 cups granulated sugar

½ teaspoon cinnamon

½ cup butter

½ cup chopped pecans

½ cup sourdough starter

1 can water-packed cherries

Pour cherries into Dutch oven or iron skillet; add one and one-half cups of the sugar, along with one-fourth cup flour. Mix well and cook over live coals or medium high heat, until the cherry juice becomes thick and the cherries are hot. Set the skillet aside for a few minutes while mixing the remainder of the ingredients.

Combine the remainder of the flour, sugars, and cinnamon, and cut in the butter. Stir in the pecans and the sourdough starter. Spoon this mixture over the top of the cherries and place the skillet back on the coals or burner. If using a Dutch oven, place the lid on and cover the lid with coals and let bake.

After the top begins to brown slightly, lift the lid and, with a sharp knife, cut a few holes in the top. This will permit the cherry juices to bubble up enough to make the cobbler much more attractive. After the top has reached a golden brown, sprinkle about two more tablespoons of sugar over the top and place the lid back on for one minute, then remove. The cobbler is now ready, so cowboys, cowgirls, and dudes of all ages: Come and get it!

R-H RANCH

OZONA, TEXAS

EDDIE AND NANCY HALE

RAISING CATTLE, SHEEP, GOATS, AND DOGS

Ozona, the county seat of Crockett, bills itself as the Biggest Little Town In The World. It's where the Hill Country meets the West. Ozona was founded in 1891 and is the only town in this eighth largest county in Texas, claiming over 3,000 square miles. Crockett County, of course, was named for everybody's hero, David Crockett. The ex-senator from Tennessee, embittered after his unsucessful run for a fourth term in Congress, came to Texas in 1836. He was looking for new adventures; he found death during the fall of the Alamo.

But in the hearts of Texans, Davy Crockett lives on. His statue stands tall on the courthouse square and he stares sternly at visitors wandering across the lawn under the tall pecan trees. In the Crockett County Museum, they have lots of information on their namesake, including the fact that he preferred to be called David, not Davy, and that he wore a foxskin cap, not coonskin, as so often portrayed in the movies. His motto, which is inscribed on the base of his statue, reads: "Be Sure You Are Right, Then Go Ahead."

We weren't sure about being that right, but we went ahead anyhow, into the Crockett County Museum, where we were greeted by Mary Hillman, one of those friendly faces for which Ozona is so famous. Mary showed us around the museum, gave us a quick course on David, and introduced us to Nancy Hale, assistant treasurer, wife of rancher Eddie Hale, and an expert on ranch living and ranch cooking. Another friendly face in a friendly little town.

HALE AND HEARTY IN HILL COUNTRY

Nancy invited us out to the ranch, gave us directions, and said she'd meet us there after dark. Dark comes early to the Hill Country in December, so we left immediately and drove south on Taylor Box Road to get a look at the country. We probably saw more wildlife on that twenty-three-mile drive than any before or since. Deer, lots of deer everywhere, darting across the road like rabbits. And rabbits, raccoons, and armadillos, the latter scurrying around like miniature kangaroos with hard shelled bodies. We began to fall in love with Crockett County.

The sun was setting in the south and we parked near a stock watering tank to watch the last rays of daylight filter through the mesquite trees. Cattle came to drink and deer stamped and snorted in the brush. Then it was quiet, the only sounds from the wildlife—birds and varmints rustling around, some settling in for the night, others preparing for their nocturnal foraging. The critters of Crockett County were preparing for another cycle of life in Texas Hill Country.

At the Hale Ranch, Eddie, a stocky, friendly, native Texan with a warm grin and hard hands, was preparing to watch the National Rodeo Finals being beamed in from Las Vegas. Ah, the wonder of modern conveniences. But this old cowboy and his lovely bride have known tougher times. Much, much tougher. "I was born in Ballinger [Texas] in 1934," Eddie states, downing a glass of iced tea. Working in the West Texas wind has a way of dehydrating a person. "Raised around Eden. That's like growing up on a ranch 'cause there's nothing there to slow you down. Daddy was a trucker who loved cowboying but never could make a living at it. But we always kept livestock, grew a large garden, and had plenty to eat."

Even though Eddie grew up at the tail end of the Depression, he never knew he was poor. To him, he was as rich as he wanted to be. "I cowboyed here and there. Broke horses. Did day work. 'Til the Army got me." When the Army released Eddie, he high-tailed it back to his beloved West Texas. "Was driving to [San] Angelo on July 4, 1957, and had a wreck. Caught a ride with a feller and ended up at the Rocker B [Ranch near Barnhart]. Had a bedroll and a borrowed saddle. That's all I had."

A "PRETTY" AND A PUPPY

And as a bachelor cowboy, that's all he needed. Well, not really. "We'd go into Barnhart about once every two weeks and get clean clothes. Troy Laundry would take in our dirty clothes and when we'd come back, have 'em all washed and ready to wear. And they had a barber shop. It'd open on Monday nights," the big night in Barnhart. There were also "pretties" in Barnhart. "I had a cousin there and her friend was Nancy and that's how we met."

Eddie courted Nancy over the next three years while he broke horses, cowboyed, and roped wild hogs on the Rocker B. "They had lots of hogs there," Eddie states. "Domestic hogs that had escaped from somewhere and gone wild. They were bad. They'd eat a new-born lamb in a heartbeat and they'd eat the

Eddie Hale and his border collies keep the wooly boogers moving on the R-H Ranch, Ozona, Texas (photo courtesy Nancy Hale).

ewe if she didn't get moving. They'd even eat baby calves. But they was death on lambs and kids [baby goats].

"So we went to catching hogs. We used to just rope 'em. Run 'em down and rope 'em, just like you would a calf. But then I got to using dogs and it was a lot easier on the horse and a lot easier on me." Eddie Hale is a natural born stock man. He loves animals and has a special way around them. Quiet and gentle, he instills confidence in young animals and they respond positively. Eddie Hale is one of the best dog trainers in Texas—and that's only because he does not travel outside the Lone Star State. He could be a world champion.

"I've always had dogs," he says. "All kinds. Curs, hounds, heelers, whatever. I just like having dogs around." Nancy's uncle saw this interest of Eddie's and gave the cowboy a border collie female. Eddie bred her, beginning his second career as dog trainer. And it was this "jip" female border collie and her pup that escalated Eddie's hog-catching program.

A SHOAT ROPER AND WILD HOG TAMER

"I had roped me a shoat [yearling pig] and had him in a little pen at the ranch. Any time we needed an eating hog, we'd just go out and rope one. But I kept this one in a pen and would take them dogs down and holler 'sooweee'. That shoat would run and I'd turn that pup loose. When he got nearly to the hog, I'd turn the jip loose. She'd bite that shoat right on the ham and he'd sit down and the pup'd grab 'im by the ear. They'd go round and round but the shoat couldn't hurt the pup and the little dog learned how to stay away from those tusks."

Now Eddie had himself a hog-catching team and they went to work. "We caught hogs weighing 250-300 pounds. I'd be ahorseback and they'd catch one that-a-way. I'd ride up, get off, grab the hog by a front leg, roll 'im over on his side and tie his legs together with a pigging string. Get up and go get another one while the hog wagon was coming." The hog wagon?

"We had a regular farm wagon with a box in the bed, pulled by two mules. We had a trap door on top of that box and we had a winch on the back. We'd just hoist 'em up and drop 'em through that trap door. We caught lots of hogs back in '67 and '68. We finally eliminated 'em off the Rocker B. Them we couldn't rope or catch with the dogs, we caught in pens. We had push-in traps all over. They'd get in and couldn't get out. Them that we couldn't catch or trap, we shot. But we caught most of 'em with dogs." Border collies.

Most people think of border collies as strictly sheep dogs, but Eddie says the border collie's natural instinct is to herd any kind of animal— horses, goats, cattle, or sheep. He also threw in another zinger. "If you just let 'em go, border collies will be world class sheep killers." For that very reason, Eddie keeps his dogs kenneled at all times. It is, perhaps, this control that makes Eddie and his son, Les, world class dog trainers.

INSTINCT, TRAINABILITY, AND FORCE

"We breed, raise, train, show, and sell dogs," Eddie says. "I have nine dogs here now; seven of my own and two outside dogs. We price our good dogs pretty high, but it's not too high for people who know dogs. A good dog will cost more'n a good horse. If you don't know dogs, the price'll just blow your hair back." And $5,000 for a top dog will surely tip a toupee or two. "Useable dogs bring around $800 to $1,500," Eddie reports, "and a good quality dog, from $1,500 to $3,000."

The secret to the Hale's success is in their training methods. First, you have to have a trainable dog and know when he or she is ready to work. "We look for instinct, trainability, and force in a pup. We want controlled force. A lot of dogs will chase and bite, but that's not force, just foolishness. If a dog is trainable and has the herding instinct, you can train it to be of some value to you on a ranch. They may not make a top trial dog, but they'll make a ranch dog—with proper training."

And proper training begins at home, early. "I start training a pup when they're about ten to twelve months old," Eddie says. "Some dogs are different. But about twelve months old, they're mentally and physically mature enough to take my training. You can train a border collie when they're three, four, or five months old, but most aren't mature enough in the mind to take the discipline, without taking away their enthusiasm. You don't want to dampen their fire. If you wait 'til they're ten or eleven months old, their mind is much more solid and they can take some discipline."

SHOWING USEABLE DOGS AND USING SHOW DOGS

Eddie says they don't ever whip a dog. Never. "They're pretty sensitive. border collies won't stand punishment like some breeds. You can scold a border collie with your voice or scare 'em with a rolled up paper sack, but you can't take a-holt of one. They quit you." Eddie socializes with the pups every day. "When I get home of an evening, I take a couple of pups for a walk. I just let 'em run and play and be a pup. I'll call 'em back to me every once in a while, just to let 'em know I'm their buddy."

And their boss. "You got to teach 'em manners. You can't have 'em rearing up on folk. And they've got to come when called. We never let our dogs run loose. Never. Their instinct tells 'em to do something with livestock. A pup will run a sheep 'til it can't run, then will bite it, and if it don't run will tear on it, and pretty quick you got a bona fide sheep killer."

The key to training, Eddie says, is in control. "I'll turn a pup loose in a pen with sheep, and if he's running and playing, bouncing around, I know he ain't ready to work. When he starts watching sheep and creeping and crawling around 'em we can start our training. It's just like working with a young horse. If you put too much on a yearling, you'll ruin 'im. But if you wait 'til he's two-past, he can work. His mind is mature. You can get something done."

Eddie uses his dogs daily. "I'm all right by myself most of the time. Just me and the horse and a dog. I'll take one dog in the morning, come back at dinner and get another dog. If you take two dogs in the morning, by dinner, you've got two tired dogs.

"We rotate and rest our dogs. When one works a half day like that, he gets three days off. This is rough country. Dogs just tear up their pads. You gotta take it easy on your dogs. In the summer, when it's 95, 100, 105 degrees, we work stock early in the mornings and late in the evenings. You can't work dogs in that heat, or they'll dehydrate and die. We take good care of our dogs because we love our dogs. We use our show dogs and we show our using dogs." And it shows. Ever since those hog-catching days on the Rocker B, Hale's dogs have been in demand.

CAMPING AND COOKING ON THE ROCKER B

Ah, the good old days on the Rocker B. Nancy fondly recalls the days of her youth. "I was just a kid," she begins, as Eddie answers yet another phone call inquiring about yet another dog or another dog show. It's a dog's life around the Hale house. And that ain't all bad. It's a lot better than it once was. "We married in 1960, when I was seventeen. They moved us to the Salt House Line Camp on the Middle Concho River." That sounds like the end of the earth, but to Nancy, being from Barnhart, it was just another day at the beach. "It was a wood-frame house and had a living room, a bedroom, and a screened-in back porch. Had ceilings about fifteen-foot high, seemed like; just an old-timey house."

But it wasn't all bad. Nancy's parents had worked on ranches, and she was well prepared for ranch life. In fact, she liked it—still does—but she admits she never was an outside person, preferring the comfort of her kitchen to the rigors of hog hunting. "It was nice out there. We didn't see many people. Just Eddie and me. The ranch furnished groceries and we could get whatever else we needed from the commissary. Our mail came once every two weeks and we didn't have a phone, but we made out just fine."

Nancy and Eddie settled into the ranch life, leased their current ranch residence in 1981, and have raised two boys and numerous sheep, cattle, horses, goats, and dogs. The boys are out on their own now, and Nancy works in town, which allows the Hales to remain sheep ranchers, a business that is getting tougher all the time. "We have to keep up a steady brush eradication program all the time," says Eddie. "But the government is getting pretty pushy about that. They're trying to stop us from pushing juniper any more. They say some bird nests in it. But junipers take a lot of water. And the mesquite is so thick around here you can't ride through it. If I didn't have dogs, I'd never get our stock gathered."

RANCHING TO LIVE AND LIVING TO RANCH

So it's just Eddie and Nancy and the dogs against the brush, the elements and the government. Sometimes you wonder why they don't just quit. "It's our life," Nancy says. "We do this because it's the way we live and it's what we live for. We're ranchers and we live to ranch." The Hales have never taken a vacation. If they get a couple of days off, they usually go to a dog show, then it's right back to the ranch and to work. But they seem very happy. Eddie gets another glass of tea, Nancy passes out more cookies; the rodeo is about to begin. It's time for the talk to stop, and the eating and enjoying Hale hospitality to begin in earnest.

Like most ranch cooks we visited, Nancy handed us a handful of recipes. For beef, for mutton, for goat, and one for venison, which we thought we'd share with you. It's pretty special and she said you can substitute beef for the venison if you like. Either way it's gooooood.

NANCY'S VENISON

2 or 3 pounds of back strap
Pinch of seasoning (salt and pepper)
1 cup buttermilk
Handful of flour
1 cup cooking oil

Slice back strap into one-half inch strips, cutting across the grain. Beat the steaks to tenderize well and season to taste with salt and pepper. Garlic salt adds a special taste. Dip steaks in buttermilk and dredge through flour. Fry in hot oil until brown, turning once to brown on both sides. Serve with cream gravy and skillet biscuits.

CREAM GRAVY

3 tablespoons venison oil

3 tablespoons flour

2½ cups milk

Drain all but about three tablespoons oil and dregs from hot skillet that venison was cooked in. While the skillet is on medium heat, stir in about three tablespoons flour and about two-and-one-half cups milk, stirring constantly. Cook until the mixture reaches desired thickness. Salt and pepper to taste.

SKILLET BISCUITS

(These are cooked on top of stove and resemble campfire bread)

2 cups flour

2 tablespoons sugar

1 teaspoon salt

⅞ cup milk

2 teaspoons baking powder

2 tablespoons oil, plus

1 tablespoon butter or oil

Mix flour, sugar, salt, milk, baking powder, and two tablespoons cooking oil, and turn out on floured board and knead a few times. Shape into biscuits or make one large loaf. Heat one tablespoon oil or butter in large skillet. Place dough in skillet and cook over LOW heat until brown on bottom, about ten minutes. Turn over and cook other side about ten minutes more. You might want to cover the skillet for the first ten minutes; it'll speed up the process and cook more evenly. Enjoy.

THE ROCKER B RANCH

BARNHART, TEXAS
RUSTY AND SHIRLEY CULP

A SPECIAL PLACE FOR SPECIAL PEOPLE

West of San Angelo, the country opens into rolling, brush-covered hills, undulating to the horizon as far as the eye can see—in any direction. This is ranch country. You won't see many people here. If you do, they're probably ahorseback, because Irion County, one of the least populated in the state, is no place to be afoot.

Mertzon, the county seat, boasts a population of 780 and was founded in 1910 as a rail stop on the Kansas City, Mexico, and Orient Railroad. West of Mertzon, at the intersections of Highway 67 and Ranch Road 163, is the town of Barnhart, population 135. About eight miles north of Barnhart, a gravel road branches to the west, and at the end of this road is the headquarters of the Rocker B Ranch.

It is immediately apparent to the knowledgeable visitor that this is a productive, profitable ranch. The headquarters complex is made of individual brick homes for the cowboys. The yards are grassy and well maintained, and deer feed nonchalantly on the lawns. Elm trees tower over the buildings, which are scattered in a horseshoe shape around the office, shop, and home of manager Rusty Culp and his beautiful wife, Shirley.

A COWBOY'S COWBOY

W. F. "Rusty" Culp is a cowboy's cowboy. Tall and trim, with work-hardened hands and a wind-sculpted face, a quick smile and a soft voice, Rusty exudes cowboy. You know instantly that you are in the presence of the real thing. It's

Saturday on the Rocker B, and most of the hands are taking the day off. Rusty is packing a door across the lawn to an empty house. He invites us to his office.

The office is spacious, clean, and well-lighted, with comfortable chairs, modern desks, and office machines. Pictures and paintings decorate the walls. Rusty slides his large frame down behind his desk and relaxes. He appears to be as much at ease riding a chair as riding the range, something he has done plenty of.

Rusty tells us he was born in 1930 in Throckmorton, north of Abilene. His father was a cowboy, who took a job in 1940 as foreman with the Reynolds Cattle Company near Kent in Jeff Davis County. Rusty attended the two-room school in Kent until the ninth grade, at which time he was transferred to Van Horn, where he promptly quit because he says he knew more than the teachers there.

At age fourteen, Rusty Culp had already seen a lot; more than fifty years later, the cowboy life is all he has known. Except for a few years in the military, Rusty Culp has been a working cowboy. Like most farm and ranch youngsters, Rusty grew up doing chores. "Anytime we weren't in school, we were working," he quips. World War II got underway when Rusty was eleven years old. With most of the eligible men pressed into military service, Texas cowboys were hard to find.

At age twelve, Rusty was hiring out as a day-worker, drawing $1.50 per day, "a lot of money in those times." At that time, Rusty was also taking in outside horses to train, an occupation that he pursued for many years as a sideline to cowboying. "I just tried it and got to liking it. Nobody ever taught me. I just watched how it was done and got to doing it. I'd take 'em [unbroken horses] and put a rope halter on 'em and stake 'em out to a log for two or three days until they started to settle down some. Then I'd take 'em in a pen, maybe tie up a foot, saddle 'em, and get on."

Rusty says he never used a snubbing post to restrain the young horses, as some trainers do. He preferred to let the horses move freely so he could get a feel for them. It was a feeling he learned to like. When he was seventeen, Rusty went to work for the Long X Ranch near Albany. "Worked for Jim Naile. We was up on the Clear Fork of the Brazos, cowboying. They had 640 sections. There was plenty of riding to do. They sent a wagon out eight months of the year. There were three line camps on that ranch. It was a big outfit."

Then, at age eighteen, Rusty went to work for an even bigger outfit. "Uncle Sam got me. I was in the Marines in California. Never liked it [California] that much. Got out after a year and went back to cowboying. Breaking horses." Rusty worked for the U Ranch near Kent for a while, then worked for Lee Graves near Fort Stockton. "Broke a bunch [of horses] for him. Left there and kept day working. Went up to Rossell, New Mexico, and rode some horses up there for Ralph Johnson."

Then the Korean War erupted and Uncle Sam called again. This time Rusty spent four years with the First Marine Division and saw heavy combat in Korea.

By now Rusty was married and figured he'd better get to making some real money, so he sold out for the oil fields. But once a cowboy . . .

"It didn't take me long to get enough of that oil patch, and in about 1963, went to breaking polo ponies. I just broke 'em the same old way." If it ain't broke, don't fix it.

A GREAT MARRIAGE FOR A GRAND OLD RANCH

Rusty rode horses in New Mexico for a while before coming to the Rocker B Ranch near Barnhart in 1967. "Started out breaking horses." The Rocker B Ranch was started by Wisconsin Senator Sawyer, who supposedly gave $100 for a section of the ranch land in 1870. Until 1954, the 172,320-acre ranch operated as the Sawyer Cattle Company, at which time it was purchased by Dallas oil magnate William Blakley. In 1964, Blakley donated the ranch to the Texas Scottish Rites Hospital for Crippled Children. The ranch is operated by a board of directors, who in 1982 named their top hand, Rusty Culp, as manager. It's a great marriage for a grand old ranch.

"When I came here they ran sheep," Rusty recalls. "Lots of sheep. But Blakley didn't like sheep. We sold 'em all in '69. We delivered 17,000 sheep off this place in two months. It's been a cow/calf operation ever since. [We] run 260 Hereford bulls. Rest are Brahman-Hereford crosses and some Charolis-Hereford [crosses]. We run around 2,700 to 3,000 mother cows."

The Rocker B puts their bulls out with the cows in January for October calves. They buy all their bulls and raise their own replacement heifers. They use Black Angus bulls and their first calf heifers. Rusty says the results have been excellent. "We tried Beefmaster bulls on our first calf heifers, but the calves were too big and we had lots of trouble. We tried Longhorn bulls on our heifers, but the buyers didn't like the calves. We like the Black Angus on our heifers."

Rusty says he also likes the Brahman on the Hereford. "That's the best breed you can get. That Brahman cross will find something to eat. We feed a 22 percent breeders cube for about two and a half months during winter, and we sell everything by contract. We start shipping in July, and our calves consistently weigh in around 580 pounds. We have a good bunch of cows." And a small herd of horses.

TOP HORSES AND TOP HANDS

Until 1969, the ranch ran their own mares and raised their own colts. Rusty wants that program back. "Getting to where you can't hardly find a good horse. So I'm going to start raising our own again. I like that old [American Quarter Horse] Hancock breeding with a little Driftwood [another AQHA foundation sire] thrown in. Just good old ranch horses. I like a horse big enough to do a job and stand up to a hard day's work and have a lot of cow [sense]."

For a lot of cow work you need not only a good cow horse, but good cowboys, and the Rocker B has nothing but the best. "We have eight cowboys here," says

Rocker B Ranch manager Rusty Culp shaking out a loop (above) and setting a heel catch (right)
(photos courtesy Rusty and Shirley Culp).

Rusty. "All married. All top hands. A good bunch of men. The best I've ever seen." All the hands on the Rocker B can weld and operate machinery as well as ride and rope. "Use to," he muses, "first thing you'd ask a hand was, 'Can you ride?' Now we ask, 'Do you have a driver's license?'"

The ability to drive a vehicle is important on today's ranches, especially one as remote as the Rocker B. "Each line camp has about forty sections, and each cowboy is responsible for that camp and those cows. We don't ride as much as we used to, but we still ride quite a bit. We still rope calves out of the herd and drag 'em to the fire. I don't ride as much as I used to, but I still like to get out with the boys."

The Rocker B boys range in age from the foreman who is sixty-four, to the newest hand who is twenty-three. Each cowboy gets a three-bedroom house and is furnished groceries, a pickup, insurance, and a retirement program. "We've got a good program here," Rusty states. "And we're proud of our operation." No doubt the hands are proud of it, too. There's not many ranches where cowboys make the equivalent of $1,800 per month and still have half of Saturday and all of Sunday off. And there are not too many ranches with a manager as understanding as Rusty Culp.

SHE'S HOOKED ON COOKING

"A man needs to spend time with his family. I know I like to spend time with mine." Rusty's first wife passed away in 1985, and he recently married a close friend who just happens to be an outstanding cook. "I love to cook," Shirley says as we leave Rusty's office and enter their spacious home, about ten steps from the office door. "Right now I'm just cooking for Rusty and myself, the cats, and the skunk." The skunk?

"I set food out for the cats, and the skunk comes and gets it. He's getting to be a pest. I was out in my shop," Shirley does ceramics "and there's this skunk with his head in the door. I screamed. I guess they thought someone was cutting my throat. But it was just the skunk. In broad daylight. I've got to figure out some way to get rid of him."

Shirley should try not feeding the skunk, but she's hooked on cooking and all visitors at the Rocker B get fed—well. "I collect cookbooks. I had this Magic Fruit Cake recipe as a sophomore in high school. Won a blue ribbon on it. Rusty likes it. I like to feed Rusty, and it's beginning to show."

But what a way to go. Shirley drew out "Old Faithful," her chock-full recipe box, and began whipping out recipes like a Reno faro dealer. "Like biscuits?" she inquired as she set a bowl of leftovers on the table. "These are delicious, but

Rocker B Ranch cowboys with ranch manager W. F. "Rusty" Culp in the middle with the white hat (photo courtesy Rusty and Shirley Culp).

my first ones were so hard you coulda drilled a hole in 'em and used 'em for a wheel. Then I discovered Velvet Cream Biscuits. Anybody can make those."

And how about venison? "We have lots of deer around here. I've got a wonderful recipe for venison. Here. Take it. And here's one of Rusty's favorites. Mexican Casserole. It's soooo easy and soooo good. Everybody loves it." Poor Rusty. Stuck on a remote ranch with a food pusher. A beautiful, classy, funny, artistic food pusher. Not bad for an old cowboy who quit school to go breaking broncs. Maybe he *was* smarter than those teachers in Van Horn. Anyway you slice it, here's one cowboy who has got it made—a fantastic job in productive ranching country, a professional crew, great cattle, good home, and a wonderful wife. Now, if he can just get back his breed of horses . . .

For a cowboy, it don't get no better than this.

As for Shirley, all she's got to do is figure out how to not feed that skunk and life will be simple. Or maybe it won't. Here's a cook who's so busy with other projects she tells us to save time when crushing crackers for a pie crust, she puts them in a plastic bag and drives over them with the pickup. "Saves time," she says. "I love to cook, but that don't mean I want to spend my whole life in the kitchen."

Only long enough to turn out those Velvet Cream Biscuits, a favorite on the Rocker B. Could that B stand for biscuit? Naw. We prefer Rusty's favorite. He says the leftover casserole can be wrapped in a soft tortilla, frozen, and placed in a plastic bag. "Next morning just throw 'em on the dashboard and by noon they're thawed and lunch is ready." Enjoy.

SHIRLEY'S MEXICAN CASSEROLE

1½ pounds ground meat

2½ cups water

1 can mushroom soup

1 can cream of chicken soup

1 small can chopped green chilies

1 small can condensed milk

1 small can taco sauce

1 large onion, chopped

1 pound round cheese, grated

1 dozen soft tortillas cut in half

Brown and drain ground meat. In a mixing bowl combine water, mushroom soup, cream of chicken soup, chilies, milk, and taco sauce. In a large loaf pan, put in layers of meat, soup mix, onions, cheese, and tortillas until all ingredients are used. Bake thirty minutes in a 350°F oven.

THE ROCKER B RANCH

177

RUNNING W RANCH

Van Horn, Texas
Lottie and Blackie Woods

A TOWN SO HEALTHY THEY HAD TO SHOOT A MAN TO START A CEMETERY

Way out in West Texas is the friendly little community of Van Horn, county seat of Culberson and the "Crossroads of the Texas Mountain Trail." The Old Spanish Trail passed through this high plateau surrounded by mountains, as did the San Antonio to San Diego Mail Route, commonly called the oldest American Trans-Continental Route. A popular stop in the area was at Van Horn Wells, about twelve miles south of the town now bearing that name.

The town was named after Lieutenant James Judson Van Horn, who commanded the army garrison at Van Horn Wells from 1859 to 1861. At that time, the Confederate Army took command of the wells and held the good lieutenant prisoner. Some twenty years after that incident and after the Civil War had ended, the last Indian battle in Texas was fought within the steep walls of Victorio Canyon, twenty-five miles north of Van Horn in the Sierra Diablo Mountains.

With the end of the Indian Wars and the completion of the Texas and Pacific Railroad, settlers began moving into the area, and the town of Van Horn was established. According to Lottie Woods, whose family immigrated to the Davis Mountains in 1884, the area was settled by hard-working, peaceable people who had come west to escape the travails of the Civil War. She says that, for many, many years, Jeff Davis County never had to convene a grand jury. "Most of the people who came here were good Christian people. Most still are."

Culberson County became known as a healthy place to live, and, in fact, one of the early residents of Van Horn, a rancher named Bill Goynes, is said to have coined the motto: "This town is so healthy we had to shoot a man to start a cemetery." Ironically, it was old boastful Bill himself who stopped the first slug fired in Van Horn, when he became embroiled in a feud over water rights with his brother-in-law.

COWBOYING TOO LONG TO REMEMBER

Lottie states that after the Civil War, her grandparents settled in West Texas because they didn't want to work as share croppers in central Texas. "The people who came West came to establish ranches and families. They came out in wagons, driving herds of cattle. Grandmother Evans said she drove mules instead of oxen. She didn't talk about it [the trip West] much, but she said one of the smartest things women ever did was shorten their dresses—to mid-calf length."

In 1934, Lottie met Beary "Blackie" Woods, who had come to west Texas from Graham with a brother in 1929, driving his 1929 Chevrolet Roadster and packing a total of $1.27 cents and the promise of a job. "Met 'im at a dance," Lottie says. "The girl he was going with introduced us. He was, and is, a real cowboy. You'll not find anyone anywhere that's more of a cowboy. We married in 1936. Fifty-seven years last August. That's the way it should be—a lifetime commitment."

Blackie started cowboy contracting so long ago he says he can't remember that far back. A tall, quiet man, Blackie doesn't talk much about anything. But when he does, the listener best pay close attention because the old cowboy speaks softly, a habit he's picked up from a lifetime of working around livestock and hunting mountain lions and other varmints that threaten his herds.

"Don't know when I started cowboying," he says. "Was raised on it. Rode bareback when I started. Didn't even have a saddle. Was six or seven. Got my first paying job on the Walker Ranch near Albany in 1927. Did everything needed doing. Did a lot of going to town. That's part of being a cowboy."

It was this going to town that got Blackie married. He and Lottie have raised five children over the years—and they've ranched. Always cowboyed and ranched. Lottie says Blackie's policy, wherever he worked, was to be allowed to run some of his own cattle as part of the salary agreement. They kept up that policy and saved money until they could lease a ranch of their own, then they kept working and ranching and saving until they could afford to buy the ranch where they now live.

FOREMAN OF RANGE RIDERS

Over the years they tried many methods of ranching, and managing, and saving, and surviving. "We couldn't afford to buy a ranch," Lottie says. "So we leased land until we bought this little place. You can't live in the country like you have town money. You can't spend money as though you already had it. You have to get by with what you have. Ranching is a way of life for us. Not all ranch children make good ranchers. It's the love of the land that makes the

Beary "Blackie" Woods, Running W Ranch, Van Horn, Texas, and hound pup.

difference. We are stewards of the land. We've leased places and have always left them better than when we moved there."

Lottie says in the late 1940s there was an outbreak of hoof-and-mouth disease south of the Rio Grande, and the USDA (United States Department of Agriculture) formed an army of cowboys and ranchers to patrol the entire border of Mexico, with orders to shoot-to-kill any cattle that crossed the Rio Grande into the United States. In 1948, Blackie hired on as a foreman of the Range Riders, who each patrolled a fourteen-mile stretch of river. Lottie and their two children moved down in 1949.

"He won't talk about it much," Lottie says. "We had two fourteen-by-sixteen army tents with board floors and sidewalls. I had a Servel gas refrigerator and a gas cook stove. We lived pretty good." Lottie says living in a tent by the river doesn't make it any less of a home. "We lived well. We managed our money well, too. When my grandmother first came out here, they lived in a tent. She had the wagonbed turned upside down and used the bottom for a table. When guests would come to visit, she'd spread a linen table cloth and set the best table you ever saw—just as she was accustomed to at Lampasas, Texas."

THE MAKING OF A CAT CATCHER

Over the years the Woods saw a lot less than the best, but they continued to manage their money well and save a little. "Blackie was a Range Rider for four years and got paid every two weeks," Lottie says. "We'd use one [paycheck] for groceries and living expenses, and put one in the bank. That way when we went back to ranching, we had enough money to buy some livestock."

At first the Woods moved to New Mexico to try sheep ranching, but the wind and the varmints soon drove the Texans home. "We spent a year in New Mexico," Lottie says. "Took us ten years to recover. We took up a little bunch of sheep, and the coyotes and cats and eagles took all the lambs and the wind blew all the time. One time it even blew Blackie's glasses off—and he wears the kind that hook behind the ears. It never rained or snowed, but the wind blew all the time."

The varmints never let up on the lamb crop. "A cat eats meat," Blackie says emphatically, his voice almost rising above a whisper. "I don't care what you hear different, a cat likes meat. Fresh meat. A bobcat will kill lots of lambs. And a mountain lion is just devastating. And I've seen eagles hauling off young lambs. They can't hurt a ewe, but they can sure take a lamb. And the coyotes just won't let you alone. They just keep digging into your profits. I've killed lots of coyotes. I just haven't killed enough."

Blackie has also killed lots of mountain lions, and according to his son Beary Junior, is something of a living legend in west Texas. "The government hunters call on him to help them. He can track a cat better'n anybody in the world. He's spent a lot of time in that old country. He knows it better than anyone. He doesn't talk about it, but he knows the country and he knows cats."

Blackie says he started hunting at about age eight, and started hunting the big cats in 1943. "Coyotes were killing our sheep and I went to find their den. I took the dogs. I've always got a couple of dogs with me. They began baying at something on a hill. I tied up my horse and walked up to see what it was. It was a mountain lion. I walked back and got my gun and shot it. That's all there is to it."

And that's about all the talk you'll get out of Blackie, but the fact is, he was hooked on cat hunting.

A CAT-HUNTING MULE MAN

Lottie says she used to go bobcat hunting with Blackie in the early 1940s, but he was so serious it took the fun out of it for her. "We'd ride out on a cliff and listen to the dogs. If you coughed or your saddle creaked, you'd get frowned at." Beary Junior echoes her sentiments: following the king of the cat killers was not much enjoyment.

"He'll eat a big old breakfast and drink a big old glass of water, then he won't eat or drink again all day. That's tough—to be out in that old desert all day like that. I can't take it." But Blackie has disciplined himself over the years so he can take the country much like the Indians who lived here and would ride all day with a pebble in their mouths to ward off thirst until they could reach the next water hole—often a full day's ride away. The lack of water and the rugged mountain terrain turn away all but the heartiest.

"It's a tough old country," Blackie admits. "But it's strong country. All we need is a little rain once in a while. Sheep do better here because cattle have a hard time getting around. But I'm out of the sheep business. The coyotes saw to that. I just run a few cattle now."

And mules. Blackie says mules do better for riding in the mountains, because they won't hurt themselves like a horse is likely to do, and because a good horse is too valuable to have up among those rocks and cliffs. "I even rolled a mule over the side once," the old cat hunter declares. Lottie says that Blackie was leading the mule around a big rock on a steep mountainside when the dirt gave way and the mule tumbled down to his death. "It was a long walk over the mountain to a neighbor's ranch. There was a jeep there with the key in the ignition and enough gasoline to get Blackie back to his pickup, so he borrowed it. The next morning, Blackie returned the jeep and left a note that he had borrowed it. This just gives a good picture of the integrity and trust between ranchers of this area."

You've got to trust your mule, too. "Mules do better up there," Blackie says. "I ride 'em everywhere I go." And Blackie is still going and says he'll continue to go "as long as I can stand up."

A COOK WITH A VARIETY OF RECIPES

Lottie doesn't have any plans to slowing down, either. She puts in a big garden every year near their modest home about five miles south of Van Horn and still does lots of cooking even though it's just for Blackie and herself these days. "I've cooked about everything there is to cook," she says. "My father was a wonderful cook and mother was also a great cook. She showed me how to cook before I could read a recipe." Beary Junior says his mother has "enough recipes to publish two books but never uses one."

"I cook a variety of things," Lottie says. "Before we got a gas range, we just had a two-burner deal with no oven. You can do a lot with a skillet. You can even make cookies in a skillet." If you know what you're doing—and there's no doubt Lottie does. She sends one of her favorite recipes she lovingly calls "Melting Moments."

LOTTIE'S MELTING MOMENTS

½ cup cornstarch

½ cup confectioners' sugar

1 cup sifted flour

¾ cup butter or margarine

In a mixing bowl, sift together cornstarch, sugar, and flour. Mix in margarine to make a soft dough. Form in one-inch balls or rolls. If in rolls, cut into three-quarter-inch pieces. Place on ungreased baking sheet. Flatten with floured fork, or dish or glass dipped in sugar. I use one with a fancy design on the bottom.

Bake in 300°F oven for twenty to twenty-five minutes or until set. Do not overbake. Makes about twenty-four cookies, and for more, you can double ingredients.

"Sometimes I put a little Tang in with the sugar. It gives 'em a little different flavor. They're sooo good."

SLASH SEVEN RANCH

FRIONA, TEXAS
M. C. AND ANN OSBORN

THE MODERN EFFICIENT RANCHERS

The country in Parmer County, especially around Friona, is flat—as a matter of fact, it's very flat. It seems you can see forever, with just the next farm or ranch on the horizon. You'll also see some extraordinary sunrises and sunsets.

One late fall evening, as the setting sun cast a bright orange glow on the western horizon, M. C. Osborn, of the Slash Seven Ranch, drove out to several of his pastures to feed a variety of registered cattle. A pretty severe drought had left the grass short, so feeding was an essential part of ranch management. It was amazing listening to M. C. rattle off the birthweights and bloodlines of his stock, all from memory—in every way the modern and efficient rancher that you need to be to make it ranching in this day and age.

CLOSE TO THEIR ROOTS

Ann and M. C. Osborn ranch just outside of Friona, an agricultural community of about 3,000 people, not too far from the New Mexico border in the Panhandle of Texas. They are in an area a little over 4,000 feet above sea level that gets only fifteen or sixteen inches of rainfall a year, much of which generally blows in in two or three storms. But as you sit in their very comfortable home, surrounded by art work and books, especially their Max Evans collection, you can tell that not only have they survived the ups and downs of ranching in this country, they have prospered.

You must understand that they do know this country and it seems, always have. Ann's dad, a former cowboy on the old XIT, first came into Parmer

Ann Osborn at the ranch near Friona, Texas

County in the early years of the century, when "the pastures were one hundred sections [64,000 acres], and the grass was up to his stirrups." Harry Whitely met a school teacher named Marye Harris, and in 1927, after an on-again, off-again courtship, they married and settled down.

M. C. was born and raised in Parmer County, as well. His mom was also a school teacher when she met his dad. Ann and M. C. knew each other as youngsters, but, as Ann says with a big smile, "We didn't like each other in high school." They are six months apart in age and they lived only a little more than a mile from each other as children.

BUILDING A SPREAD

When they were in college—M. C. at Texas A&M and Ann at Texas State College for Women (now Texas Woman's University)—they fell in love. They married two weeks after graduation, in 1957. It wasn't too long after their wedding that they moved back "home" and set up to build a ranch. As M. C. explains, and anyone who is thinking of starting a ranch knows, there are really only three ways to get a ranch: "You inherit it, you marry it, or you make enough money doing something else to buy one." Well, fortunately for the young couple, M. C.'s dad was a farmer and helped them get started. M. C. took the money he made from farming with his dad and began to buy ranch land, a process he is still engaged in. Today the Osborns have more than 5,000 acres of dry ranch

M. C. Osborn feeding cattle at the Slash Seven Ranch.

land. They used to irrigate but stopped in 1979 because the water table was getting low and pumping it became too expensive. He says that today, irrigating "is all work and not much return." They farm nearly 1,000 acres of wheat, milo (grain sorghum), and some hybrid sudan grass hay, some for sale to the huge feedlots in the area.

Still, their main operation is their cattle. They run registered Herefords, Simmentals, Tarantaise, Brangus, Longhorns, and Beefmasters. They run a cow/calf operation, with the calves hitting the ground in April and May. The Slash Seven also runs a good number of cattle at the feedlots. They always have about 1,000 head there, and they buy and sell each month. In principle, it's very simple—you try to buy low and sell high—sort of like playing the stock market. Anyone unsure of what they are doing can take a real beating in this high stakes cattle game. But the feedlot cattle do augment the cattle on the ranch without having to own additional land.

A drought in 1990 forced the Osborns to sell most of the cattle at the ranch, so they are, in fact, in the process of rebuilding—a very slow process. As M. C. says, "We are very conservation-minded when it comes to saving the soil and trying to make the place better than when we found it. I stock at a very conservative rate."

The ranch also has some land in the Conservation Reserve Program (CRP), putting farm land back to its natural state for ten years. That acreage is not used—for anything, including grazing. It's just grass. The Osborns intend to graze the land when the ten years are up, and they know now that the grass will help reduce soil erosion. But the new range also will allow them to increase their cattle herd and maintain the land at the same time.

THE COWGIRLS DO THE JOB

The Slash Seven is a family ranch, and Ann and M. C. have had great help from their five daughters—Paige, Shawn, Nikki, Lacye, and Tiffany—girls who are now grown and away from the ranch. "They did their share," their parents proudly state. When they were still at home "they did everything that was to be done—a boy couldn't have done more. . . . A girl can do everything a cowboy can do and a whole lot he can't." Enough praise from their smiling parents.

In addition to the cattle, the ranch also has some fine American Quarter Horses, for both ranch work and competition. Tiffany has amassed enough trophies to cover the walls from floor to ceiling in a good size room. And there are also the Angora goats who are "cute and fun," according to Ann. The goats produce mohair on their place down in Hamilton County, west of Waco.

TIMES DO CHANGE

Like all modern ranchers who have been on the land for a considerable amount of time, the Osborns have observed all the recent changes in ranching. They believe that today they are more efficient, the tractors are better and the cows are tougher and can take better care of themselves. In fact, they breed better cattle. The ranch used to have to hire five hands during the summer, but now Ann and M. C. are able to get the work done by themselves. They have better all-around ranch management and get better use of the land, by their own figuring.

Although he doesn't much care for farming, M. C. realizes that farming and ranching "really go well together" in this Texas country because "you always have feed, have a little wheat for pasture, and the stubble to graze in." But one good hail storm can easily wipe out a crop.

The Osborns are very optimistic about the future of cattle ranching. When asked if ranching would disappear, M. C. smiles and says quietly, "It'll never happen. Everybody wants to own a cow—they think because you own a cow there is something magical about it." And Ann adds that it was a wonderful way to raise their five daughters, even though the girls didn't always think so. Their friends were in town, "and they didn't get to drag Main Street every day after school." It's difficult to keep kids on ranches today because "it's hard work and the pay's not very good." They point out that their own daughters are all doing very well financially in city jobs.

But for Ann and M. C., ranching is what they do and what they want to do. "It's new every year. Every morning you get up there's something new out there. It's the cattle—it's intriguing—the science of cattle breeding. I don't think it gets more interesting," says M. C., a thoughtful and very intelligent conversationalist. Ann says she loves ranching. "We've grown up in this sort of life and it's just our way of life." Ranchers will survive, they figure, because their love of the land is so strong. M. C., who has a degree in economics, says he didn't have to come back to the land, but he chose to do that. And it just seemed natural that when Ann and M. C. were married, ranching would be their future together. He adds proudly, "I had to do a lot of undesirable things, like very intensive farming, to get where I am today."

COMMUNITY LEADERS

Today Ann and M. C. Osborn are almost models of the modern ranchers and are intricate members of their community in Friona and Parmer County. They belong to many ranching and cattle organizations, and Ann has been president of the Library Board, helped start the Meals-on-Wheels program, and in 1984, was selected as Woman of the Year. Over the years, they have both been president of the Chieftan Parents, the high school booster group. And don't ever underestimate the influence of high school sports in Texas. Because all the girls played sports, particularly track and basketball, there were several weekends when mom and dad logged 1,000 miles going from one competition to the next, sometimes taking in six or seven games a week. That is real dedication, but it might just explain why the girls still like to come home whenever they can.

GOOD EATS

Sitting around the Osborns' dining room table—it seems almost all the ranchers entertain at the dining room or kitchen table—having coffee and feasting on good pie, it was only natural to talk with Ann about cooking. She says she only learned to cook "because I got married and had to feed M. C." Her two favorite recipes are her Mexican Pile-On and Marinated Eye of Round Roast. The Mexican Pile-On is "what the girls asked for most of the time. But generally the girls were light eaters; they ate like birds."

The Roast, as it is fondly called, is the whole eye of round, marinated and slow cooked, then cut like it was a fillet. One of the stories that the boyfriends liked to tell is that they'd ask each other, "Did Ann cook you The Roast when you were visiting? Well, you've got it made if Ann cooked you The Roast."

The Osborns, with M. C.'s spur collection adorning the walls of his office, and his own sculptures in the living room, their old tool collection hanging in the garage, and the books, art work, and trophies throughout the house, let you feel their ties to their place and the land. And there sure aren't any doubts that you are going to love Ann's recipes.

MEXICAN PILE-ON

2 bags corn chips
1 large box instant rice, cooked
1 pound grated sharp cheddar cheese
2 heads shredded lettuce
7 diced tomatoes
3 diced onions
1 jar chopped olives
12 ounces chopped pecans
1 8-ounce can flaked coconut
1 large jar hot sauce

MEAT SAUCE

4 pounds hamburger
3 chopped onions
2 18-ounce cans tomatoes
1 large can tomato sauce
2 small cans tomato puree
4 tablespoons chili powder
1 large can ranch-style beans
$^2/_3$ tablespoon garlic powder

Brown the meat and onions. Then add the remaining ingredients. Simmer for two hours. Serve in bowls. Arrange the chips first, followed by the rice, meat sauce, onions, lettuce, tomatoes, cheese, olives, pecans, coconut, and hot sauce. Serves sixteen.

MARINATED EYE OF ROUND ROAST

Whole eye of round
½ cup salad oil
½ cup tomato catsup
½ cup wine vinegar
1½ teaspoons salt
1 teaspoon black pepper
1 clove garlic

Combine all the above ingredients and pour them over the roast. Marinate in the refrigerator overnight. Cook covered at 275°F until the meat is tender. Slice and pour the sauce over the meat or serve the sauce as gravy.

THE SLOAN SISTERS RANCH

SAN SABA, TEXAS
KEITH AND CHRISTINE BESSENT

RAISING FAT CATTLE, FAST HORSES, AND FATTENING PECANS

San Saba, which bills itself as the pecan capital of the world, is a beautiful small town, established in 1854 and named for the river that flows through the area, providing the water and rich soil that produces all those pecans. We pull into San Saba one bright December afternoon, and not knowing anyone, stop at the county courthouse and speak with Joyce Marshall in the County Extension office. Joyce tells us the most famous resident in San Saba county is the movie actor Tommy Lee Jones, but a phone call lets us know that the costar of Lonesome Dove is not available.

"But if it's history you're after," Ms. Marshall says, "you really should visit the Sloan Sisters Ranch. It's been here forever, and one of the descendants works right across the street, in the library."

Librarian Christine Pool Bessent is busy, as she has been from the day she was born. Husband Keith has just returned from elk hunting in New Mexico, and the last thing they want is to be interviewed by some wandering writer. But being from good Texas stock, the Bessents aren't about to turn away a visitor. That Texas-bred hospitality runs deep.

Keith is wasted from that elk hunt, so he just settles back and listens. Christine jumps right in. "What exactly is it that you want?" she inquires. When we tell her we want her life story, as well as the story of the ranch, she takes to it like a cutting horse after a cow.

"The ranch was started by my great-grandfather, T. A. Sloan. He married a Henderson and a lot of the [ranch] property was grandmother's, particularly the property on the river. And they bought a lot more property. There were nine Sloan children—seven girls and two boys. My grandmother was the youngest. She died last April at 105. There's a lot of history at that old place."

To say the least. Christine's mother is Patsy Marshall and her maternal grandfather was John O. Meusenbach, originally from Germany, who settled in the Texas towns of Fredericksburg and New Braunfels. John O. Meusenbach also made a treaty with the Comanche Indians in the area. That treaty was signed by a peaceful pond, shaded by centuries-old live oak trees, on Henderson property then, later owned by the Sloan sisters, just up the road from the current Sloan sisters' house.

IT'S THE WATER

There are at least two books written about John O. Meusenbach and another book that has an entire chapter devoted to Christine's ancestors. Retired San Angelo cattle buyer, Wade Choate, published a little book about his life's work titled *Swapping Cattle,* which looks at fifty years of Texas ranching and Texas ranchers. Choate relates a time in San Saba when he was riding with Tom Allen Sloan, who shot a deer out of season and dumped the buck in the trunk of Wade's company car. Later, when Choate opened the trunk, the deer jumped out and ran toward town. Sloan killed the buck in downtown San Saba. Still later, Tom Allen invited Choate out to meet his cousin, Sloan Pool (Christine's father). When they pulled up at Sloan's house, he wasn't there, so they decided to wait. While they were leaning against the car, bullets started ricocheting around their feet. Sloan was executing, from afar, the old west tradition of making dudes dance. Choate recorded, "Those boys around San Saba and Pontotoc and Lometa have a different kind of water to drink or something."

Perhaps it is the water. Or the minerals in the water. Collectors come from all over the world to study the various minerals and rock formations in the area. Whatever it is that motivates the Sloans, visiting with Christine, you get the picture that here's a different breed of cowgirl. "When I was growing up, I couldn't wait for summer, so I didn't have to go to school," she tells us. "But I did have to get up at 4:30 in the morning and go gather goats. Still, it was better than going to school. We had lots of goats then. Angora and Spanish, but mostly Angora. We had 'em for brush control."

Christine says she and Keith quit the goat and sheep business five years ago and now run a cow/calf operation, which they like much better. "My family has always had cattle. My grandfather ran registered Herefords. When Daddy took over, he started putting gray Brahman bulls on 'em [Herefords], and that gave us the F-1s. They do good. The buyers like 'em, but it was hard to replace those Herefords. We liked 'em."

Christine and Keith now run commercial Beefmaster and like them even better than the Herefords she grew up with. "We use a Charolais bull on Beefmaster cows and it's working great," she says. "We tried Salers for a while. Most of 'em were wild and the buyers didn't like 'em so we went to the Charolais. We can't afford to keep anything around here that doesn't turn a profit."

*Horse handler Keith Bessent and Nolan Ryan, the Sloan Sisters Ranch running wonder. Sloan Sisters
Ranch, San Saba, Texas.*

CRAZY ABOUT HORSES

What Christine's ancestors could afford was good horses, and the Sloans
always had some of the best. "My family has always been into race horses. My
mother's family was crazy about horses. I got to work with them [race horses]
some. I'd go out ahorseback and gather goats. When I was little, I'd start from
the house. Later we'd take a truck and trailer and haul to the back of the pasture.
That cut down on our riding and gave us more time for other chores. There's
always something to do on a ranch."

Like spraying for ticks or burning needles off prickly pear cactus. "I started
driving a spraying truck when I was in the second grade," the librarian reports.

"I was doing ranch work even before that. They [my parents] trusted me to be by myself. I have one brother and one sister and I didn't take to house work. I still don't. I much prefer to be outside. I've worked hard all my life, but I don't mind it. Lots of folks have worked a lot harder."

Only a little, perhaps. "I never got to participate in any rodeos or anything like that when I was growing up. If we rode horses, it was to do ranch work. But I do love horses. Horses are my weakness. Dad raised running quarter horses and thoroughbreds. We'd bring horses that couldn't win to the ranch and make ranch horses out of 'em. Most of 'em made it pretty good. But I was the only one light enough and stupid enough to ride 'em.

"There were times we'd get a horse in and he'd still have racing plates on and I'd bail on 'im and go gather goats. Sometimes it was a little scary. I'd put about anything on their head. As I got older, I got a little smarter and would wrap a hackamore with baling wire to slow 'em down a little. I also learned later—way later—to work with 'em in a pen before just taking off across country. Before, I'd just jump on and take off. It was dangerous, but I never got hurt bad."

Just scared badly. "We were gathering Spanish goats, and you should never do that with a horse right off the track. The goats were running everywhere, and people were running by me on all sides, and this horse just took off and I like to have never got it stopped. Race horses are that way. Daddy put a new shadow roll on one we had, and I rode up to this little trap to try 'im out. When we hit a trot, that thing starting bouncing and scared that horse and away we went. I couldn't begin to stop him. We were going faster and faster and my life was flashing in front of me.

"That horse hit the fence in front of grandmother's house and that shadow roll must have caught on top of the wire because we just turned a flip and landed in the yard. I went skidding across the carpet grass but wasn't hurt hardly at all. It about scared me to death, but I came out of it all right."

A GRADUATE OF THE SCHOOL OF HARD KNOCKS

Christine lived to tell about that wreck and more. She is the quintessential cowgirl, growing up ranching, getting her education in the school of hard knocks. "Nobody ever showed us kids how to do anything. They just expected us to get it done. We never had a riding lesson. Our hired hand, Soap Hardman, had five kids, so there was always a bunch of us kids goofing off somewhere. One time we were sorting cattle and we kids got to playing around. Daddy got out a buggy whip and we didn't let any more cattle get by."

This school of hard knocks prepared Christine well for ranch life, if not for life in the big city, or big colleges. "I went off to college for two years. It was a big change for me. I didn't like being off the ranch. I'm just a country girl. I didn't like being stuck in a little room with all those little rules. I was used to coming and going when I wanted to. I love to learn, but college wasn't my deal, so I came back home and went to work on the ranch."

Historic Sloan Sisters ranch house, San Saba, Texas.

In 1974, Christine married Keith Bessent in San Saba, and they lived in a trailer house in a pasture until recently, when they moved into the Sloan sisters' house. As the sun began to sink behind the courthouse, Christine locked the library and we adjourned to the ranch.

"Just follow me," Keith says as he crawls into his new Chevy pickup. He's been a long time away from home and is in a hurry to get there. We turn off Highway 190 onto Ranch Road 2732, a winding, narrow strip of asphalt where the words "cut and fill" are unheard of. The sun is setting right on the road and visibility is next to nothing. It was one of the wildest rides of the entire Texas trip. The Chevy is visible only occasionally. However, there is no mistaking the Sloan sisters' house. Hard by the highway, the two-story ranch house, shaded by towering trees and surrounded by a wrought iron fence, dominates the landscape.

MODERN RANCH LIFE ON AN OLD RANCH

Being back at home pumps new life into Keith, or perhaps it was that stimulating drive. As Christine changes into evening clothes and prepares to drive to a Cattle Womens' meeting in Lampasas, fifty miles away, Keith takes care of evening chores and gives us a run-down on the old ranch house. "The Sloan sisters' house was built in 1883. All nine kids, a bunch of hired help, and orphaned kinfolk lived here. Some of the hired hands lived in the basement. They had only cold water to bathe in.

"They pumped water up to a metal tank and it gravity-flowed to the house. They also collected water off the roof and it went into a filtering system and they used that. The main water comes from this ditch behind the house that comes from the Sloan Springs Branch south of here. That spring has never failed. Even in the worst droughts, it's always provided plenty of water for the ranch."

Keith was born in San Saba in 1951, and he and Christine remember the drought years. "I hope I never see that again," Christine says the next morning at breakfast, as she prepares to go into town early, to another meeting. "When I was a kid [back in the drought of the fifties] we had to burn pear for the cows. I was too little to pack those propane tanks they had then. This last drought, just a few years ago, we used those big tanks pulled behind the pickup, and the burners had hoses about 200 feet long."

During that drought, while Keith gathered pecans, Christine and Malvin Hector, their neighbor, friend, and hired helper, who worked for the Sloan sisters about all his life, burned the needles off the prickly pear cactus, in the mornings, before Christine left for her job in town. "I open the library at 11:00 [A.M.]," she says. "I work before I go to work. I'd burn pear most of the morning, then go straight [to the library] without stopping to take a bath. Many a day I went in smelling like propane and burnt pear. I hope I never have to do that again. We won't if we're lucky."

A FLOP-EARED RUNNING HORSE

The Bessents have recently been lucky in weather and in the horse business. Carrying on a family tradition, Christine and Keith raise race horses, and even though it's a hit and miss proposition, last year they made as much off their horses as they did their cattle. That takes some shrewd trading and lots of luck. "We've had good luck," Christine reports. "I bought my first [race] horse at an auction in New Mexico a few years ago. We looked at over 700, and soon as Keith walked away, I bought one. It was a flop-eared mare. Ugliest thing you've ever seen. I cried. I'd used all my savings. The only good thing I heard was Daddy said he'd never seen a flop-eared horse that wouldn't run.

"She surpassed my wildest dreams and won over $75,000. Now her babies are running." And winning. And making the news at home and abroad. Christine bred the mare Caralot to the stallion Ronas Ryon. When the bay colt was born, Christine began to cast about for a proper name. Keith suggested Nolan Ryan, after the famous pitcher for the Texas Rangers. "I didn't even know who Nolan Ryan was," Christine says. "Then I saw him in an ad for Wranglers in the Progressive Farmer, and I said, 'so that's Nolan Ryan. He looks all right.'"

So she fired off a letter to the future Hall of Famer. You have to get permission to name horses after famous people. Ryan was in spring training at the time and his office sent his signed baseball card. So Christine wrote back and explained again what she wanted, and this time got a personal letter with permission to proceed. She said if she had known how much publicity it was going to cause, she would not have named the horse Nolan Ryan "because you want the horse to live up to his namesake, which in this case is a pretty big undertaking."

As it turned out, Nolan Ryan—the horse—began burning up the track and winning about the time Nolan Ryan, the pitcher, was throwing heat across the plate and winning. And pundits were quick to notice the juxtaposition of horse race and pennant race and the ink began to flow. Wire services picked up on the story and the phone started ringing. Every time Nolan Ryan, the horse, won and Nolan Ryan, the Ranger, won, more stories were generated. But then in 1993, the forty-seven-year-old pitcher injured his arm and announced his retirement and the three-year-old colt injured an eye and had to be pulled from training.

Christine and Keith are now doctoring the bay gelding and say he is responding very well. Some day soon they hope to put him back on the track, but both say they'll never again name a horse after a celebrity. "Too much pressure," Keith says. "We've got enough to do around here without answering the phone all the time." However, Christine adds that they weren't so busy they couldn't be polite to people; it's just that they stay very busy.

PICKING PECANS, FIXING FENCES, AND COOKING

During our visit, Keith is in the middle of the pecan harvest. He says because 1993 was a dry year, the crop was not as good as usual. In a normal year, he gathers about 100,000 pounds of pecans, another nice addition to their horse and cattle business. The pecan trees are native to the area and do well in the flood plain of the San Saba River. Pecans were gathered by hand for years, until one Bill Burnham of the San Saba area invented a mechanical gatherer, a device that looks like a snowblower with hundreds of rubber fingers that roll the pecans onto a conveyer which then dumps them into a box. A labor-saver that Keith, admittedly a little lazy, admires greatly.

"There's constant chores on this place," he laments. "The two things I hate most is fixing fence and fixing water gaps. Every time the river comes up, it wipes out the river bottom fences. The last time I'd just got around to getting everything fixed and it rained and the river come up and took out all the fences. That's the reason I just take off sometimes and go hunting. But about four days of that getting up at 3:30 cures me and I'm ready to go back to the ranch."

On normal days, when they're not calving or foaling or burning pear, the Bessents sleep in 'til daylight, a luxury that Christine relishes. "My aunts [the Sloan sisters] always got up at 5:30 in the morning. I finally figured out why. They had to clean this damn house. I'll tell you right away I ain't much for cleaning house. Or cooking. When I was little, Momma would say something about cooking and I'd hit the door. I'm still a little bit that way."

Who, then, does the cooking on the Sloan Sisters Ranch? Keith would rather be hunting and Christine would rather be riding. Who does the windows and the dishes? They both do. Christine can cook. She just doesn't put a lot of time into it. She's figured out recipes that can be thrown together in short order; Keith is on his own during the day. He eats a lot of pecans. You can pick 'em up everywhere you walk. "Here, have one," he says, as he cracks one against another in a large fist. "They say these things will help your rheumatism. I don't know. All they've done for me is make me fat." And smart.

"We try to work smart around here," he says. "There's just the two of us, and with Christine gone a lot, we have to make every minute count. Our ancestors used to rope calves and drag 'em to the fire. That was fun, but now we just can't take the time. It took a lot of people. We run 'em through a chute and we brand, doctor, castrate, dehorn, and inoculate, and we're through. We're free to go do something else. We feed [cubes] with an automatic feeder that's mounted on a truck. Anybody who can drive can feed. You back the truck under the bin, pull a lever, and it loads the hopper. You drive out in the pasture and pull another lever and the feeder spreads the cubes and you're done."

Christine's father is close by to help the Bessent couple should they need it. "Daddy's installed a hydraulic squeeze chute," Christine says. "It can be operated by one person. Everything on the ranch is designed to make the work more efficient and less expensive. You have to be innovative to keep up with the changes in ranching today. The price of beef is up, but so is the price of pickups and gas and tractors or any kind of machinery. Way up. Out of proportion. It's not easy being a rancher today. But we still love ranching. We love the life. We've always been ranchers and we'll always be ranchers, I reckon."

We can believe that. What you probably won't believe is that Christine, the non-cooking rancher, gave us a fist full of recipes, one for a sauce for pasta she calls Pesto Presto, and another for pecan pie. Being as she hails from the Pecan Capital of the World, we thought we'd share that one. It is tasty. It's good for what ails you, and if you don't pig out, you won't get fat. Enjoy.

CHRISTINE BESSENT'S PECAN PIE

3 eggs

1 cup sugar

½ cup corn syrup

½ cup melted butter

1 cup pecans, chopped or whole

Beat eggs in a bowl and stir in sugar, syrup, butter, and pecans. Pour this mixture into an unbaked pie shell. Bake in center of 350°F preheated oven for thirty-five to forty minutes, or until pie turns light brown. Be careful not to bake too long or you'll burn 'er up.

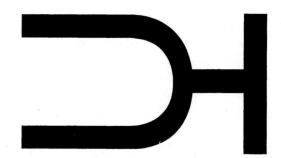

SPUR RANCH
SPUR, TEXAS
EILEEN DIXON

FIFTY YEARS AND STILL GOING STRONG

The Spur Ranch is another of the great historic Texas ranches, started in the post Civil War era, that has not only lasted through the past one hundred years, but has managed to prosper. It is located in the same general area of the Panhandle as the Four Sixes, Matador, and Pitchfork. The ranch has changed over the years, but they still run fine horses and cattle. In addition, they have added tens of thousands of wild turkeys, chukars, bob-white quails, and ring-necked pheasants.

The Espuela (Spur) Land and Cattle Company, in the late nineteenth century, was almost a million acres of Texas real estate. Originally, the Spur was a corporation of several westerners, headed up by A. M. Britton of Denver, the same Britton who had been instrumental in creating the Matador Ranch before he sold out for a generous profit to a Scotch syndicate. The Spur group bought thousands of acres, and then Britton set sail for the British Isles to seek out investors who would "buy at once and repent at leisure." This seemed to be the investing mood in merry old England. He did find investors, who then formed the Espuela Land and Cattle Company, Limited, of London. In 1885, they bought the Spur Ranch. At the time of the sale, the ranch had a "book count" of 40,000 head of cattle.

A VIRGINIA GENTLEMAN

The Espuela Land and Cattle Company became a success, due in great part to the ranch manager, a Virginian by the name of Spottswood Lomax. Lomax presided over the ranch from 1884 to 1889. Although he was respected by the men who worked for him, his wife found the isolation and lack of amenities on the ranch unpleasant, and spent almost all of her time in Fort Worth, where Lomax maintained a home for his family.

Lomax received $7,500 a year from 1884 to 1889, but hard times forced the owners to cut his salary to $3,750, raising it to $5,000 when Lomax threatened to resign. The handwriting, however, was on the wall. When a bank in Vernon, Texas, offered Lomax a job, he accepted rather than take the paycut from the Espuela.

Still, the ranch was prospering, and the new manager, Frederick Horsbrugh, understood what a gem he had. The following are a few excerpts from a letter he wrote in 1905 describing the ranch:

"The west pasture has seventy sections [44,800 acres] of the north end in Crosby County fenced off. This is a very fine pasture, being shut in by brakes of the plains, and has natural water and windmills. It is well watered and sheltered, without being too rough, and has some of the finest stretches of farming land you ever saw. I call it the best cow and calf or steer pasture in America . . .

"All over the grass is fine, and though we had some trouble two years ago and last year because it did not rain, there is a very fine coat of turf all over the property this year, which bids fair to last, due attention being given and constantly directed towards shipping out old cows, enough, as well as annual draft of steers, so as to prevent overstocking . . .

"As a cow ranch, I don't know its equal, and I believe I am within the mark when I say that two-thirds of the entire land is capable of being farmed; growing cotton, kafir corn, milo maize, etc."

THE COWBOYS ARE BORED

Life on the big Texas ranches, as on ranches all over the West, was hard. The Spur cowboys worked seven days a week. At Christmas they did get three or four days off, but they were usually bored, because they had no recreation to fill their time. Surprisingly, they liked to testify in court trials because they were paid for their time away from the ranch, and because it broke up the cowboy's daily routine. They also liked dances, although the Spur apparently did nothing to make these galas more accessible. Ranch records for the period from 1885 to 1907 list only one dance staged by the management.

Mostly, these old-time cowboys, much like their present day counterparts, enjoyed hunting and fishing, and spent as much time in these pastimes as they could spare.

Today things have changed, and then again, not really changed all that much. The ranch, now much smaller, is owned by Jim and Cisco Barron. They raise good quarter horses, Senepol cattle, and the wild turkeys, chukars, bob-white quails, and ring-necked pheasants that are sold to game farms all over the nation.

The Barrons met while they were both high school students in Spur, Texas, and they were married right after Cisco's graduation in 1966. They have two sons, James and Matt, both in their twenties. The Barrons have managed to maintain this historic and beautiful ranch, and yet still keep up with all the latest innovations in ranching, right down to the computers that share the ranch office with some beautiful western art.

KIDS COME TO THE RANCH

In addition to the usual ranching activities, Cisco Barron, with great pride, says that the ranch is "special, because we participate with the children in the area. We have kids from Lubbock that come and we have children from special education classes. They actually get to participate in the brandings. That makes us more unique [sic] than some of the other ranches in the area." She says that most of the children are learning disabled. But they also have had a private school in Lubbock bring their students and "we have a barbecue for them—we let them eat with the cowboys, and if it's the right time of the year, we let one child at a time either hold the branding iron or participate somehow in the actual branding." The Spur Ranch hosted these kids on a regular basis for more than ten years. The children seemed to enjoy eating with the cowboys and asking questions about why they wear their big hats, questions many people from all over the world would probably ask if given the opportunity. Unfortunately, there are usually too many of the youngsters to let them get on the horses, but Cisco says that she always enjoys receiving letters from the children after they've visited. She is "always interested to read what most impressed the guests."

COWBOYS AND BUCKLES

The working ranch itself still raises prized quarter horses with their own brood mare band and their four stallions. These horses are sometimes sold, but the cowboys on the ranch do much of their work ahorseback, headed up by Bill Smith, ranch foreman since 1973. Bill's dad ranched south of Spur, Texas, and he grew up in the area. He knows horses and cattle. Bill now lives on the ranch with his wife, Dana, and son Billy. His wife rides often with her husband, although she's not officially on the ranch payroll. In fact, both Bill and Dana are very knowledgeable about horses. They have even judged horse shows together. Billy is one of the Spur's cowboys, working for his dad.

The Spur cowboys are all excellent horsemen, and they're pretty good at working cattle, too. Recently, a team from the ranch won the exhibition team penning competition put on by the American Quarter Horse Association and the National Cattleman's Association in Reno, Nevada. Their winning time of thirty-nine seconds is good in any league. Bill headed the three-man team and proudly sports the championship buckle that they won.

Senepol bull, Spur Ranch.

A NEW BREED

The cattle on the ranch are the relatively rare and exotic Senepol, and the Barrons are quite proud of their herd. In fact, Jim is a national officer of the Senepol Cattle Breeder's Association, based in Kentucky. The breed is fascinating to most western ranchers.

In the late 1800s, Henry Nelthropp brought a small herd of N'Dama females from Senegal in Africa to St. Croix in the Caribbean because he wanted to increase the heat- and insect-resistance of his native herd.

In 1918, while visiting Trinidad, he saw two Red Poll bulls, imported from England. He admired their conformation, polled character (no horns), general disposition, and red color so much that he bought them and added some others to begin a breeding program. This eventually would result in the Senepol breed of cattle.

Nelthropp and his descendants crossed the two breeds, the N'Dama and the Red Poll, until they reached the right blend, in 1948. The resulting cattle were mated as purebreds from that time on. It wasn't until 1977 that the first load of Senepol cattle were imported into the United States. They are the most popular in the South and the Southwest because, among many of their interesting characteristics, they tolerate the heat well. The African N'Dama contributed the heat-resistance, while the Red Poll gave the breed their excellent carcass quality, fertility, lack of horns, and gentleness.

WARTIME RANCHING

Going along with all the innovations at the ranch are the enduring traditions that give a long overview to the rich history of the Spur. No one better represents these than Eileen Dixon, who has been cooking for the cowboys for more than fifty years.

She first came to the Spur in 1942 with her husband, Bob Dixon. It was during World War II and cowboys were hard to find. Dixon had to "see about this ranch by himself. . . . When we moved out here, it was just us, and when we could, we had a hired hand." Bob wasn't from a ranching background, but he did love horses. And anyone who knew him will readily tell you that he eventually became one of the best cowboys in the area. In 1925, he came to the ranch, and in 1937, he and Eileen were married. She has "cooked a little on and off since I've been here . . . at times we've had as many as twenty cowboys."

THE EARLY KITCHEN

Looking back over the years, Eileen says that to be a good ranch cook you've "got to cook what the cowboys like. They don't go for a lot of fancy stuff. Just beans and potatoes—things that'll stick to their ribs while they're working."

Life in the kitchen has changed in some ways, at least as far as the tools of the trade are concerned. "When I first came out here we cooked on a wood stove and had kerosene lamps and used the fireplace for heating—we burned up on one side and froze to death on the other."

In 1946, the ranch installed electricity and gas. "Things were a lot simpler and easier. When we first moved out here we milked fourteen cows, my husband fed fifty hogs, and we raised chickens. We also raised registered Hereford bulls out here. He liked to have died when they put a mixed black with the Herefords." Bob Dixon, like many of the old-time cowboys, loved the purebred Hereford cattle.

Maybe the biggest change Eileen Dixon has seen over the years is the change in the way cowboys do their work. "My husband rode all over this pasture ahorseback. He did not have a pickup. He fed with a wagon and team in the wintertime. Now the cowboys have their pickups and horse trailers. They haul to a pasture and work that pasture and load up and work another pasture." Of course, you must realize that on these ranches a pasture is thousands of acres, not some small enclosure.

Eileen says that "things are more modern now." But on the Spur they still ride a lot of horses. Often that is dictated by the terrain, and with the rolling hills and breaks, horses just seem to work better.

When it comes to the cowboys, Eileen has a warm spot as big as a Spur pasture. This is, no doubt, part of the love and admiration she still feels for her husband, who passed away in 1973. As she explains, cowboys "are still good people. These boys would do anything for me that I ask." With her warm smile she says that Bill Smith, the ranch foreman, is one of the best cowboys in the

Bob Dixon ropmg calves at the Spur Ranch in 1940s (photo courtesy Eileen Dixon).

country. However, she is very thoughtful when she adds that, over the years, the cowboys just aren't as good as they were thirty or forty years ago. "They've had it so much easier. They haven't had to learn the hard way like the old cowboys did. I just don't know how they'd do in real tight places." She doesn't think they are as tough, but she says that the Spur cowboys are as committed and understand the cowboy life as well as the old-timers.

One quality that she does miss is the courtesy of the older cowpunchers. "These younger boys don't always understand that." It does seem that many of the older hands had an almost courtly manner about them, perhaps a reflection of the times.

#1 COWBOY

Although he has been gone for more than twenty years, Eileen still speaks lovingly of her husband. In fact, she rates him number one as a cowboy. "He was an all-around cowboy. He was a roper. I went to watch him, and out of three hundred head, he wouldn't miss a loop. And he knew cows; he knew horses. He was a smooth rider. He knew his job well." You definitely get the feeling that in Eileen's eyes, all cowboys are judged by the standards set by Bob Dixon. They are mighty high standards.

CUT THE CHOLESTEROL

Over the years, Eileen has enjoyed the "fellowship, learning about all the boys." There is no longer a bunkhouse on the ranch—it burned down—so all the cowboys live at home. This makes life a little easier for the ranch cook, since she now only has to cook one meal a day—lunch.

As the cowboys have changed, so have their eating habits. "We used to butcher the hogs and have pork and sausage." Then with a big laugh she says, "Now we go for things that are not as high in cholesterol. But I still serve lots of red meat." She quickly adds that, in the old days, they didn't hear so much about cholesterol "because the cowboys worked harder—we worked off the food we ate."

Eileen's favorite foods, at first glance, seem to be the traditional ranch fare—chicken-fried steak, cobbler—but then she added one to the list that really came out of nowhere—broccoli corn bread. "It's really delicious, but these boys don't think so because it's got broccoli in it. Bill Smith won't touch broccoli." She enjoys making this tasty bread for her company and family. "It's sort of a meal within itself." And, she quickly adds, "I've learned to take short cuts in cooking. I used to go the hard way. Now if there's a short way, I'll take it." She gives, as an example, baking cakes. "When I used to bake cakes I'd bake them from scratch. Now I use a lot of mix cakes. And Jim [Barron] just nearly dies 'cause I used to make biscuits. The baking powder didn't agree with my husband's stomach, so I stopped making them." Jim, who is a wonderful cook himself, wanted her recipe but she just told him, "I can't do that."

In addition to the recipe for broccoli corn bread, Jim, who is a champion chuck wagon cook, offers one of his favorite recipes, "Cowboy Fiesta," a beef dish that's a must for any good cattleman.

BROCCOLI CORN BREAD

2 boxes Jiffy Corn Bread mix

1 cup cottage cheese

1 medium onion, chopped

1 package frozen chopped broccoli, thawed

4 eggs, beaten

2 sticks oleo, melted

1 small can whole corn

Mix all the ingredients, making sure that the broccoli is completely thawed. Bake in a thirteen-inch x nine-inch greased pan at 350°F for about thirty-five minutes, or until it turns brown.

Round steak
Picante sauce
Blue cheese dressing
Sour cream
Monterey Jack cheese
Flour tortillas

Pound a piece of round steak to one-quarter-inch thickness, making it a little larger than your flour tortilla. Brown the meat in a large iron skillet with a small amount of oil until it's done. Lay a hot tortilla flat and place the meat on top. Mix the picante sauce, blue cheese dressing, and sour cream, according to your taste. Slightly melt the Monterey Jack cheese and put it on top of the mixture. Top all of this with another hot flour tortilla. Roll the tortilla tight, using the cheese to help it stick together. This will form a log. Slice into one-inch pieces and serve. This can be heated at about 250°F for about ten minutes.

SUMMEROUR HEREFORD RANCH

DALHART, TEXAS

JOHNNY AND JOWAYNE SUMMEROUR

TRADITIONAL LIVING ON A FAMILY RANCH

The entire area around Dalhart, Texas, is so rich in ranch history that it seems that on every road, in every direction, there is a good ranch with fine looking cattle and horses. This is, of course, the edge of XIT country, and even the museum in Dalhart, although officially the Dalhart-Hartley Counties Historical Museum, is known far and wide as the XIT Museum. Heading northeast out of town, on the road to Stratford, it's only about eleven miles before you hit the turnoff to the Summerour Hereford Ranch. There are several highway signs to help keep the traveler from getting lost. The signs also help the many cattle buyers get to the ranch on time, each November, for the annual bull production sale. They come from all over cattle country to attend this much awaited fall event.

Overseeing part of the ranch operation are Johnny and JoWayne Summerour. JoWayne is a vivacious, outgoing woman, who is a wonderful spokesperson for the ranch. She is native to the area, having grown up in Stratford, just north of the ranch. She met Johnny Summerour while they were both in high school there. He went off to college at what was then Oklahoma A&M in Goodwell, and after college, in 1954, they were married. They have two daughters, both married. Melody Sample is a school teacher, and Stephanie Sanders works in a corporate office; both live in Fort Worth, where they went to college. Neither married men with ranching backgrounds or interests, and as JoWayne talks about her daughters, there is a wistfulness because they are off in the big city and will not, in all likelihood, continue the family's ranching tradition. She says, "They just never went with ranchers."

The ranch is run by the three Summerour brothers. Johnny ramrods the cattle division, and Jimmy is in charge of the farming where they raise wheat, milo, and corn, some on irrigated and some on dry land. E. B. "Buzz" Summerour, the youngest of the three, farms his own place and does some of the farming for the ranch.

THE SUMMEROUR TRADITION

The ranch has been in the Summerour family since 1916, when Johnny's father and grandfather bought some land and began the operation. His father had worked as a cowboy on Charles Goodnight's JA, so there is a long ranching tradition with the Summerours. In 1929, he married Dorothy Pronger, whose family still ranches just southeast of Stratford, and as a wedding gift they received a registered heifer. This started the Summerour ranch on its way to being one of the very prestigious Hereford spreads in the Panhandle. By 1936, they were in the registered business full time.

The Summerour brothers have increased the size of the ranch considerably from the original twenty-one sections (13,440 acres) that their father and grandfather started. Their father passed away in 1969. Johnny is also part owner of the Nortex Feedlot in Dalhart, where they feed some 15,000 cattle each day.

CITY GIRL AND COUNTRY BOY

JoWayne is not from a ranch family. Her father had a small business and she lived in town, although she says, "I always loved the country and the animals. I used to spend the summers with my grandmother in Oklahoma and stay a month. I love ranching and I'm not going anywhere. I'm not moving to town. Dalhart's too big for me. If I could have any house in Dalhart, I wouldn't move." Sitting in her roomy, very comfortable home, JoWayne says that she "loves the privacy" of ranch life but that she does like to travel, and even when on ranch business, like at a big show, "I like to get out and about and see the museums and whatever there is to see," whether it's Denver, Fort Worth, or San Antonio.

Even though the ranch is known far and wide as a registered outfit, they also have a sizable non-registered steer herd. They run about 350 registered cows and registered bulls, but they also have about 1,500 commercial steers. They buy outside cattle all the time, and run them on the land just north of the home ranch. The registered herd is breeding stock, and the commercial steers are for beef. The registered Herefords calve twice a year, in August and September, and in March and April. The Summerours don't have a big branding because there are relatively few calves and the calving season is spread out. They have enough help all year so they don't have to add any crew for the branding. They just pull all their hands from the farming and cattle operations and get the job done.

Johnny Summerour at his house on the Summerour Ranch, Dalhart, Texas.

RANCH PRIDE

One thing that really stands out in talking with JoWayne is her pride in the Summerour Ranch. "I hope I never live long enough to see the place go down. We love our land and where we live." And that pride is obviously shared by her husband. He looks, as so many of these Texas ranchers and cowboys seem to, the way you might imagine a rancher should. As he drove me around the ranch and explained some of the ranch operations, I could almost feel the family tradition from this quiet, articulate spokesman.

The foreman on the ranch, Alan Rickston, who is married with two children, has been with the Summerours for over eighteen years. He is in charge of the registered cattle.

THE BULL SALE

In 1971, they started having the bull sales and have had them every year since. It is now one of the premier sales in the region, and the ranch has "focused on developing size, growth, and performance numbers without losing the thickness or meatiness . . . that bull buyers have always come looking for," says the New Mexico Stockman. The sale is right at the ranch in their own sale barn, not something every ranch has. JoWayne's sister, Lori Funk, wrote the poem, "Bull Sale," which gives a pretty good account of what goes into making this a success, and a success it surely is. They get lots of repeat buyers, the prices are good, but "never as high as we want." The buyers come from as far away as Alabama and Florida, and, of course, from all over the immediate area.

BULL SALE   by Lori Funk

It is two weeks before the bull sale date—
Each bull's in his pasture
    looking for a mate
Johnny is anxiously awaiting this big event.
He really wishes it had "come and went!"

It is one week before the bull sale date—
Each bull has been brought into the lot,
    breaking down many a gate.
Fences are flattened and bulls are crippled—
Tempers are short and bulls are rippled.

It is three days before the bull sale date—
Johnny is tense and he thinks the bulls
    are thin—
If Johnny was a female,
    you'd think PMS had set in.

It is two days before the bull sale date—
    Time is getting near
The phones should be ringing—
Buyers voices you want to hear.
    Sleep is hard to come by—
    Johnny gives a SIGH!

It is one day before the bull sale date—
He has heard from many but still does not know—
    If the day of the sale they'll
    show up with the dough!

It is 12:00 the day of the sale—
    the dinner bell sounds
    and people gather round.
It is 1:00 and the sale begins—
It's 500-now 600-a 1,000 now make it 2.

It's 3:00 and the sale is through—
Thank God for family, friends,
    buyers, and cow punchers, too.
If it wasn't for all of these—
This sale just wouldn't be such a breeze!

JoWayne says that as much as she's interested in the ranch and cattle, she's never worked with them. "Mr. Summerour [Johnny's dad]—he had all these boys—never had to call on women to work outside so none of us—not one of us—has ever worked with cattle." The men did all the cowboying and the men didn't even like the women to ride with them.

UPS AND DOWNS

Ranching has had its ups and downs. "When we married there was no rain, no grass, and it was about three years before anything was good. And still, I can't imagine living in the city. There are no ups and downs compared to what it would be like if your husband had to go nine-to-five in the city. . . . Our life has had its hard times, and there isn't always money. Sometimes you're deep in debt. And the bankers don't really like registered cattle. They think we could make a lot more money running steers on a turnover operation." She quickly adds, almost in defiance, "This is something my husband had always loved. He started showing cattle when he was eight or nine years old . . . he loves it today." Johnny even judges at the big January show in Denver. He was born eight miles from his present home, on the Pronger Ranch, and has lived just about all his life in the house he shares with JoWayne today.

The Summerours don't feel there have been very big changes in their ranch operation over the years. "We have pavement right up to the ranch," JoWayne says with a big laugh. But most of the changes are mechanical, like better machinery, irrigation equipment, and quicker ways to do things. They still use horses for ranch work, although JoWayne doesn't ride anymore. The ranch buys all the horses they need and, as on most traditional spreads, they don't have any mares and they don't do any breeding. "Johnny's dad used to say that 'a man in the horse business would soon go broke.'" A lot of things on this ranch seem to have their origins in an earlier time; things are both traditional and modern, all at once.

THE OLD WAYS PREVAIL IN THE KITCHEN

Even the cooking at the ranch is traditional. "My daddy was a meat and potato man. I never had a casserole served to me in my home. Then, when I married Johnny, Mrs. Summerour made lots of casseroles, so I learned mostly from her. She lived out here together with three daughters-in-law and you talk about a neat woman—she got along with all of us."

Johnny will eat anything. "He was brought up to eat anything that was set down before him. Those kids called their daddy 'the Boss,' and I will guarantee you that if they said anything bad about their mother's cooking, they were gone. And they ate what was put in front of them. Mr. Summerour was the boss and he made the rules. He brought his boys up to be ambitious and very frugal. He set rules and made the boys stick to them." When Johnny was in high school, his dad made him choose between playing ball or working at the ranch with the cattle. "Nowadays, the parents want their kids to do everything: play ball, do this and do that. And daddy is home feeding the steers. And we all know that steer shows have gotten out of hand because daddy is doing it anyway. Johnny Summerour was brought up to work. He worked, and we had a date usually on Saturday night and Sunday afternoon. But I really liked that. I knew that he was going to amount to something. . . ." The Summerour boys never rodeoed. Their daddy wouldn't have it.

In the ranch house, the display of family antiques, especially the crocks in the kitchen, are hard to miss. "They're not easy to find," JoWayne announces proudly as she takes us on a little tour of her collection.

And getting back, finally, to those casseroles. JoWayne says that she particularly likes to cook casseroles—all kinds, from vegetable to hamburger to beef. At one time she also liked to cook desserts, "but now nobody eats them. We certainly don't need them." And, surprisingly, for a cattle rancher, the recipes she wants to pass along are all without beef. Here's hoping the Hereford Association doesn't get too angry.

BLACK-EYED PEAS

4 or 5 slices of bacon

1 cup chopped celery

1 chopped onion

1 chopped green pepper

2 large cans black-eyed peas

1 can stewed tomatoes

2 bay leaves

Fry the bacon until it is crisp. Then drain and save the grease. Into the grease add the celery, onion, and green pepper, and sauté. Pour this mixture into a big pan and add the peas and the stewed tomatoes, bacon and bay leaves. Slow cook for about one hour. Take bay leaves out before serving.

BREAD PUDDING

2 cups torn bread pieces

4 cups hot milk

2 eggs

$^2/_3$ cup sugar

¼ teaspoon salt

1 teaspoon vanilla

2 tablespoons melted butter

½ cup raisins

Soak the bread in hot milk and then mash well. Separately beat the eggs with sugar and salt. Add the bread and the milk to this mixture. Add vanilla and butter. Bake in a greased pan or dish at 350°F for thirty minutes, or until a knife comes out clean. You can add raisins. Serve with whipped cream with rum or Kahlua.

THE 33 CATTLE COMPANY

Sierra Blanca, Texas
Ben and Dora Vance

RAISING THE BEST HORSES IN THE WORLD

Along the far reaches of Highway 80, which follows the old Overland Stage Route in West Texas, sits Sierra Blanca, named for the nearby Sierra Blanca Mountains and county seat of Hudspeth, the third largest county in the state. Hudspeth County was named after a Texas cowboy who eventually served twenty-nine years in the state legislature. The county is still one of the least populated in the state, averaging two square miles of clean, fresh, arid air for every Texan.

These Texans are tough. Their ancestors fought off Indians, Mexican bandits, dust, scarlet fever, and an almost total lack of water in this 5,000-foot-high plateau, bumped against the base of five mountain ranges. And these people are proud. Proud of their heritage and proud of who they are and what they do. And what most of them do is ranch and raise cattle and horses.

Just off the on-ramp to I-10 East is the 33 Cattle Company, which is in the process of producing some of the best horses in the world. If you don't believe us, just pop in and visit with fifty-eight-year-old Ben Vance, owner, operator, long time cowman, all-around cowboy, and horseman extraordinaire.

Visiting with Ben was something akin to climbing to the top of the mountain and talking with the guru. In this case, a horse guru. A native son of Texas, Ben speaks with that soft flow and click that Indians so often use. He never raises his voice, and when talking horses, puts a lot of hand and body movement into the descriptions. Here is a man who knows as much about ranch-type horses as anyone in the world.

A YOUNG ATHLETE ON A RUNAWAY HORSE

Both Ben and Dora were raised in East Texas around Houston, where Ben rodeoed for years. Dora, who's been married "to this same old cowboy for forty years", says Ben and his partner, Wilber Steadman, won so many ropings and doggings that rodeos in that part of the country fixed it to keep them from winnng quite so often. Ben says they did everything the hard way back in the old days. He hasn't got much good to say about today's rodeo cowboys.

"When I come up you dogged [steer wrestled], roped, milked wild cows, and done it all with one horse. Now these silly bastards got to have a different horse for every event. And them damn bronc riders. Got to put all that goop on their hands. Hell, we never done that. You crawled on the sumbitch, maybe took a mane-holt, and rode 'em. You know. That's the truth."

Ben's a big man. Maybe six-foot-three. When he was dogging, he carried about 240 pounds, and he got down and got the job done. In a hurry. "You didn't have time to worry about hitting the ass end and turning a flip. You just got down where you could and turn 'im, otherwise he'd run off with you. We was dogging 700-pound steers. These people today are getting down on steers weighing 350 pounds. Shit. We used to rope calves weighing more'n that. They rope these little old 150-pounds calves today. You know. Ain't nothing but a young athlete on a runaway horse roping a goat."

Ben comes down equally hard on the new Professional Rodeo Cowboys Association's rule that prevents jerking down calves. "I want a horse to stop a calf. That's what you rope 'im for. To stop 'im. Now they penalize you for jerking a calf 'cause he won't get up. Hell, he ain't big enough to get up. Damn, you better have a horse that'll jerk the sumbitch over where you can get down and get a-holt of 'im. You know."

THE MAKING OF A BEN VANCE HORSE

We know that after Dora became pregnant with their first boy (they had two; one died in a car wreck), they decided they had better settle down and earn an honest living. So, in their words, they came out west. Ben went into partnership with a cowboy friend and they leased a 400,000-acre spread near Sierra Blanca, where they were in the cattle business for the next thirty years. They always had a few good horses, and Ben broke and rode and sold horses. In 1985, they decided to go into the horse business full time, so they built up the little place by the highway.

They live in a 100-year-old adobe house surrounded by elm trees. Dora plants a big garden every year and Ben and the "boys," Julio Marta and his sixteen-year-old son, Jerry, take care of the horses. The Vance's surviving son, Bit, drives trucks, does day-work for ranches, and hauls cattle. Bit's wife, Ruthie, works at the County Extension office; she's the one who directed us to the 33 Cattle Company.

Ben is working with a young colt when we drive up. Ben starts all his horses himself. He's throwing a loop over the colt's head and the colt is a little bug-eyed, but he isn't running back or doing anything stupid. This is a quintes-

All-around cowboy Ben Vance at his 33 Cattle Company, Sierra Blanca, Texas.

sential Ben Vance colt, alert, but not panicky; just attentive, ready for anything that takes place in front of him. He stands and takes his medicine, the makings of a top-notch ranch horse. A Ben Vance horse.

"This is a two-year-old out of Freckle's Flint [Ben's own stallion]," he introduces us. "All these colts just come in off grass." He gestures at the line of colts standing tied to the pipe fence, soaking up the morning sun. "We halter break 'em as weanlings, then turn 'em out 'till they're coming two. We bring 'em back in at two. I go through 'em and start 'em on cattle. We sell the cutting and reining futurity prospects as twos. I pick up the other colts at the end of their second year and start 'em on barrels, roping, dragging logs, cutting, whatever it takes to make a ranch horse. We always got cattle to look at. We turn out some of the best ranch horses in the world."

RANCHING MARES AND RANCHING COLTS

One of the things that contribute to the development of these world class ranch horses is Ben's lease of a very large ranch in the mountains. All his mares and all the yearling colts run on that 70,000 acres, free as the breezes. It is well known that horses raised in small pens and backyards where they never get enough exercise never develop into outstanding horses. All you have to do is follow the racing industry and observe the number of horses that break down each year. These horses are raised in paddocks and pampered and just never develop. This is not the case with Vance's horses.

"I ranch all my mares," he states. "And I ranch my colts. We don't bring nothing in unless we're training on 'em or weaning 'em. They get no handling a'tall. Mares foal on the ranch and they never come to the corral. I think we're about the only people around that run a bunch of mares like we do. That's what makes my horses so good. We raise 'em on the ranch, we wean 'em on the ranch, and we work 'em on the ranch. These colts are raised to take care of themselves. We're not out there every day packing feed to the sumbitches. They're doing it themselves. They're making their living out there."

And down along the interstate, Ben and Dora are making their living. "We built everything just the way we want it," Ben says. "These colts are broncs when they come in off the range. We can run 'em in the pens and into alleys and never have to get off and close a gate. It's all pipe construction and it's the best I've ever seen. It works well for us. We're real proud of our operation. It's making money for us."

Ben makes his money by starting with good blooded mares, then raises good colts and puts a good foundation on that colt. "You leave out a step anywhere," he says, "and it'll come back on you. You won't have an outstanding horse. You might have an okay horse, but you'll never have a great horse." Ben handpicks all his mares, and all his mares will do ranch work. He's got twenty-eight gray mares and admits he's partial to a blue horse. But he's also got palominos, grullas, and sorrels. And he starts all the colts himself.

"I start 'em in a bozal. Get 'em to bend and flex and give their heads. I step on and off a few times and pull their heads around, then I turn 'em over to Julio. Ain't a better horseman anywhere. I brought him and his family up from Mexico. Fine people. He's my number one horseman. Ain't none better."

SMILE WHEN YOU SAY HORSE TRAINER

Ben carefully avoids using the words horse trainer, and when he does he spits. "Horse trainers are what ruined the horse business back in the early eighties. Oil prices were up. People were buying ranches, hiring trainers who had a sign out, 'I am a horse trainer.' . . . Most of 'em couldn't train a horse to go get a drink of water. They get maybe thirty colts in their barn and take one good one and go the world with him. Hell, that ain't horse training. Anybody can train a good horse. A horseman has to take anything that comes down the alley and make a good horse out of him. That's what we do here. We take these colts and make outstanding horses out of them."

After the colt begins to flex and bend, Ben and Julio will put a snaffle bit in the young horse's mouth. If he fights that, it's back to the bozal. That's the way the Spanish started their horses centuries ago, and that how the vaqueros of Mexico turned out some of the world's best ranch horses. They stayed off the horse's mouth until the horse learned how to bend and flex and give to pressure. It's a tradition that continues at the 33 Cattle Company.

"I got twenty-one horses here that I'll sell between now [December] and May. Then we'll be hauling horses to the Fort Worth Show in February. They've invited twelve of the top horses and horsemen in the state to show. I don't show horses. Ain't no money in it. I sell horses to people who want to show. But in Fort Worth, I'll be showing a horse to sell, and we're going there to win. I train a lot of horses, but I ain't no horse trainer. I'm an all-around cowboy. An all-around cowboy can train a horse. He can ride and rope and read a cow and out-think a cow. That's what being a cowboy is all about, reading a cow. But you can't hardly hire good cowboys any more.

"I've hired lots of boys here and put 'em on a colt and sent 'em up checking on the yearlings. They [yearlings] need to be checked every day or so, and you can ride for over thirty miles up there and never open a gate. But after a few trips they [cowboys] get tired of it and go back to town. Then it's just back to Dora and me and the boys."

KEEPING A COWMAN ALIVE

While Julio took the kinks out of a snorty two-year-old, Ben watched from the fence, and Jerry mucked out stalls and put horses on the walker, we went inside to visit Dora. "I been with him so long," she says, "I just never could figure out how to get away from him. We've had a very good life. I came from a big family and we ranched. I've always ranched. It's all I know. When we had the big ranch, I had to cook for the crews. I don't know where I learned to cook. Ben asked me that. But I've always cooked.

"I love to bake. Cowboys like their sweets. You know. I bake lots of cakes and pies and stuff like that. But since Ben had a heart attack last year and open-heart surgery, I've had to change his diet a lot. I feed him lots of chicken, and he don't like chicken. Not even a little bit. He's a cowman. Through and through. A real cowman."

The real cowman decided to take us out for lunch and gave a running commentary on the town. "There's the grocery store. They got good groceries in there, but we can't afford 'em. We shop in El Paso. We got lots of choices in horses here, but only one place to eat." The rest rooms are out of order. "Can you just hang out an old dirty rag so's I can wipe my hands off?" the cowman inquires of the waitress. "And we want fresh meat. None of that stuff you got in the back room."

Ben cuts no one any slack. Except Dora. "I never been seriously hurt on a horse," he begins table talk, then wilts under Dora's stern stare. "Oh well, there was that one time my horse hit a badger hole. I was gonna rope this old stud horse and was a-bailing to him when my saddle horse stuck both front feet in a badger hole and we went a-flying."

"They brought him to the house all covered with dirt and blood," Dora interjects. "We took him to the hospital and they wanted him to go take a shower, but he wouldn't. They tried to keep him in bed, but he kept getting up and walking around asking, 'Where in hell am I?' Finally they just let him go." And here is a cowboy/cowman/horseman who has seen both heaven and hell in one lifetime. And heaven, Ben says, looks a lot like West Texas to him.

"I died," he says of his heart attack. "I died and went to heaven. Not many people can say that. But I done 'er. Was the prettiest place in the world. Reminded me of home. Prettiest grass. Rolling hills. Pretty mountains. Beautiful place. Lot better'n I thought it would be."

But then Dora ended the out-of-body trip into the celestial with a little down to earth CPR. While Ben was beginning to enjoy heaven, he is happy to spend a little more time in Texas. "I'm real happy here. I got a good wife. Good help. Good facilities. Got everything I want right here. This is a little one-horse deal. We built 'er ourselves and we're pretty proud of it. All we know is work. We've lost more money in ranching than most folk ever make. But we're doing what we love to do. I love turning out good horses and I'll keep doing it 'til the day I die."

And Dora will keep turning out those good meals, albeit with a little less fat and cholesterol. She sends us a couple of good old ranch recipes that are favorites on the 33 Cattle Company. She says they're quick and easy and anyone can throw 'em together. And together they make a wonderful meal. A real West Texas meal from real West Texas ranchers. Enjoy.

DORA'S COWBOY STEW

1½ pounds hamburger meat.

Pinch of salt and pepper

3 or 4 potatoes, cubed

1 onion, chopped

1 can ranch style beans

Brown hamburger meat and season to taste with salt and pepper. In another pan, brown potatoes and onions together. Add ranch style beans. Simmer for about five to ten minutes.

DORA'S BISCUITS

1 package dry yeast

1 cup warm water

¾ cup Crisco oil

½ cup sugar

½ teaspoon salt

3 tablespoons baking powder

½ teaspoon baking soda

7 cups flour

2 cups buttermilk

Dissolve yeast in warm water. Mix yeast, water, oil, and sugar together. Sift baking powder, baking soda, and salt together with flour, and add alternately with buttermilk into yeast mixture. Dough will be a little sticky. Roll dough on floured board and cut or pinch off biscuit-sized pieces. Bake in well-greased pan at 350°F until biscuits are golden brown. Extra dough will keep in refrigerator for two weeks in a covered container.

VALDINA FARMS

UTOPIA, TEXAS
DAN AND PEGGY WILSON

A BIT OF OLD KENTUCKY IN TEXAS HILL COUNTRY

West of San Antonio along the Sabinal River in the heart of the Hill Country, south of the little town of Utopia, is Valdina Farms, one of the most interesting of all ranches in a state known for big, open, unusual ranches. The 18,000 acre ranch straddles the Uvalde and Medina county lines, hence the name Valdina. Emmerson Woodward, a thoroughbred horselover, put millions of dollars into the ranch, building barns, paddocks, and racetracks along the lines of a Kentucky horse farm, and tacked the name "Farm" onto this fabulous operation.

Dinosaur tracks are clearly visible, embedded in rocks along Hondo Creek, just north of the town of Hondo, the county seat of Medina. We stopped in Hondo and talked with Fred Graff at the local western wear store and got caught up on some local history. Then we drove across the county line to Uvalde and visited with Barbara Baily in the Chamber of Commerce office. Barbara, we learned, was a soul sister who had lived in Whitefish, Montana, and we became immediate friends. She invited us to visit her at home so we backtracked to Sabinal.

Barbara and her husband, David, live in the oldest home in Sabinal, which they say is haunted by the ghost of prior residents who lived and died there. It is also right next door to Beth Woodward Davis, the great-granddaughter of Emmerson Woodward. David Baily was born in Sabinal in 1950, grew up cowboying in the area, and now works for Valdina Farms. He filled us in on what it's like cowboying in Texas Hill Country.

THE REAL COWBOYS RIDE IN TEXAS

"I was born at the beginning of a seven-year drought," Dave begins. "I was about seven, first time I saw rain. Liked to have scared me to death. Mud was caking up between my toes and I went screaming into the house." After that, the rains came more frequently, and David learned to ride to stay up out of the mud. He says he and his younger brother Bill grew up cowboying for their grandfather, who was one of the best cowmen in Texas. "He was of German descent and could guess a calf's weight within five pounds. He was just uncanny. I wish I was a third of the cowman he was."

Dave may have a way to go to be the cowman his grandpa was, but both Dave and Bill are top-notch Texas cowboys—Hill Country Cowboys. "I'd like to get some of them old boys down here from Montana and turn 'em loose in the brush country," Dave says. "We'd find out in a helluva hurry who the real cowboys were."

The real cowboys in the brushy hill country of Uvalde and Medina counties ride small, 14.2-hands horses packing double-rigged saddles with toe fenders, and not much excess leather to hang up and collect brush. They carry twenty-eight- to thirty-foot ropes, they tuck their loops under their arms, and they don't swing a loop. "When you see an opening, you just dab it on 'em," Dave says. "There's jungles out there where you can't get through on your hands and knees. But the cattle can. They got trails. Only way you'll get 'em out is with dogs."

Dave left Sabinal for a season and cowboyed out of Marfa in West Texas, a place he dreams of returning to some day, even though it was almost the death of him. "A rancher up by Fort Davis had some wild steers he wanted gathered, and me and an old boy went up to do the job. I was a-bailing off this hill, right behind a big old steer, just about to drop a loop, when the steer tripped. My horse fell over the steer and we went down in the dust. Next thing I know, it's three days later and I'm in the hospital. I got a bad broken arm and several teeth knocked out and I'm bruised up all over. Was out of work for seven months."

BUILDING A HEAVEN FOR HORSES

These days, Dave works regularly at Valdina Farms. It's a pleasant drive up Highway 87 to Ranch Road 1796 and four miles of gravel road, across a bridge into the courtyard of the ranch headquarters. The most impressive thing about Valdina Farms' headquarters is the size and construction of the buildings. The bridge across the dry creek is made of concrete. The barns, bunkhouse, mess hall, and grain silos are all made of concrete. Built in the early 1930s by Mexican labor, all the concrete was packed and poured by hand.

The second cowboy at Valdina Farms is Mike Colvin, whose father, Charlie, was foreman here for thirty-five years, and his father, Ralph, worked there before that time and married Woodward's daughter. Mike relates the story of his ancestors at Valdina Farms. "The old man [Woodward] bought this place for his son, Harley, who had emphysema. Harley crashed his private plane and was killed. The old man and his wife were killed by a train when their car stalled on a crossing in D'Hanis. Harley's wife is still alive and resides in Dallas, and this place is kinda deteriorated now, but it used to be one of the best horse ranches in the world."

*Valdina cowboys and cowdogs:
David Baily (left), foreman Dan
Wilson, and Catahoula hounds.*

Mike says that Woodward probably had over 200 people working there when the buildings were under construction. The buildings are impressive, and one only has to stand in the sun and look around to get a feel for what it was like, packing cement in five gallon buckets up and down ladders, helping mold the buildings that slowly grew up out of the Texas Hill Country. The training barn has twenty stalls measuring sixteen-by-sixteen, and the entire top level has a concrete floor; all the better to store hay. The mare barn has twelve stalls that are twenty-four feet down each side, with a sixteen-foot aisle down the middle. There is a swimming pool, also built of concrete. And finally, there are those eight silos; about twenty-four feet across and fifty feet deep.

Mike says each silo was filled with grain to feed the race horses. A tripod was placed over a silo and the hands used mules to pull up fifty-five-gallon drums of grain. "Even after the construction was completed, they had over forty people working here full time. Of course, that was during the days of screw worm infestation, and those cowboys rode every day. Dad said they'd wear out a set of shoes on a horse every two or three days. That's a lot of riding."

The cowboys at Valdina Farms don't do nearly that much riding anymore, but they still go out on horseback, and they each still keep a string of good old Texas cowponies. The foreman of Valdina Farms, Dan Wilson, is a typical Texas cowboy. He came to the ranch with the new owner, Virgil Boll, a businessman who also owns other ranches as well as a feedlot, and does a lot of buying, feeding, and selling of stocker cattle. He'd recently flown through the windshield of his vehicle and wasn't available for interview, so Dan filled us in.

RIDING HERD ON FOUR-WAY COMPOSITES

"I was born in 1954 in Yancey, USA, on a ranch about thirty miles from here. Cowboyed all my life. It's the only thing I've ever done, except the two years I took off to go to school [Southwest Texas Junior College in Uvalde]. I didn't like school very much and got to doing day-work, making $100 a day, so I dropped out. Lots of times I wish I'd gone ahead and finished, but I was having too much fun cowboying."

Dan has cowboyed on lots of ranches, and admits Valdina Farms is just a little different. "We usually run around 700 mama cows and 750 stocker cows. But this year [1993] it's been awful dry, so we've cut back some. We do some preconditioning on calves, getting 'em ready to go to the feedlot, and our hunting lease is a big part of the operation. There are some trophy deer here, but all the hunting rights are leased. I really don't get involved in the hunting part."

Just the cattle and horse part; and the hogs. "Our main herd [of cattle] consist of Brahman-Hereford-cross cows and Simmental bulls. Virgil has been working on a four-way composite breed by using F-1s [Brahman-Hereford], Tuili, and Braunvieh [a meatier Brown Swiss]. Tuili [an African breed], he likes for small calves and heat resistance; Braunvieh for high grading and fast gain. We're planning to switch from F-1s to Brangus."

Dan says most of their horseback work comes when they're preconditioning calves and moving cows from pasture to pasture. They also feed hay during winters, and have trained the cattle to come to the sound of the horn on the truck. That cuts down on the wear and tear on men, horses, and dogs; wear and wrecks that Dan is well familiar with.

"I've lost a couple of good horses working people's spoiled cattle," he relates. "One time the dogs had this Brahman cow bayed in a white brush thicket and I went in to push her out. She was facing me and I could see she was real mad. As I turned to leave, she charged and hit my little dun horse broadside. Stuck a horn right in him and he died about an hour later. That was a good little horse. I once roped a big old F-1 off that same horse, and the cow came right up the rope. Hooked a horn in my stirrup and tipped us over backwards."

There's no going backwards at Valdina Farms. Dan and Dave and Mike have converted the old concrete mess hall into their tack storage. The kitchen that once housed a mad cook, who had to be disarmed by Mike's father, now stores grain for cow horses. The race horses which once ran on tracks in California and Kentucky, and even won a Kentucky Derby, are no more. The barns are empty, used only for storing hay. The swimming pool is overgrown with weeds, and the race track has been plowed under.

A GAMBLING HALL AND A SNAKE DEN

Besides being a race horse lover, Emmerson Woodward was a gambling man. In the rambling ranch house where Dan, his wife, Peggy, and three children reside, are remnants of the wild and woolly days of prohibition in Texas. "They had a big bar in the basement where they produced homemade beer and had an elaborate warning system," Dan says. "There was a switch upstairs that rang a bell in the basement if a raid was coming, and supposedly there's an escape tunnel that leads out to the creek, but we haven't been able to find it."

What Dan and Peggy did find when they moved in to the old ranch house/casino-on-the-prairie was the resident snake. Peggy Rothe Wilson was born in 1958, just seven miles from the ranch, and grew up doing ranch chores. Still, she said she wasn't prepared to share a house with a snake. "He was a big—five-feet long or longer—blue snake, and at first we didn't bother him because they're good about killing rattlers. He was right at home here. You were likely to find him anywhere. The kids would go out to play and that snake'd be lying right in the way. They'd yell, 'Mom, come move the snake.' I'd go chase it under the house and everything would be okay." For a while.

"Then one morning, I went zipping out the door, not thinking, and there's that snake, lying right on the step. I went straight up and let out a big scream and when I came down, I starting figuring out a way to get rid of that snake." The Wilsons now use the standard Texas ranch trick of letting cats take care of the snakes. That gives Dan more time to trap pesky hogs that tear up fences and feeders and gives Peggy more time to cook, something that she says she loves to do, but learned only because she grew up in a large family and had to cook.

BEATING THE HEAT WITH BEER BREAD

"It seemed like the cooking never ended," she says of growing up with five brothers and a sister. "I remember Mom just going from one meal to the next. I learned to cook from her. I don't use prefab things. I can make anything I like. I cook lots of meat. Venison. Beans. Chili. I cook for the crews here. Big pot of beans. Chili and rice. Stew and corn bread. My favorite thing is coconut pie. And bread—I love to bake bread. Beer bread is my favorite. Dan'll come home for lunch and there'll be an empty beer can on the counter, and I'll say, 'Just baking bread, Honey. Just baking bread.' I enjoy baking bread."

Both Dan and Peggy say they really enjoy working and living at Valdina Farms. And David and Mike both say they have never worked for a better boss. Now that Dan is getting the hogs trapped, he can give the cattle proper attention, Dave and Barbara can entertain their ghost, and Mike can reminisce with his dad about the old days. Peggy has eighty-sixed the blue runner and can concentrate on cooking, and that makes for a bunch of happy cowboys. You'll be happy, too, with Peggy's beer bread.

PEGGY'S BEER BREAD

3 cups flour

1½ tablespoons baking powder

1½ teaspoons salt

2 tablespoons sugar

1 12-ounce can beer, at room temperature

½ stick butter or margarine

Preheat oven to 375°F. In a large bowl, mix flour, baking powder, salt, and sugar. Pour in ALL of the beer, except maybe a few sips for the cook. Stir to make a soft dough. Put mix into greased loaf pan and pat to fill all corners. Melt butter and pour over dough. Bake forty-five to fifty-five minutes until top is golden and crusty. Remove from oven. Cool ten minutes before slicing. Slice with electric knife, if possible. One loaf makes about eighteen slices. Enjoy—and don't drink all the beer.

BRAD WHITFIELD

FREELANCE COWBOY
FORT DAVIS, TEXAS

JUST A PLAIN OL' COWBOY

On most ranches we visit, our focus is on the country, the ranch, the rancher, the cattle and horses, and finally, the cowboys and the cook. Occasionally we'll come across a cowboy who, for one reason or another, does some cooking, but hardly ever do we find a cowboy who fits the image made popular by the old dime novels and "B" movies—a hand who can ride and rope and cook and play a guitar and sing. In Fort Davis, we ran across Brad Whitfield, a tall, handsome man who is a real working cowboy. Brad possesses all the skills necessary to make a top hand anywhere. He also writes and records songs—and he can cook.

Brad is true to the title of his first album, *Just A Plain Ol' Cowboy*. If you can ever use the word "just" to describe all Brad can do. He is more than just a plain ol' cowboy. Much more. Brad Whitfield is a real working cowboy.

COWBOYING IN EL DESPOBLADO

Brad was born and raised near Odessa, which is in the northeast quadrant of Big Bend Country, an area Spanish explorers called *el despoblado*—the unpopulated desert. "Years ago, it was some of the better cattle country in the world," Brad begins his description of his home range. "The grass was as lush as it could be. But mesquite took over and the oil [wells] came in and now there's roads and pumps and oil patches as far as you can see. But there's still some good ranches. There just ain't no scenic value around Odessa."

Brad's father worked on ranches in Coleman county "for years and years" until he decided he could make more money in the oil fields—undoubtedly the truth, but young Brad decided he would always be a cowboy. And he decided wanted a little more scenic value in his life. "I took to day-working when I was in high school, and I worked on most of the ranches in that part of the country.

It's strong old country. The cattle do well up there, but it just ain't good country where a cowboy wants to live and work."

The problem with cowboying around Odessa, Brad explains, was oil field workers. "Time and time again, we'd throw a dab of cattle together and get a little drive going toward a set of pens and here'd come a roustabout crew, or a drilling crew, and a company man or two, and there'd go your cattle. It was just like working cattle in town. A helluva mess is what it is."

So in 1976, when he graduated from Odessa High School, Brad went east to a ranch near DeLeon and started his post-graduate cowboy career. "Worked for OBBCO Ranches down there. In that country, ranches are pretty small and we ran commercial cows, yearlings, and registered cattle. I took care of the yearlings. Received 'em., straightened 'em out, and put 'em on pasture. It was a good job."

But when you're just out of high school, good jobs don't necessarily parlay into steady employment. "When you're young you want to see new country, ride new horses, do new things." So when a friend called and said there was a camp job open at the Long X Ranch near Kent, Brad jumped at the job. "I'd always wanted to be out here. I came out and have been here ever since." Brad worked at the "X" for several years, and that's where he fell in love with cowboying in the Texas Davis Mountains, in an area the chamber of commerce refers to as the "Switzerland of Texas."

DOING THINGS THE OLD WAY IN THE TEXAS ALPS

A unique area where the continental divide crosses Texas and colorful mountains rise up from lush meadows, the population in the Big Bend country is confined to small towns like Marfa, Kent, Alpine, and Fort Davis. And the primary residents of the country, other than the native deer, javalina, birds, and snakes of all kinds, are cattle and horses and the men and women who make a living caring for them. The American cowboy is still very much alive in the Texas mountains.

"I like the mountains," Brad relates. "I like the way they do things out here. Things haven't changed out here. Before I came to this country, I had branded lots and lots of cattle. It was always down an alley into a chute. Came out here—we throwed cattle in a corner, made a wing with trucks and trailers, put a fire in the middle, and two men rode into the herd and started roping and we started branding calves.

"That's the way they do it out here—rope 'em and drag 'em to the fire. [We] cut 'em ahorseback. Pair 'em up ahorseback. Things are done out here the way they was done 150 years ago. I've worked cattle both ways, and this is the way I prefer to work cattle. That's what them horses are for: ride and use—not standing there tied to the fence. This is my country. This is where I want to work and live."

'Course, being the typical cowboy, Brad didn't stay at the "X" forever. He worked for most of the big outfits around Kent. The U-up/U-down, the Mayor, and, for several years, the "U" near Balmorhea, where he was elevated to

Fort Davis freelance cowboy, Brad Whitfield.

foreman. Brad says the life of a cowboy, especially a young cowboy, is something akin to being a bird: "You're about as free as a man can get." Then he got married. "My wife wasn't liking all that moving too much. We had a few kids on the ground, so I settled down"—near Fort Davis where Kelly, Mrs. Brad Whitfield, works for the Prude Ranch, as does Brad, part-time. Ever the cowboy, Brad still refuses to wear any one brand. He freelances, doing day-work for area ranches.

Recent labor studies have shown that about 30 percent to 40 percent of the workforce in America is now made up of temporary employees. Studies also indicate that this is a fast growing trend, with some 50 percent to 60 percent of the total labor force being "temps" by the turn of the century. Brad probably doesn't know he's a trendsetter. He does know, however, what it takes to be a good "temp" in Texas. "The secret of being a successful day-work cowboy is to have a wife with a good job," Brad quips. He could have added having an understanding wife, which Kelly, lovely, outgoing, and hardworking, most certainly is.

That frees Brad up for day-work, and with his experience, he is like any professional "temp" anywhere—he is in constant demand. "Just a few weeks ago, my friend, James, and I were helping an outfit preg-test some heifers, and there were five we couldn't get penned. So we just roped 'em and bedded 'em down and tied 'em up and let the vet check 'em right there."

HOW TO BED DOWN A BAD BOVINE

Roping and bedding down takes a real cowboy with a real good horse. It's called 'tripping a critter,' and it's common where a cowboy is working alone with just his horse and perhaps a dog and has to doctor a sick or injured animal.

"When I rope 'em, I don't care if it's around the head or the horns, I just throw my slack down his right side, get two or three dallies, go by 'em on the left side, and jerk 'em down.

"They'll lay there pretty good if you really bed 'em hard. They'll stay bedded down and you can step down and tie 'em. I've always got two or three pigging strings on my saddle. They're about six-foot long with a loop on one end. First thing I do is put my knee on the neck and pull a front foot up. Put the loop around that foot, and with your off leg and other arm, pull the two hind feet up and dally around all three feet. If I have to go get a trailer and leave the cow tied, I'll cross-hobble 'em. That way they can get up and move, but can't go nowhere. You can't leave a critter tied down very long. They'll die."

Brad uses a thirty-five-foot nylon rope, three-eighths inch in diameter. When a rope gets old with use, he'll unravel one strand, leaving two that become his pigging strings. He says he uses rubber on his horn, unlike the buckaroos up north. "Up there they use them sixty-foot ropes and have mule hide on their [saddle] horns and play them cows like a fish on a string. When I rope something, I want it to stop. That's the reason I rope it. To stop it."

In the Texas brush, a cowboy and a horse have to be be quick to stop a critter. "Thirty-five foot is a big plenty of rope. I carry a small loop. Fold it under my arm until I'm ready. You don't want it hanging up in the brush. You wait till you see an opening, and swing twice and rope. If I can't rope 'em in the brush, I send in my hired man."

Brad's hired man was a yellow, catahoula-pit bull-cross, sitting in the back of his truck. "I can tell her 'catch' and she can catch a full grown bull and hold it till I get there and get a rope on it. She'll get 'em right by the nose and just set there until I say 'that's enough.' [Then] she'll quit. A good dog like that is worth two or three men. 'Specially [men] that don't know how to work cattle in the brush."

PROPERLY OUTFITTED FOR BRUSH POPPING

Brad not only knows how to work cattle in the brush, he knows how to dress for the brush country. "I wear shotgun leggings laced all the way. I step into 'em just like a pair of britches. Summertime I wear a brush jacket over a T-shirt. I wear tall-top boots. Handmade. Got a pair of Mingos, made in El Paso. And two pair of Mercers, made in 'Angelo. When I'm working, I tuck my pants in my boots so my leggings will slip over my jeans. And I don't care where you're working, there's gonna be ants in them pens. That's another reason I poke my pants in my boots."

For horses, Brad prefers the American quarter horse, or some mix of quarter horse. "Just good old ranch type horses. Most important thing in my work is to have a horse with heart. I don't care how big they are, if they ain't got the heart, they'll quit you. Lots of horses won't take this brush. That catclaw is tough. You gotta have a tough horse. Right now, my main horse stands about 14.2 [hands] and weighs about 1,200 [pounds]. I'll rope anything off that horse. He's a grandson of Doc Bar, and he'll eat a cow alive. He's got heart. He's the right kind."

It's important for a cowboy to have the right kind of horse, especially working cattle in the mountains. Even then, there's no guarantee that your day won't be ruined by some bad bovine. "You know when the fun goes out of roping a bull?" Brad asks, then answers, "When you catch him. Then you got to do something with him. You can't be too careful when you're roping bulls."

Or heifers. "Things happen. To me, that's a wreck. We was up at the "X" roping heifers, and I was chasing one down the side of a mountain and was just ready to rope when my horse stuck both front feet in a badger hole. That's the last thing I remember. I woke up and still had my rope in my hand and my horse was okay so I got back on."

But didn't go anywhere. "Ol' Allen Fry, the guy with me, asked what happened and I said I didn't know. Then I asked him, 'What're we doing?' And he said, 'Whata you mean? Whata we doing? We're roping these remnant heifers. Do you know where you are?' I looked around and said, 'There's the J. D. headquarters; we're in Running Water Draw. Why are we roping these heifers?'

"He said, 'Get off that horse.' When I did, I seen my knee was about the size of a basketball and he took me to the house. I'd just bought a new Chevrolet duallywhat's this? and it was setting there in the yard. I asked my wife, 'Who's visiting?' She said, 'What'd you mean?' I said, 'Who's truck is that?' She said I was worse than a drunk. About drove her crazy."

But Kelly drove Brad to Van Horn where, much to his chagrin, he was hospitalized. "They thought I might have blood vessels bleeding into my brain and they was talking about doing surgery. I thought, 'In Van Horn, Texas? Naw. I don't think so.' So I walked around that hospital all night. I ain't went to sleep yet."

CENTER-FIRE SADDLES AND STREAMLINED HORSES

Nor quit cowboying yet. But things do happen. Brad's next wreck took out his saddle. And a cowboy is pretty useless without his saddle. "We were up on the U Ranch doing a work, and that place is 144 sections. We was hauling clear to the other side and gathering. I hauled six horses over the evening before [the work started] and hauled six the next morning. Those six horses we hauled saddled, and threw the rest of the saddles in the back of the truck. The truck didn't have a tail gate, and we left way before daylight and was a going along and I heard this whump-a-whump-a-whump and yelled, 'Settle down back there.' I thought the horses were jumping around."

It wasn't horses jumping. "I laughed and told the guys, 'It's probably my damn saddle fell out.' Sure 'nuff, we get to the pens and I start feeling around for my saddle and it's gone. I went back and it was just torn all to pieces. That gooseneck had run over it and drug it. It was in sad shape. I almost cried."

But cowboys don't normally cry. They just suck it up, or cowboy up, as they call it, and go on with life, and work. "I took it to Big Bend Saddlery there in

Alpine and they rebuilt it. Did an excellent job. It's just as good as new. I was lost for a while there without my saddle."

While he was saddleless, Brad borrowed a center-fire rig from a friend, and that convinced him that his old double-rigged Olson-Stilser was worth it's weight in gold. "I'd heard about how good them things [center-fire saddles] fit a horse, and how good they felt, and I'd always wanted to try one. We was working Beard Mountain and it was straight up, switchbacking all the way. We'd been riding them horses pretty good, and they was pretty streamlined, and I didn't have a breast collar. That saddle kept slipping back, and I grabbed a mane-holt to stay on, but the saddle went right back over the horse's butt.

"I finally had to take a pigging string and make a breast collar for the damn thing. I figured out that if you're riding a center-fire and have to rope something, the best thing to do is send someone else to rope it. I was sure glad to get my saddle back."

RIDING ALONG, SINGING A SONG

And glad to be able to occasionally day-work for the Prude Ranch, an outfit that can use his cowboying skills and also gives him an opportunity to practice his song writing and picking and singing. "First time I was there, we'd just come in from working cattle and I was dusty and sweaty and they wanted me to get up and sing. 'Course, everywhere I go I pack a guitar, hoping somebody will ask me to sing. Well, I got up and apologized for looking the way I did, but the next day John Robert [Prude Ranch manager] told me, 'No, that's just the way we want you to look.' I never thought you had to look a certain way to sing."

You just have to sound a certain way. Western preferably. And Brad certainly is that. "I got started in high school. Me and some friends were in FFA [Future Farmers of America] and we entered the "Talent Team" contest, went to state and won third [place]. I kinda been at it ever since. I like to write songs. I like old ballads. Marty Robbins-type. That's what I'm working on now. Old western type ballads. That's what I do best."

On his *Just A Plain Ol' Cowboy* album, Brad sings two songs he wrote: "Ride Outlaw Ride" and "You're Just A Memory." To fill out the album, "just to have something to sell," Brad recorded several old Ray Price classics and does justice to them all. Brad is a regular at the Prude Ranch Elderhostel programs, and has performed for several television commercials and documentaries. In fact, Brad indicates he's getting about too busy to write and almost—almost—too busy to cook, a skill he picked up in his bachelor cowboy days.

"I got married back in '78," he says. "But in '76, '77, and part of '78, I was batching with another old kid and had to learn how to cook." A skill that he resisted learning as long as possible. "When we'd get a paycheck, we'd run into the Dairy Queen there in De Leon and eat us a good supper most of the time. If we was running way low on money, then we'd go to cooking."

COWBOYS DON'T DO DISHES

But not doing dishes. "We had us a deal where we wouldn't wash dishes until there was just nothing left to eat out of or cook in. Lot of times we'd have friends come over and they'd just shake their heads. We weren't much for housekeeping." What actually got Brad into cooking real food was a stint at the U-up/U-down.

"I met Bob Hendrick there. He was a camp cook and one of the best. He taught me a bunch of stuff about making bread and stuff, and I got to cooking pretty good. Now I cook for people regular."

And for competition. "After Chip [Prude] quit going to cookoffs, I teamed up with Glenn [Moreland] and we got to taking the chuck wagon to them poetry gatherings where they have chuck wagon competitions. My specialty is bread. I can cook anything, but bread is my specialty.

"Just put in some flour, 'bout a cup of oil, and a cup of sugar, and dissolve a pack of yeast in some warm water, and put a little sugar in the water where it'll be like sourdough. Mix 'er all together and let 'er rise and punch it down. Pinch out your biscuits and set 'em in the Dutch oven and let 'em rise. Set 'er on the coals, put the lid on, put coals on the lid, and let 'er cook."

Like most camp cooks, Brad says there's no measurements to any of his recipes. "But it always comes out pretty good. I like it." Brad shares his recipe for beans, and we think you'll like them, too.

BRAD'S BEANS

2 cups beans, pinto beans preferred

½ cup bacon bits or salt pork chips

1 clove garlic, chopped real fine

1 tablespoon onion, minced

1 pinch chili powder

Salt to taste

Soak beans overnight. Next morning, start cooking 'em. Cook 'em in the same water you soak 'em in. Add your bacon bits or fry up some bacon or salt pork and chop it up real fine. Add your garlic and onion and just a pinch of chili powder. The chili powder is for color, not for taste. Use plenty of salt and cook beans fast. Keep 'em at a constant boil for three to four hours until the beans get just soft. They're sure good eating.

Brad has won cooking contests in Ruidoso, Fort Worth, Lubbock, and other places with this bean recipe. He says he enjoys cooking and is having the time of his life. After sampling his fare, you will, too.

XIT

GONE BUT NOT FORGOTTEN

XIT

BIG! There just isn't a better word to describe the XIT, in the 1880s the largest range in the world under fence. And it was all in parts of ten counties in the Texas Panhandle. The ranch's more than three million acres ran from the old Yellow House headquarters, near what is now Lubbock, northward to the Oklahoma line in an irregular strip that was more or less thirty miles wide.

Even by Texas standards that sure is big. And Texas, at that time the largest state in the Union, used the land to pay for its red granite capitol in Austin, still the biggest state capitol, with a dome that rises seven feet higher that the nation's capitol in Washington, D.C.

Back in 1875, the Texas government felt squeezed in its old building and decided it needed new space. The Texas Constitutional Convention had set aside three million Panhandle acres to be used to get a new capitol. The legislature cut a deal with Charles and John Farwell, two Chicago contractors, to do the work. In exchange for the land, they agreed to build the state a new $3,000,000 capitol.

⚜

The fencing of the XIT range began in 1885 when Bill Metcalf was given the first contract to fence the 476,000-acre Buffalo Springs pasture. The fence cost $35,000 and was made of cedar posts (cut illegally on Federal land near Cimmaron, New Mexico). It was strung with Brinkerhoff Lance (twist) and flat ribbon wire. The XIT eventually built over 1,500 miles of fence to enclose ninety-four pastures. The fencing was all four strands of barbed wire with a post set every thirty-feet and a gate placed every three miles.

Ultimately, the ranch used 6,000 miles of barbed wire, enough to cross the United States twice, at a cost of $181,000. They used over 300 railroad boxcars

F. A. (Finley Alonzo) Bradley (second from right) was ranch foreman at the No. 1 headquarters of the XIT Ranch 1910-1913 at Buffalo Springs, 30 miles north of Dalhart (photo courtesy Dessie Hanbury).

of wire, 100,000 fence posts and one boxcar of staples, and another boxcar for gate hinges.

Although the ranch really just existed from 1881 until 1912 when the owners began to sell off the land, it has had a lasting impact on ranching, not only in Texas but throughout North America.

In 1885, when the first of the eventual 150,000 head of cattle were herded onto the XIT range, the XIT began to define big ranching. From Buffalo Springs, the number one division headquarters thirty-two miles north of Dalhart, to Escarbada ("Shallow Water") and the Yellow House division in the south, ranching was changed forever.

A big outfit like the XIT had to have rules, and in 1888, the ranch manager, Abner Taylor, posted a list of twenty-three "General Rules of the XIT Ranch," that read like Hollywood's Code of the West. But in a more realistic way, the rules epitomized much of the moral and ethical conduct of ranchers and cowboys. The following are some of the rules the XIT cowboys had to abide by.

The abuse of horses, mules, or cattle by any employee will not be tolerated; and any one who strikes his horse or mule over the head, or spurs it in the shoulder, or in any other manner abuses or neglects to care for it while in his charge, shall be dismissed from the Company's service.

Employees are not allowed to run mustang, antelope, or any kind of game on the Company's horses.

No employee of the Company, or of any contractor doing work for the Company, is permitted to carry on or about his person or in his saddle bags, any pistol, dirk, dagger, sling shot, knuckles, bowie knife, or any

Dessie Mae Hanbury, daughter of XIT ranch foreman F. A. Bradley. Dessie is being held by her father in photo opposite.

other similar instruments for the purpose of offense or defense. Guests of the Company, and persons not employees of the ranch temporarily staying at any of its camps, are expected to comply with this rule, which is also a State law.

Card playing and gambling of every description, whether engaged in by employees, or by persons not in the service of the Company, is strictly forbidden on the ranch.

Each outfit of men that is furnished with a wagon and cook is required to make its own camping places, and not impose on the other camps on the ranch unnecessarily.

Employees are strictly forbidden the use of vinous, malt, spirituous, or intoxicating liquors, during their time of service with the Company.

It is the duty of every employee to protect the Company's interests to the best of his ability, and when he sees they are threatened in any direction, to take every proper measure at his command to accomplish this end, and as soon as possible to inform his employers of the danger threatened.

Employees of neighboring ranches on business are to be cared for at all times, and their horses fed if desired (provided there is feed in the camp to spare); but such persons will not be expected to remain on the ranch longer than is necessary to transact their business, or continue their journey.

Bona fide travelers may be sheltered if convenient, but they will be expected to pay for what grain and provisions they get, at prices to be fixed from time to time by the Company, and all such persons must not remain on the company's land anywhere under any pretext whatever.

It is the aim of the owners of this ranch to conduct it on the principle of right and justice to everyone; and for it to be excelled by no other in the good behavior, sterling honesty and integrity, and general high character of its employees, and to this end it is necessary that the foregoing rules be adhered to, and the violation of any of them will be considered just cause for discharge.

🔥

The era of the XIT is being kept alive today by the annual XIT Rodeo and Reunion, which was started in 1936, and by the Dallam-Hartley XIT Museum in Dalhart, Texas. And no one is more responsible for the success of the fine small museum than Dessie Hanbury. Her roots at the XIT are very strong . Her father, Lon Bradley, was ranch house foreman at the Buffalo Springs division. Burton Hanbury, her father-in-law, was an XIT carpenter for twenty years. She also says, "My mother cooked for the cowboys when we lived at the Springs, and the corn pudding recipe was one of her favorites." So here is a little bit of ranching tradition: Mrs. Bradley's corn pudding recipe from the Buffalo Springs division of the XIT. She says it makes a "great sidekick for fried or broiled fish." We are also including from the ranch, a classic recipe—cowboy biscuits. "These deep-fried 'beauties' are chuck wagon classics. Without ovens, the only way trail cooks could make biscuits was to fry them in kettles called Dutch ovens." Give them a try!

CORN PUDDING

2 tablespoons butter

¼ cup chopped onion

2 tablespoons flour

1 cup milk

1 cup fresh, canned, or defrosted corn kernels

1½ teaspoons salt

¼ teaspoons pepper

1½ teaspoons sugar

2 eggs

Preheat the oven to 350°F. Butter a seven-inch baking dish. Melt one tablespoon butter in a small skillet and sauté the onion in it. Set aside.

Melt the remaining tablespoon butter in a saucepan and stir in the flour. Pour in the milk gradually, stirring until smooth. Bring the mixture to the boil, stirring frequently. When thickened and smooth, add the corn, sautéed onion, salt, pepper, sugar, and eggs, beaten until light and foamy. Mix well. Pour into the prepared dish and bake for thirty-five to forty minutes, until lightly browned.

Yields four servings.

1 cup all-purpose flour

2 teaspoons baking powder

½ tablespoon sugar

¼ teaspoon salt

1½ tablespoon butter

1½ tablespoons solid vegetable shortening

⅓ cup milk

Vegetable oil for frying

In a bowl, sift the flour with the baking powder, sugar, and salt. Cut in the butter and shortening until the mixture resembles coarse meal. Stir the milk into the mixture with a fork, using just enough milk to make a soft dough.

Turn the dough out onto a well-floured board and knead gently for half a minute. Either divide the dough into eight portions, roll into balls, and flatten to one-half-inch thickness, or roll out to one-half-inch thickness and cut into biscuits with a two-inch or two-and-one-half-inch biscuit cutter.

Heat one-inch of oil in a large, heavy skillet. Drop the biscuits into the hot oil and fry for four to five minutes, turning once halfway through the cooking time. Do not crowd the biscuits in the pan. Drain on paper towels and serve hot.

Yields about eight biscuits.

INDEX